The Center for South and Southeast Asia Studies of the University of California is the unifying organization for faculty members and students interested in South and Southeast Asia Studies, bringing together scholars from numerous disciplines. The Center's major aims are the development and support of research and language study. As part of this program the Center sponsors a publication series of books concerned with South and Southeast Asia. Manuscripts are considered from all campuses of the University of California as well as from any other individuals and institutions doing research in these areas.

RECENT PUBLICATIONS
OF THE CENTER FOR SOUTH AND SOUTHEAST ASIA STUDIES:

Prakash Tandon
Beyond Punjab: A Sequel to PUNJABI CENTURY (1971)

Surinder Mohan Bhardwaj
Hindu Places of Pilgrimage in India:
A Study in Cultural Geography (1972)

John Larkin
The Pampangans: Colonial Society in a Philippine Province (1972)

Daniel S. Lev
Islamic Courts in Indonesia:
A Study in the Political Bases of Legal Institutions (1972)

Robert Lingat
The Classical Law of India. Translated by J. Duncan M. Derrett (1972)

David N. Lorenzen
The Kāpālikas and Kālāmukhas: Two Lost Śaivite Sects (1972)

Gordon C. Roadarmel
A Death in Delhi: Modern Hindi Short Stories (1972)

A. M. Shah
The Household Dimension of the Family in India (1972)

Elizabeth Whitcombe
Agrarian Conditions in Northern India. Volume One:
The United Provinces under British Rule, 1860–1900 (1972)

Information and Behavior in a Sikh Village

This volume is sponsored by the
Center for South and Southeast Asia Studies,
University of California, Berkeley

Information and Behavior
in a Sikh Village

Social Organization Reconsidered

∽∽∽

Murray J. Leaf

University of California Press
Berkeley, Los Angeles, London

University of California Press
Berkeley and Los Angeles, California
University of California Press, Ltd.
London, England
Copyright © 1972, by
The Regents of the University of California
ISBN 0–520–02115–0
Library of Congress Catalog Card Number: 78–172390
Printed in the United States of America
Designed by Dave Comstock

Contents

Tables

Figures

Preface

The theory put forth in this book has grown out of ideas that led me, seven years ago, to a field study focusing on marriage rituals in a Punjabi Sikh village. The pattern of growth has been erratic and would be difficult to explain, but it has certain points where certain intellectual debts are due.

My basic method for delineating systems of concepts (which I call conscious sociological models), together with the closely related approach to the analysis of rituals, was the first component of the work to reach its present form. This took shape before the field study, largely under the tutelage of Professor David M. Schneider of the Department of Anthropology of the University of Chicago. The second component, slightly less old, is the use of information theory to interpret statistical results—an approach in which I received help and encouragement from Professor Harrison White, who was then also at Chicago. At first, the approach to structure and ritual was not integrated with the approach to statistical description. I am deeply indebted to Professor Harold Garfinkel for the concept of "everyday behavior" that bridged this gap by providing a common focus that both subsidiary analyses could be referred to. These three key developments led to the field project.

My research proposal was supported by a grant of the United States Public Health Service, Mental Health Division (No. MH 08194), and I arrived in India in May of 1964. In New Delhi, Dr. Indera Paul Singh of the Department of Anthropology, Delhi University, graciously served as my host and adviser. Later, Dr. S. R. K.

Chopra, chairman of the Department of Anthropology of Punjab University, was similarly helpful in extending the hospitality of his department and in arranging for an appointment as Honorary Lecturer therein. Mr. A. L. Fletcher, the Financial Commissioner of the Punjab Government, and Mr. M. S. Gill, then District Commissioner of Ambala, likewise offered their personal understanding of the project and the full support of their offices. R. L. Anand, Director of Census Operations for Punjab, gave freely of his time and experience in ethnographic field work in the region. I am further grateful to Mr. S. J. Sandhu, Deputy Director of the Punjab Government Economic and Statistical Organization, and to Justice Harbans Singh of the Punjab High Court for their suggestions.

For the components of the present scheme that have been developed since the field study was completed, I owe a great deal to a group of economists who meet occasionally under the rubric of the Committee on Problems of Economic Change. Professor Walter C. Neale, Professor Anne Mayhew, and Professor John Adams have made particularly important contributions to my recent thinking. More than anything else, it was the effort to meet the questions and critiques of this group that led to the last major transformation, and integration, of the scheme. They forced me to examine and reject many minor distinctions between classes of phenomena and, eventually, to see information theory not merely as a convenient framework for interpreting statistical analysis but as a comprehensive scheme for explaining the function and structure of systems of concepts and of the contexts that affect their use as well. Information theory seemed to be a near-perfect general frame within which "economics" and other social systems could be compared. Now, after I have been constrained to modify slightly some basic assumptions of the formal theory to fit the present problem, it may even be more than that.

The Statistical results used in Chapter 6 were obtained from computer analysis of village data supported by grants from the Academic Senate of the University of California, Los Angeles Division, and from the Wenner Gren Foundation for Anthropological Research (grant number 2457).

The contributions of the villagers of Shahidpur to the present work have been enduring and pervasive. Each of the six substantive chapters, three through eight, was drafted before I left India and was read out or paraphrased, mainly in Punjabi, to interested villagers for discussions and comment. In addition, beside providing "data," these villagers demonstrated, and even told me, that there is a discernible common humanity among people that lies behind their cultural differences, even given that these differences include all their explicitly held and shared values and beliefs. This "humanity" includes the integration of emotions, desires, fears, and faith into their explicit cultural conventions as part of their fabric of life. I found this first when I realized that the predicted logic of marriage rituals held true only when we included a father's concern for his daughter and her security in the equation of costs and gains, and when I saw that such concern was in fact part of the social structural model. I found it again when I left the village at the end of what had seemed a long game of cat-and-mouse, for I was made aware that I was leaving a group of people who had, for no discernible practical reason, made me and my affairs a part of their own lives.

While the villagers of Shahidpur were generally considerate and helpful and almost always hospitable, I must mention by name Bakhtavar Singh and his son Naranjan Singh, and Inder Singh and his son Netar Singh. Both houses gave freely of their food, their knowledge, and their confidence.

In the preparation of the manuscript I have received invaluable and expert help from the Central Stenographic Bureau of the University of California at Los Angeles, and from Miss Carole Deets, who has worked as my general assistant under the UCLA work-study program.

The index was prepared by Mrs. Roberta W. Goodwin.

My wife, Michelina, has been a constant support and help in all phases of the study.

Any omissions or errors that may appear here are my own responsibility.

Murray J. Leaf
Los Angeles, California

Chapter I

Introduction

This is a social analysis of an agricultural village in Punjab State, India—a community of about 860 people who are for the most part adherents of the Sikh religion. Like most anthropological village studies, this one makes use of a "theory" and of a concept of "method," and it makes certain claims for its own value on the basis of the originality and importance of the theory and method it uses. But, even though there are unique elements both of theory and method presented here, and though Sikhs are but slightly represented in the modern anthropological literature, the principal claim this study makes upon the attention of social scientists is based not so much on the content of theory, method, or fact alone but rather on a broader and more general consideration of the pattern of relationships among them. The individual points of theory, method, and fact are presented in service to this larger vision and, in part at least, have been generated by it.

Typically, anthropological theories propose to describe society or culture in general, by finding one type of phenomenon or set of principles that controls or encompasses the whole. The theory to be presented here pretends not to generality in this sense, but rather to a level of specificity not usually sought. This aim represents a basic overall reorientation of research strategy.

Since Durkheim, anthropologists have by and large accepted a very specific conception of social theory, built on two distinct elements. The first and most important is a general view of theory itself. What is now called theory is the direct descendant of what was called natural law in the nineteenth century. This was thought of on the pattern of Plato's world of "forms" (logos) as distinct from matter, as that which is abstract and general, distinct from what is concrete and particular. Such law was considered to be determinative of the characteristics of any particular actions in the phenomena they "governed," even though they were "ideal" components in the minds of human observers. Hegel's "world reason" that determined history, and Spencer's "superorganic" law that governed social phenomena, are both patterned after this ancient fashion. Durkheim added the second major element of the modern theory when he equated such theory with "society" itself, conceived of essentially on the model of Comte's "organic" state. This synthesis permitted Durkheim to claim to discover deterministic "natural law" empirically as it appeared in social rituals and all other actions that he construed as manifestations of the "collective consciousness" that was "outside and above individual and local contingencies" (1957, p. 444).

Durkheim's contention was that "man is double." "There are two beings in him; an individual being which has its foundations in the organism and whose activities are therefore strictly limited, and a social being which represents the highest reality in the intellectual and moral order that we can know by observations—I mean society. ... This duality of our nature has as its consequence . . . , in the order of thought, the irreducibility of reason to individual experience." For Durkheim, literally all concepts, all regularity in cognition and experience, were imposed on the individual from without "by the authority of society" (p. 17), which was itself a "reality *sui generis*" (p. 16). The entire edifice of this argument—the social determinism, the equation of society with the "collective consciousness" and with all thought, and the radical dualism between mental phenomena as general and biological phenomena as particular—rests entirely and squarely on the dichotomy between form and matter.

Radcliffe-Brown (1961, pp. 1–5) kept all Durkheim's basic elements and the ideas of theory they were based on. He backed away only from Durkheim's rigid, causal determinism and adopted the newer but closely related language of the logical positivists to describe his new position. His was the view that social theory was a logically connected "set of analytical concepts" (p. 1). It was derived from a comparison of "forms of social life." But it was not clear that it *caused* the forms except in the sense that it embodied them. However, the idea of a one-for-one relation between social structures and patterns of action was retained, along with the paradoxical idea that social structures, though mental phenomena, were not known to the natives whose behaviors they directed. (See Levi-Strauss 1962, p. 322.) Despite their commitment to the idea that scientific theory had to have such a relation to action, which was consistent with the broad idea that individual behaviors were inherently "particular," proponents of this theory have never made a systematic effort to connect specific elements of theory to specific types of phenomena, or to specific observational procedures.

Notwithstanding its long pedigree, the view that the difference between theory and fact corresponds to the distinction between form and substance has not been without serious challenges in Western philosophy and, more recently and importantly, in the study of academic science. The most important relevant current philosophical tradition directly attacks the distinctions both between "form" and "matter" and between "reason" and "phenomena." Kant denied absolute reality to both "form" and "matter" in the older senses and turned the older tradition inside out. He argued that the formerly "absolute" realities, the substantive "things in themselves," and categories of pure reason from which perception had been thought to be derived, were in fact entities hypothecated by people under pressure of acting on the basis of their perceptions. Perceptions themselves were neither form nor matter in the old sense; they were more basic, not only intellectual but also emotive and conditioned by practical necessities. In effect, Kant's was an empirical and pragmatic (in James' sense) approach to metaphysics and to theory. He rejected the attempts to derive knowledge from unknowable absolutes, logical first principles like the distinctions between form and matter, or theories of the relation between qualities and real objects in themselves. He tried instead to describe, explain, and assess the kinds of "absolutes" men had postulated by analyzing, precisely if abstractly, the way men act and speak.

Subsequently, Wittgenstein treated a wide range of traditional problems in epistemology, ethics and esthetics as though they were rooted in and referrable to a "language game" (1965, pp. 5^{e}ff.). This continued Kant's mode of analysis on a less abstract and far-ranging, more precise and in some ways more forceful plane. Over and over, in each area, Wittgenstein made Kant's point: the established "absolutes" to which traditional problems were referred were but hypothecations, esoteric elaborations rooted in the common communicative actions of men. The problems were insoluble only in relation to the hypothecations; they were not obscure if they were referred to their empirical context in communicative practice. For example, people spoke of "goodness" not because there was some absolute reality, "the good," but because it was consistent with the conventions of communication in normal life to do so. The basic rule of the "language game," repeated on almost every page of Wittgenstein's investigation, was to avoid "confusion." One played the game in a certain way, such as speaking of moral and ethical qualities as if they referred to "substances," because the alternative would create confusion among those one communicated with. Or, more positively, the order inherent in the playing of the "game" was that of taking part in the communicative conventions in such a way as to maintain ordered social intercourse. Wittgenstein also made it plain that this language game was not mere play, divorced from the realities of daily life. Neither was it restricted to the use of words alone. Knowledge of the game was demonstrated not only by the unconfused use of words in academic discussions but also by the unconfused connection of actions of many kinds with the uses of words in ordinary circumstances. He did not fall into the trap of the logical positivists in attempting to replace the metaphysical dichotomy between form and matter with an equally untenable radical dichotomy between language and objects. Insofar as Wittgenstein advocated a general philosophy or theory, it was intertwined with the empirical concept of the language game itself and his closely related operational and comparative techniques of analysis.

In the philosophy of science, Thomas Kuhn's (1962) view of the role of theory differs from that of the logical positivists in the same way that Kant's and Wittgenstein's approach to epistemology differs from Hume, Hegel, and Spencer. The differences were recognized in Kuhn's unusual preface, which in part explained how his analysis came to be published as part of the *International Encyclopedia of a Unified Science*, which had been established as the principal vehicle of the logical positivists (including Leonard Bloomfield in linguistics). Kuhn suggested that though his analysis was not quite appropriate for the vehicle, its publication was in response to earlier commitments, undertaken when he was of a different frame of mind.

Theory, for Kuhn, is articulated in reference to a "paradigm," and a paradigm is something very much like the "game" of Wittgenstein. Although Kuhn offers no comprehensive definition, he does indicate that a "paradigm" is a general picture of key phenomena imbedded in a key "achievement," an "example of scientific practice" (p. 10). These paradigms are prior to specific rules of practice, theory, laws, and so forth that are "abstracted from them" (p. 11). As such, paradigms are inextricably associated with analytical and descriptive practices, devices for observation and measurement, and conventions of community behavior and communication. Within a field, ruled by a broad paradigm, subfields develop through reference to the general theory for parameters and through use of theories and other such conceptual devices to delineate a system of activities that can be made relevant to the whole around it. Activities in subfields can be independent of each other, although their mutual interrelations can be changed by a "revolution," a change in the ruling paradigm that occurs when a substantially new theory with associated practices and devices is accepted.

The present view of theory is very much like Kuhn's. This study does not propose a new set of abstract statements in place of a former set, as two different ways of "analyzing" a set of phenomena that is given or defined independently of either theory. Rather, first of all, it proposes part of a paradigm, a part of a picture of a new way to conduct a study that includes an integrated picture of both theory and phenomena. Within this, it introduces some new theoretical concepts—concepts not of completely general relevance, but only of specific application within the framework of this type of study. In this context, the theory is closely associated with specific techniques of analysis and description of its specific set of social phenomena. Some of these phenomena have been dealt with by others, and some are delineated here explicitly for the first time. The purpose of "theory" is to enable us to delineate each type of phenomenon from others, in the way that statics implicitly defines a domain separate from dynamics or high-energy physics. No whole of social theory, which might correspond to the whole of physical theory, is offered here. The present analysis does suggest, however, how such a theory might be built up by successive developments of related paradigms in areas adjoining that delineated by this analysis.

Theory in Radcliffe-Brown's sense was intended to abstractly summarize complexity, to represent complex and dynamic activities by means of stable and enduring formal statements. So conceived, as Bailey accurately observed, theory was inherently removed from the dynamics of daily interaction to the extent that it became "scientific," elegant and easily comprehended (1960, pp. 13–15). Barth recently recognized that this view of theory is not the only one possible for anthropologists. An alternative existed in theoretical statements (social structure) that could generate, or predict, the complexity encountered in field analysis from simpler basic elements. Paradigms, in Kuhn's sense and in the present sense, can be made to operate in this latter way. If the paradigm refers to a situation that is essentially dynamic, the theory abstracted from it can refer to and articulate this dynamism. The theory can describe the mechanism that generates the complexity and it can indicate means of isolating that complexity. By so indicating the way complexity can be generated such a theory automatically suggests the operational means by which it can be applied in analysis and prediction. A dynamic processual paradigm can give theoretical statements dynamic and generative implications.

The most basic element of theory in this analysis is a modified version of the analytical model of the communicative process proposed by Weaver (Shannon and Weaver 1964). Although the modifications have no bearing on the mathematical definitions of noise, of feedback, and of a "bit" as the unit of measure of information, they permit the general conceptions of information and entropy to be applied to different systems of cultural artifacts that affect behavior and are in turn affected by behavior. These include ecological and economic systems, as well as several ideological systems normally brought under the heading of "social structure."

Weaver's essay lays the foundation for the mathematical theory by describing information as a property of a transmission from a "transmitter" through a "channel" with an inherent source of "noise" to a "receiver" and finally to its "destination" (p. 7). The message was described as "selected" by the transmitter, or for the transmitter, from a "message source" that is spoken of as the "set of possible messages." "Information" was formally defined as "a measure of one's freedom of choice when he selects a message" (p. 9). This sees communication as essentially a one-way process and envisions the message source as a fixed list of possible communications. This is a perfectly appropriate and useful set of assumptions, with empirical content, for engineering purposes, but it is not precisely adapted to the description of face-to-face interaction in social situations.

Weaver's theoretical model can be modified for social analysis by two principal substitutions. Instead of a fixed list of possible messages, a message source is to be thought of as a paradigm in its own right—a picture of a key element of reality, associated with analytical techniques and referred to in forming the recognizable communications of a community. The second change is substitution of the idea of "constructing" messages for Weaver's idea of "selecting," as in the formal definition of information. The new definition of information would be "the measure of one's freedom of choice when he *constructs* a message."

These modifications permit the process of communication to be thought of as cyclical, not linear. The initial message source that specific communications reflect can also be seen as their "destination," their ultimate point of reference. Weaver's model thus comes to describe the process of creation and maintenance of information, as well as its transmission. If we consider, for example, the basic phonological and morphological structure of English as a message source, we can see that it is referred to in the construction of verbal communications in English, as in the linear model. But we also can see that its proper use by individuals (who serve as transmitters and receivers) contributes to consensus on the structure. Its use becomes part of, or reinforces, the structure and contributes to the organization and content of the message source for the next communication in that set of users of the source. "Noise" in this scheme assumes the properties of Wittgenstein's "confusion" in many respects. It becomes that part of discourse which interferes with the effective maintenance of regular order in the relevant message source.

One value of this scheme derives from the utility of the concept of "entropy" that Weaver applied both to messages and to the "sets" of messages from which selections were made. The concept was similar to the same concept in physics and was closely related to the concept of "information" itself. "Thus, for a communication source one can say, just as he would also say of a thermodynamic ensemble, 'this situation is highly organized, it is not characterized by a large degree of randomness or of choice—that is to say, the information (or the entropy) is low' " (p. 3). This applies as well to a message source thought of as a paradigm as to a message source thought of as a list. Message sources can be compared with one another with respect to their relative amounts of entropy and to the type of integration of their elements into highly organized or less highly organized patterns.

The connection between the amount of entropy in a message source and the information content of a message that may be "selected" or "constructed" from that source is the heart of the mathematical theory of information as such. If a message reflects a choice from a large number of options, its information value is high. If it reflects a small number of choices, its value is low, to the extreme where no choice is possible so that the one output is constant, unvarying, and "meaningless"—incapable of directing a differentiated response. According to Weaver's reasoning, a high-entropy (low-organization) message source would be capable of producing messages of high information value because it allows a wide latitude of choice among possible communicative acts. Low organization means that there are many different elements that can be selected or reflected in messages and that can be chosen independently from one another. In a low-organization source, a choice of one communication element does not determine the choice of another. Conversely, a highly integrated, low-entropy source is one with few choices to make, or one wherein the choice of one element predetermines the choice of many others. A message constructed in response to a completely integrated source, no matter how superficially complicated it may appear, can mean no more than "yes" or "no," "send" or "not send." High-entropy sources do not necessarily give rise only to messages of high information value, but low-entropy sources, sources that are highly organized, necessarily produce low-information messages. This is because the maximum number of choices that any given symbolic construction can represent, in referring to the source, is low.

Shannon and Weaver were aware that this concept of "information," though it was purely formal in terms of the theory, seemed to be saying something important about "meaning" as it has been investigated in our scholarly tradition since its inception. In fact, there are many obvious similarities between the idea implicit in information theory that "information" is what results in an expected practical effect in the receiver and Wittgenstein's notion that we are deemed to understand matters if we play the language game without causing "confusion." The relationship between information, in terms of the theory, and meaning, as it is generally understood in pragmatically oriented systems of philosophy, is strengthened in the context of the present modifications of the theory. It will be seen that the highly organized sources produce messages that not only are low in information in a formal sense, but are very "general" or vacuous in a semantic sense; empirically, they have little importance for the direction of detailed action, and their importance and general function in society derive directly from this particular property of vacuousness. Other systems that are less highly organized, and have therefore higher information in a formal sense, are utilized in constructing communications that have very detailed importance in directing practical behavior—high "meaning" in at least some of the sense of ordinary usage.

This is a much simpler use of communication theory than what is usually proposed for the social sciences. The general practice is not to focus on the properties of message sources and the information value of the messages produced in each as such, but rather to try to focus on interpersonal relations as if they were "channels" of communication and, subsequently, of feedback (Wiener 1961; Miller 1965), in the formal sense. The goal of this approach has generally been to define, mathematically, specific structures of channels or networks the society may have and to relate them to different organizational potentials to process new types of information. The complexity of any actual example of such an analysis would be beyond belief, and we really do not have a firm enough grasp on what a social relationship is or how it is constructed to warrant such an application. It is therefore not surprising that this approach, however promising it may sound, has never been developed beyond the stage of programmatic suggestions. Norbert Wiener, himself one of its more prominent advocates, freely pointed out that if an analysis of this type could be implemented it could not apply to anything like a whole society, nor could it ever be expected to obtain the kind of power and precision that similar analyses have attained in engineering applications (pp. 162–164). This use of information theory is in fact analogous to social theories on the pattern of those of Radcliffe-Brown and Durkheim, with the goal of scholarship again seen as the production of a set of abstract statements that corresponds to and directs a realm of behavior.

The formal relationship between the information of communications and entropy in message sources on the one hand, and between information formally defined and meaning as we commonly understand it, on the other, gives this modified information theory the capacity to serve as a framework both for comparing different systems in each community that affect the creations of meaningful behaviors, and for describing a method of analysis whose relationship to the systems analyzed is itself rationalized in terms of the detailed and dynamic properties of the systems it is applied to. The process of communication envisioned in the modified scheme describes both the nature of the systems and the way those systems can be scientifically and operationally delineated.

The present analysis describes six message sources in this community, and their relation to behavior. The point in each case is not that information theory is a broad system of abstract terms that can be made to cover each one—as an exercise in classification like Nadel's "calculus of social relations" based on his adaptation of Russell and Whitehead's calculus of propositions or like Parsons' theory of action (1959)—it is that these things *are* message sources. The modified conception of a message source describes them better than any other I can find or invent. The differences in form and function between them are differences in their properties as message sources and not as some other sort of phenomena.

This description of the six sources is a description of only "part" of a village community, in two senses. First, though they are the major sources, they are not the only message sources that affect communication in the village. Second, it describes a "part" of the village in the sense that there are many important phenomena, traditionally of interest to anthropologists, that are not message sources in the present clear and direct sense. An example of one such phenomenon is given in chapter 9, which goes beyond description of message sources into the analysis of their combined function in communicative behavior

—an analysis that is also a schematic analysis of communicative behavior itself. But aside from this, there are several important areas that cannot and need not be treated systematically here at all, even though they can be given theoretical form that will show their relation to message sources in the present sense. Some of these are indicated in passing—various types of activities and various systems of physical, biological, and epidemiological phenomena that affect behavior without being subject to conscious choice and selection through symbolic devices like the present systems. In addition, language, considered in its semantic and not its phonological aspect, is treated implicitly here as a complex vehicle for utilizing such sources, one which contains arbitrary symbols (words) especially defined to designate parts of each source, but which is not structured as a single source in itself. This is an important issue, deserving of extended treatment. But attempting to deal with it here would not be practicable and is not necessary. Also implicit here is the idea that the different message sources are utilized by actors, who stand outside them, in accordance with some general purposes that cannot be reduced to elements of the sources themselves. But again, no systematic effort can be made here to provide a theoretical analysis of such a behavioral strategy in this context. These secondary problems, however interesting they may be, need not be dealt with in order to advance the present argument, because a number of alternative solutions to each would fit perfectly well with the specific analysis here offered of the broad types of social phenomena that communicative behavior responds to and affects.

Focusing on information systems and their maintenance, in place of social structures in the traditional sense, permits a new level of analysis to be added to one of anthropology's most important traditional questions. Generally, we ask What is the nature of the reality surrounding the native, that influences or determines the character of his behavior? To answer this question, we attempt to "put ourselves in the native's shoes"—to look at society as a participant. Anthropological accounts attempt to describe what it is the native sees, and to say whatever can be said about its resemblance to what other natives in other societies see. The present analysis, however, forces us to take what I can only think of as a step backward, from the position of the native's shoes to the point where we see the native standing in them himself. The basic question we now ask is How does he come to believe that he knows it is there, how does he know others will share his beliefs? Information sources are a reality the native "sees," but they are also realities that exist in the context of a more inclusive system of usages and forces that maintain them. This broader system includes natives as living human beings with constant needs for cooperation and material support. Message sources are part of the human "tool kit," and exist in the context of human actions, purposes, abilities, and predilections.

Since there is at the moment no wide discussion explicitly directed toward the present view of theory or the present concept of an information source, it will be necessary to enter into a number of discussions of more specialized theoretical issues that are in, or that cover, areas now considered to be unrelated. With the partial exception of the division of labor, and the major exception of the analysis of behavior in chapter 9, the subject matter of each of the separate chapters has been the concern of distinct sets of scholars in specialized theoretical debates whose central issues have often been far afield from the present one and from each other. It will be necessary to separate the issues in these discussions in order to indicate the empirical and methodological support the present orientation has already found. While views that concur with the present theory are generally minority positions within the several relevant disciplines and subdisciplines, their findings taken together add up to a full-scale alternative theory of society and behavior. One reason for this is that dominant theories tend to replicate each other, but do not have an additive effect across the different subject matters. In some cases, as in kinship and political analysis, they reproduce in each area roughly the same range of analytical difficulties and problems. In other areas, notably in economics as compared with the dominant versions of social structural analysis, they generate sharply and irreconcilably opposed interpretations of behavior and what orders it.

Each substantive chapter that follows attempts to indicate the relationship of the present analysis to positions that have been developed within the social science disciplines or anthropological subdisciplines that have been chiefly concerned with its subject matter. In addition, the Appendix provides a general overview of the different threads within various subareas of anthropology that seem to lead to and tie in with the present theory taken as a whole. Although, again, this is no more than a sketch, anthropological readers may want to consult this section before proceeding into the body of the arguments. In reality, it would be impossible to detail all the influences and arguments that are relevant to the present scheme. To do so would take us to every major writer in almost every area of the discipline, and to writings in philosophy, history, and economics as well.

In the absence of an elaborate framework of comparative remarks, the organization of the chapters is intended to provide a frame of reference for readers to facilitate comparisons between chapters and comparisons of any chapter with other works in the general problem area. Chapters 3 through 7 each describe one message source, and indicate three most important things about it: the major elements that make it up, its relation to behavior, and the operational means by which it is to be observed. In chapters 3, 4, and 5, which deal with high-information sources, major subsections each describe one of the major elements along with its relation to behavior. In chapters 6, 7, and 8, which describe the highly organized, low-information sources that cannot be easily divided and that do not have such precise relations to action, major subheads describe first the source as a whole, and then its principal manifestations or uses in behavior. In each chapter, specification of the operations by which the analysis can be verified consists in specification of the relevant behaviors in terms that will permit any future scholar to find them or similar behaviors if they wish to undertake a similar study in the future. The summary section of each of these chapters provides a review of the description that points out the formal properties of message sources in terms of the basic theory. In addition, as these summaries proceed they provide progressively more comparisons of the sources to each other with respect both to form and to function, so that it is possible to obtain an overview of the argument by reading these sections in order. To save space while taking advantage of certain relevant areas of inquiry that have developed in different disciplines, each chapter also emphasizes one special aspect of information systems for special treatment: their organization, their relation to behavior, their relation to hypothetical "referents," and so forth.

Building on the descriptions of the several systems, and following from the summary comparisons of their organization, chapter 9 draws the several sources together into a coherent overview, and attempts to provide the outlines of their interrelationships. Since they are interrelated in individual behavior, and not in some "superorganic" universe, this necessarily involves presenting a schematic general analysis of ordered individual behavior and behavioral groupings. Finally, the concluding chapter returns to a wider perspective and sketches briefly the place of this scheme of social organization in our academic tradition.

The overall intent is to present the concepts and data in enough detail to indicate their utility and power in the different areas of inquiry that have too often and too long been regarded as separate, and also to present the material compactly enough to show the fundamental simplicity and power of the basic concepts.

Chapter II

The Village and Its Setting

*T*he content and structure of the several message sources in the village are influenced by several factors that derive from its location and its climatic patterns, although location and climate themselves are not message sources or discrete elements of such sources in their own right. They are not maintained by the actions of the villagers and do not, strictly speaking, provide structured choices for the villagers to make in their daily rounds of activities. Location and climate do, however, help provide the specific content of the message sources and affect their several structures and uses.

Location

Shahidpur is a relatively old and well-established village. It lies at approximately 76°20′ east longitude and 20°43′ north latitude, in the rich and densely populated east central portion of the Punjab plain. Its elevation is about nine hundred feet above sea level, and it lies at a distance of about fifteen miles from the nearest edge of the Himalayan mountain system. This location determines the village's local climate, its water table, and its access to communication networks, to government services, and to useful items of commerce produced in urban centers. It also determines the access of government and some commercial services to the village.

The Punjab plain abuts against the Himalayan mountain system, its north and northeast boundary. At the juncture of plain and mountain, the low and level alluvium, always below a thousand feet in elevation, gives way abruptly to a hill zone of high erosion, then to the mountains proper, whose first ridges are often over five thousand feet above sea level. They begin a wide belt of high broken country, which gains gradually in elevation until it forms a ridge of the Great Himalaya, many of whose peaks reach over twenty-five thousand feet. Behind them lies the Tibetan plateau, about 250 air miles north and northeast from the edge of the plain in Punjab.

The summer monsoon, a mass of moist air moving northwest from the Bay of Bengal, reaches Punjab after being deflected and concentrated by the Himalayas. This far from the sea, the rain precipitated by the cooling and rising of the air mass falls soonest, heaviest, and longest on the hills leading to the great ridge, and from them it nourishes the Ganges and Jumna, and the four rivers flowing into the Indus that give Punjab its name (from Persian *panj*, "five," and *ab*, "river"). It falls on the plains most heavily and early in proportion as they are close to the mountains and close to the point of origin of the winds, with the former distance becoming more critical as the latter increases. Since Punjab is over nine hundred miles from the Bay of Bengal, the proximity of the mountains is the most important influence on the local pattern of rainfall. Kangra Town in Kangra District, which lies within the first hills, receives an average of 59.37 inches of rainfall a year. Ambala, on the plain below these hills, receives 34.24, while Ferozepore, about eighty miles into the plains, receives an average of 14.56, according to official records. The average annual rainfall for the area of Shahidpur, in Rupar Tehsil of Ambala District, is 33.11 inches.

As distance from the mountains increases, and rainfall decreases, the surface water running from the mountains is collected into fewer and fewer major streams, the groundwater table goes down rapidly, and the proportion of years in which the monsoon is inadequate to sustain a crop increases. This means in part that as rainfall goes down, so also does the efficiency of wells as sources of irrigation, with the result that both the driest areas and the wet mountain tracts traditionally rely on rainfall farming and on canal systems, while farmers in central Punjab and similar areas in Uttar Pradesh use wells and the ubiquitous Persian wheel. This middle ground, from the line just far enough from the mountains to avoid erosion, to the line not too far for regular rainfall and a high water table, is the home of the great Indo-Gangetic cities, and of north India's principal farming communities—Muslim Jats, Sikh Jats (here translated as "Farmers"), Thakurs, and so forth. It is a tract of rich and densely populated land that extends outward from sixty to thirty miles from the mountains and runs parallel to them from Allahabad to Lahore. Shahidpur lies somewhere north of the center of this tract, in terms of distance from the mountains, and at a point where the tract enters the westward-sloping Indus system after leaving the area of the eastward-sloping Ganges drainage.

Communication Facilities

The favored zone that contains the major seats of civilization of north India also contains the traditional centers and routes of trade, as well as the modern Grand Trunk Road and major railways. It is, and has been, the zone where "civilization" is felt most strongly in the rural areas. Regular police surveillance, trade, and administration have been reflected in village life since ancient times. Accordingly, there can be no occasion to speak here of an "economic frontier" such as F. G. Bailey (1957) attempts to define in the Kond area to the south, no "rational" and mercantile system newly impinging on an old "traditional" structure of isolated villages. Nor does it make much sense to speak of distinct urban and rural traditions of religion or political thought or of a "great tradition" somehow independent of "little traditions," and vice versa. Although the villages have an ecological self-sufficiency, as villages have elsewhere, this does not keep their residents from being intimately involved in the political, social, and economic affairs that characterize this region as a whole. The villagers participate widely in many long-established regional systems of communication and in shared concerns and ideas.

Shahidpur is covered by radio from Indian and other stations, has daily mail service, and is within the reach of an active publishing industry in regional languages and English. All of these affect village activities. The highly organized, low-information systems of concepts current in the village are affected by the wide-reaching channels by which ideas and concepts enter the village. Both these systems and the loosely organized, high-information systems are directly affected by the communicative systems that facilitate physical movement of material goods and face-to-face contact between villagers and outside friends, businessmen, and officials. Roads are the chief "channels" of such latter communications, and distance is a major determinant of the usefulness of different communicative options. The most influential places, accordingly, are those that are nearest. With a few exceptions that will be noted as they become relevant, villagers conduct their trade and other business personally, at the closest possible points. For most purposes, these are the nearby villages and towns of Chamkaur, Rupar, Kurali, Morinda, Machli, Dinpur, and Samrala.

Chamkaur is a village of about a thousand people, almost due north of Shahidpur and about four to seven miles distant by road, depending on the route. It contains a higher secondary school, several large Sikh gurdwaras (*gurduārās*) (temples), and the headquarters of the Block Development Officer (BDO) who serves Shahidpur. This official accepts applications for agricultural development loans. These loans carry very low interest charges and can be applied to capital improvements such as digging wells and purchasing pumps. In addition, the BDO distributes certain fertilizers and, from time to time according to conditions, special feeds—such as chicken feed—which are also in high demand. Chamkaur can be reached in less than an hour by bicycle, and in four hours by oxcart.

Rupar is about fifteen miles northeast of Shahidpur, on the south bank of the Satluj River where it reaches the plain. It contains the headquarters of Shahidpur's tehsil, its immediate administrative subdivision of Ambala District. (See Potter 1964 for a general description of the administrative system.)

The tehsil headquarters keep and maintain the revenue records for the village and the tehsildar's court adjudicates disputes with respect to them. The revenue records are the only systematic official delineations of the landholdings of the villagers, and function like the deeds and titles in the Western system to certify legal ownership. They carry a presumption of truth in a court of law, and therefore can only be changed with duly established legal procedures. Their importance to the villagers cannot be overstated, and with it the importance of the offices and institutions that maintain them.

Rupar also houses a branch of the government-related Bank of India, to which payments must be brought on loans issued by the BDO. Finally, regular civil and criminal courts, now separate from the formerly monolithic revenue structure, are also established in

Rupar, and matters of concern to villagers in connection with revenue records not infrequently flow over into activities that come before these branches.

Because of its courts and offices, Rupar provides something of a battleground where villagers contend for control of land in the intense competition that is concomitant with its intense population pressure and high capitalization of land. Certain prominent villagers are well known in Rupar, and the principal officials in Rupar are known in the village. Although Rupar has a small *mandi* (*manDī*) or market square, where villagers occasionally trade, its importance in this respect is minor.

South of Rupar and almost due west of the village is Kurali, with a large *mandi*. It is here that most villagers market most of their crops, buy a few agricultural commodities, and buy and sell cattle. Kurali is a legally designated "market town," structurally different from a village. It is run by a legally constituted market committee, not a panchayat, and its activities center on the *mandi*. The shops of the jobbers who deal in grain and dominate the life of the town surround the *mandi*. Their houses are generally attached to their shops. Each farmer in Shahidpur generally deals with just one jobber in a long-term relationship. The farmer sells the jobber grain, and both borrows from the jobber and leaves money with him. The jobber is an important source of marketing information, telling farmers what to plant, and sending word when to bring specific commodities to market. As Darling noted some time ago (1947, p. 191), the houses of the jobbers are rather modest, as are the other aspects of their establishments. The farmers themselves, at least in Shahidpur, seem to value their jobbers' services. Although the interest jobbers charge is high by Western commercial standards, ranging upwards of 12 percent per year compounded annually, it must be noted that the interest jobbers pay to farmers and other depositors ranges from 7 to 9 percent per year compounded annually.

The Kurali cattle market is not based on the *mandi* system; it is organized through periodic fairs held in an open area nearby. Buyers and sellers gather for the occasion with whatever they wish to trade, and officials of the market committee and government attend to certify the records of the transactions.

Kurali is on both a rail line and a major motor road, running north to Hoshiarpur and south into Uttar Pradesh. Crops generally go out by the railroad. The metaled road affords the means for Muslim buyers of cattle, apparently connected with the meat and hide industry in Saharanpur, Uttar Pradesh, to herd cattle bought in Kurali to their destinations.

Morinda is east and slightly south of the village, about seven miles away by an asphalted road served by regular buses. It is a road transport center of some importance, and has a small *mandi* and numerous light industries and shops, beside the recently built government-owned sugar mill. The shops and light industries provide some cloth goods, tools, and hardware. The mill has had important effects on land prices, crop practices, and labor prices, which will be described.

The metaled road to Morinda passes through the neighboring village of Machli (a pseudonym) not far south of Shahidpur. The town of Samrala is about eight miles west of the bus stand on the same road, and provides a somewhat larger selection of shops for household and agricultural goods and hardware, more often visited than Morinda.

Machli itself adjoins a second small village called Dinpur (a pseudonym) that elects members to the same panchayat. Dinpur houses a higher secondary school that serves forty surrounding villages, including Shahidpur. The importance of the school in local religious and political affairs is already great, and its impact will be increasingly felt as more and more graduates take jobs in government service. It seems to draw local residents in this area into some kinds of political conflict with those of Chamkaur. Both schools are part of the well-developed educational system supported in part by the Sikh religious organization.

Among the roads villagers take to reach one or another of these towns are those associated with the canal system of the region. A minor of the Bhakra canal cuts through the village lands, and the road beside it links the village both to the Morinda-Chamkaur road at a point near Rupar, where the Bhakra mainline crosses the Sirhind Canal, and to the Morinda-Samrala road at a point between Machli and Samrala. Chamkaur and Rupar are connected to each other by the canal road on the bank of the Sirhind canal, taking off from headworks at Rupar. Although unpaved, these canal roads are all-weather

roads of superior quality. They are maintained by the canal department itself, whereas the usual roads between villages are maintained
only by the villagers whose lands they cross. It sometimes happens
that one village does not find it in its interest to maintain its section
of local road, and thus the utility of the road for heavy vehicles may
be lost for many. This happened, in fact, in the case of the road from
Shahidpur to the metaled road to Morinda and Samrala. The farmers
of Machli, on the metaled road, did not need to maintain the road
back through their lands toward Shahidpur. The result is that the
canal minor road provides the only means by which trucks, which
now bring bricks and similar heavy goods, can be brought in. The
village roads are narrow and susceptible to flooding, since they are
at field level. The canal roads, except along the minor channels, are
on the canal's raised banks.

Finally, the canals themselves are important both directly and
indirectly. They bring water directly to a portion of village lands,
and also affect the water table of the entire village and its region.
Even though they are of recent introduction, they, like the other facilities of the region, are woven into the distinctive fabrics of several
village information sources.

Climate

The influences of the place of the village in its socioeconomic
setting merge with the influences of its climatic setting. The monsoon
wind that brings the annual rains is part of an extremely regular and
predictable annual time-table of climatic events. There is practically
no day-to-day "weather" in a European or American sense. Variation
consists chiefly in year-to-year differences in the "strength" of the
monsoons, in the total amounts of water that fall, rather than in its
overall temporal distribution.

The principal native calendar (*vikram* calendar) divides the
year into twelve months, beginning in mid-April. These are grouped
by villagers around Shahidpur into six seasonal phases of two months
each; their names, and principal characteristics, can be translated as
summer, rains, cold, rains, fall, and spring. The "summer" and "cold"
seasons are dry periods, and come before the onset of the summer
and winter monsoon rains, respectively. Of the rainy seasons, the
greatest portion of the local average of 33.11 inches annually falls

in the summer monsoon—about 25 inches between June and September, with 10 inches concentrated in July. The winter rainy period is both less intense and less concentrated, with February the wettest month at 2 inches, and about 6 inches the total average rainfall for the general period of October to May. Annual temperatures reach a peak in the "summer," just before the rains, and may be about 105°–115°F in the shade. The annual lows are reached in midwinter, in the rainy season, and run about 70°–80°F during the day.

Farmers have adapted to the cycle of the rainy periods and dry periods in their selection of crops and practices of planting, harvesting, storage, and transporting. All crops have to be harvested in dry weather, and have to get rain at some critical but variable point or points in their growth cycle. The growth cycles themselves differ in length. Each crop grown has to be planted at such a time in advance of the expected rains that the water will come neither too soon nor too late for its particular needs.

The different conditions created during the annual sequence of climatic changes provide many opportunities for the intensive multiple cropping that has evolved as an integral part of the village social and economic system in Shahidpur and in similar villages all throughout north India. Tropical, subtropical, and temperate crops, together with arid-land crops and crops requiring large amounts of water, are all worked into the overall annual cycle at some point. Fallowing, in the densely populated zone, is seldom used. Two crops a year are the general rule, although some land is devoted to perennials, principally sugarcane, while three crops or more are grown in a few cases. This particular mode of adaptation to the climate and setting results in a very efficient use of land and human labor, and it naturally has certain attendant costs.

Conclusion

It may add precision to the concept of a message source to note that there is no suggestion that location and climate, which are not sources, are therefore not consciously before the villagers or do not affect their conscious decisions in some way.

Villagers are well aware of the effect of their location, and not infrequently elect to leave the village in response to this awareness, as will be described. Similarly, they are well aware of the distances to markets, and act in accordance with their knowledge. The point is rather that location, for all this, is not an "ensemble" that has entropy (or "information") and that it is therefore most strongly not an organized system of elements that call for differentiated action and that in turn reflect actions. Although it is true that if one goes to Rupar one doesn't go to Kurali, the choice that villagers actually make is in terms not so much of the relative *location* of these two places as such as their relative *significance* in the context of local ecological, economic, or other systems of benefits and needs. The effects of location on decisions are not free or "direct" effects. They are, rather, mediated or contextual. Villagers who migrate out to buy land elsewhere, for example, leave the village not because its location places it with a zone of intensive agriculture and high populations but because these conditions within the economic system provide certain advantages that can be exploited by selling out and moving to a less intensively developed area where money can be reinvested more profitably under certain circumstances. The key to the reasoning to move in such a case is thus the economic notion of differential profit rather than location per se. In other contexts, or rather in the context of other message sources, other elements would activate the decision.

Chapter III

The Village Ecology

*T*he concept of "information" does not replace our established understanding of ecology, but rather adds precision to it and avoids certain confusions. An ecology is commonly considered to be a system of homeostatic relationships between biological populations and nonliving objects in an environment. The additional concept of information—specifically of high information—adds precision to this definition by providing a consistent focus on the exact ways in which humans respond to and influence these relationships.

Any species, individual, or group of biological organisms can be described as the focus of a system of homeostatic interrelationships of populations they depend on and affect. For plants and very simple animals, relationships with and among surrounding organisms and the overall environment can be accounted for mechanistically. Each population can be seen to have chemical and mechanical effects on the others, and their numbers can be seen to interact and balance out through these effects. Too many of any one functionally related population will have one direct effect, too few, another.

As we move to animals of more complex biological and social organization, mechanistic explanations become increasingly insufficient. More and more actions are triggered by social and symbolic stimuli, and produce results at increasingly remote points of time by more and more indirect means. Mechanistic explanations come to refer only to remote possibilities that the triggered actions either forestall or ultimately create. These possibilities are cast in increasingly larger temporal frameworks.

Generally speaking, the expansion of time perspective and of responsiveness to remote or contingent events seems to be proportional to the expansion of symbolic intervention in natural processes. In this respect, humans appear to be at one extreme of a natural continuum. They show maximum responses to symbolic stimuli and maximum expansion of the time perspective within which actions and their causes and results are related. It is in this sense that human ecologies, as Julian Steward (1955), Clifford Geertz (1966), and others have stressed, are characteristically *cultural* ecologies. To those who initiate action within them, they have a pervasive conventional and symbolic character, bound up with complex language usage as well as with a degree of systematic manufacture of tools to produce tools, that is lacking in the ecologies of nonhumans.

The concept of information characterizes the precise way in which human ecologies inherently involve systems of conventional restraints laid upon the physical elements that humans react with, and the way that humans in turn actively place their own constraints on the purely biochemical and mechanical aspects of surrounding biological populations and physical objects. Humans—including the villagers of Shahidpur—lard their environment with symbols for what they find. But they also selectively encourage some elements in their surroundings to flourish, and discourage others. They select, import, and protect ecologically related species, and even create them, on a scale unknown elsewhere in nature. Even the "hardest" objects in the ecological system of a village like Shahidpur are as conventional and cultural as the most abstract terms that "refer" to them or otherwise direct differentiated behaviors. Each object, physical or conceptual, in the village ecology is a repository of information in the specific sense that it presents or connotes a set of choices of effective behaviors. Each differentiated element represents a set of differentiated actions: the past actions that have created it, and the future actions of similar character that will maintain it. These actions are known and are necessarily tied to, or are represented by, other objects that are "symbolic" in more usual senses: there are special words that are used to refer to the ecologically significant objects, rules for their use, tools made to aid in their exploitation and traditions of lore and art that are handed down among those who maintain and depend on the system.

In the context of the ecology, "knowledge" of the season, of its importance for different crops and actions, moves people to behave in certain ways just as direct effects of cold, heat, scarcity, or abundance move simpler nonhumans to behave. Villagers react not so much to what *does* happen as to the *significance* of what happens or could happen. In this sense, they approach the entire ecology as a system of symbols. The villagers' own actions directed toward the ecology are "symbolic" in precisely the same sense—their significance lies not only in their direct results but in remote consequences that those who perform them expect in terms of their own verbalized and experiential knowledge. Biochemical and mechanistic laws and forces serve as sanctions, as threats behind the demands for certain actions, precisely parallel to sanctions that lie behind other symbolic systems that demand conventionalized responses. Such sanctions can be applied without human agency in the event of the "wrong" response to what is expected. A mismanaged crop will fail; a mistreated cow may die. If the conventionalized actions were consistently inappropriate to the conventional human ecology, or if they were appropriate but did not occur, the ecology would deteriorate. Ultimately, as Steward noted, it could deteriorate to a point where the human population itself was reduced. This ultimate sanction seldom comes into play directly, mainly because there are other information systems that establish competitive relationships among the people within the community, through which ecologically ineffective individuals are forced out or effective people are encouraged to enter the system. In effect, these systems set up mechanisms whereby the sanctions of the ecological system can be applied selectively, and thereby forestall their being felt generally.

This chapter describes the major populations that subsist in Shahidpur as components in a message source of high information, or entropy, in terms of Weaver's definitions. Since Shahidpur is primarily an agricultural village, I will concern myself primarily with agriculture—the agriculture, in general outlines, as practiced and described by the more successful farmers of the village.

The large groups of biological entities on which Shahidpur depends are crops, cattle, and men. Besides them, it is convenient to regard the ecology as containing developed nonbiological resources that they closely depend on and that in turn closely reflect their peculiar needs: the developed water supply and the farmland of the village. To say specifically that the village ecology is a source of "high" information, or low organization, means that the choices structured by one element do not bear a direct or rigid relationship to the actions in response to other elements in the system. The way that laws of biological relationship and growth, among the more rigid we know, can give rise to a system providing free choice among structured options will be discussed in context.

Developed Water Supply

Figure 1 shows the general plan of the village area, with its populated area, agricultural area, and principal roads and irrigation sources.

Although canals and wells are not biological objects, all the village populations respond to them and they (unlike rain) respond to the populations. The land-revenue record compiled for the village in 1956 (current through the time of the present study) listed 69 percent of the total 440 acres of agricultural land as either well irrigated, or well and canal irrigated. An additional 11 percent was watered by canal alone. At the time there were twenty-two wells in the village. By 1965, the time of the present study, three new wells had been built, one with a diesel pump, bringing the total proportion of land irrigated to at least 80 percent.

The water from all the wells (with the exception of the one with the diesel pump) is lifted by Persian wheels turned by draft animals. Eighteen of the wells have one wheel, three have two.

Since there is no effective bedrock beneath Shahidpur (a characteristic of the Indo-Gangetic plain) the water level in the wells responds closely to local conditions of rainfall and to canals. The table now stands at about twenty feet, having risen from thirty following completion of the canals in the area. This follows what is apparently a common pattern, attributable to percolation from the canal main branches and minors (Prashar 1965, p. 8). The major channel of the Bhakra main line near the village is paved only with a rather porous brick, while the minor channels are not paved at all.

The village canal minor is part of the perennial flow portion of the Bhakra canal system (southern branch), and contains water all year except when it is under repair. Its raised channel produces a

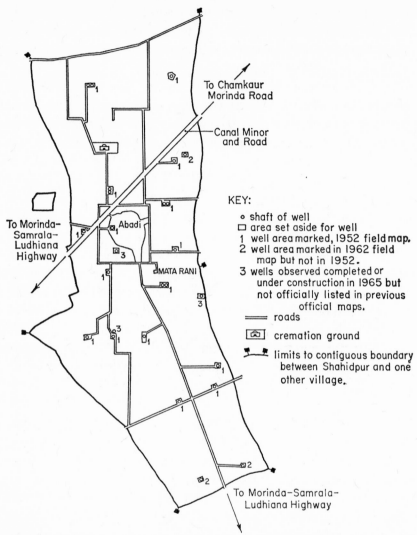

Figure 1. Village area showing wells, roads, and public lands.

strong flow of water in the fields, which can be tapped without limit by the farmers, who pay a flat fee based on acreage and land productivity rather than a rate on volume of water as such. Canal water differs from that of wells in that it requires no draft power.

Domestic water for the houses in the village is now generally supplied by hand pumps in the household compounds. Families still lacking such pumps draw water from one of two public wells in the central populated area, which is called the *abadi* (*abādī*). The water level lies about forty feet from the lip of the higher well, indicating that the village mound is raised twenty feet above the level of the fields. Most of the house pumps are driven down as deep as possible to assure the cleanest water possible.

There are several tanks (ponds) in the populated area. They are now used only for washing buffaloes in the rainy seasons, when the water is relatively clean. At other times, the canals are now used for this purpose. The few fish, ducks, and turtles in the ponds are not ecologically important.

Land and Soil

The ecological effects of the climatic cycle and water supply take form in relation to the village soils and land form.

The village soil is a uniform, brown clay-loam, completely free of rocks or stones, which farmers report to extend down fifteen to twenty feet before water-bearing sand is encountered. Through use, it has been made level, and because of the farming practices it is also free of organic matter.

The clay content of the soil, which is so high that water jars and pots can be made from it, makes it relatively impermeable when wet, so that in a rain or during irrigation, water quickly collects on the soil surface and sinks in slowly. Such land is susceptible to local flooding, and flooding can itself damage some crops at some stages of growth. Further, the soil has very little strength when it is wet, therefore shallow roots, such as those of wheat, can easily lose purchase, allowing the plants to fall and lodge in the ground. Finally, as it dries this soil loses the open structure obtained in plowing and hardens into a compact mass, generally in the form of a surface layer two to five inches thick. This makes it still more susceptible to subsequent flooding. In addition, the surface thus formed is too hard for young plants of certain species, particularly wheat, to break, and it chokes off their growth. On balance, however, it must be added that such soil is easy to work, retains moisture well, and is well adapted to accepting the wide variety of village plants and fertilizers. The special features of the soil are taken into account by farmers in timing, planting, and watering, and they are reflected in the village tenure system and technology. For example, tenancy arrangement includes provision for immediate inputs of fertilizers; and the light, shallow,

double-edge plow is easily guided with one hand in the dry clay,
throws up a low furrow suitable to the pan-type flood irrigation that
is used, runs deep enough to cut the surface hardpan, and yet does
minimal damage to the natural soil structure below it.

Crops

The character of the village ecology as a message source is most
apparent from the perspective of its crops. Villagers respond to the
"information" of their water sources, energy supplies, and land types
by allocating their crops to these more durable portions of the overall
system. Then they respond to the crops by deciding on the allocations
of their own time and resources to them, in performing the operations they require. The outcomes of these latter actions, in the form
of good or bad harvests, are thus the product of several levels of
response, and they provide in turn the resources that develop or
maintain the system as a whole. At the same time, even while crops
are enabling the ecology as a whole to go through its cycles of con-
straining and reflecting action, the individual crops themselves are
being cycled in the same way. Each time a farmer harvests a crop
he modifies the population it represents by acquiring new experience
and by selecting, often deliberately and carefully, his seed for the
next cycle.

The overall pattern of interaction of each crop with all other
elements of the ecology is too complex to be analyzed and summarized by present means. It is easy, however, to describe the general
features of the individual crops that farmers take into account in
producing the pattern.

Crops are grown the year round. Most of them are worked into
either a summer array of fast-growing hot weather crops or a winter
array suited to the longer, milder, and drier season from October to
April. The first group is called kharif (*kharīf*) crops. The second
array, harvested in the April–May season, are rabi (*rābī*) crops. A
few crops, among them the important sugarcane, do not fit precisely
into either category. Some condiments and vegetables are grown for
more rapid harvest; cane is harvested all through the winter slack
season for three winters after each planting.

Tables 1 and 2 estimate the average amounts of land devoted
to each summer and winter crop, respectively. As a practical matter,

I was unable to measure crop patterns directly in the field because of the lack of equipment and because of the way such activity would have been interpreted in the village context (where the only similar activity was for purposes of taxation). The estimates of the pattern of crop acreage are based on figures collected by the Revenue Department for the Shaia Circle of Rupar Tehsil, the geographical tract of "good loam soil" that contains Shahidpur and approximately 170 similar villages (Caprihan 1962b). I discussed this report with its author, and am confident that his figures are superior to what I might have compiled myself. In addition, the figures accord with my own rough estimates based on photographic surveys and on proportions of the crops paced off along the roads of the village in the different seasons. Finally, farmers in the village repeatedly expressed the opinion that government figures on acreage may be considered reliable, although yield and location of specific farmers' plots are gen-

Table 1
KHARIF CROP PATTERN BY LAND TYPE

Crop	Well	Canal	Well-canal	Rainfall	Total all types
Maize	23.3	23.6	5.8	16.0	20.9
Mung and mash	2.1	3.6	0.4	2.6	2.3
Cane	38.4	16.2	71.5	7.6	30.9
Chilis	1.4	—	0.5	—	1.0
Fodder	4.3	17.9	2.4	41.5	12.4
Cotton (desi)	10.1	7.6	13.0	1.5	8.3
Cotton (American)	10.7	16.3	2.9	3.7	9.4
Other	8.8	14.4	3.3	23.4	14.2
Failed	0.9	0.4	0.2	3.7	1.6
	100.0	100.0	100.0	100.0	100.0
Area of each land type as percentage of total area sown	67.5	10.0	3.9	18.6	100.0

SOURCE: These figures represent a ten-year projection of average crop patterns for Shahidpur, based on proportions of land of each different water supply type as recorded in the village Land Revenue Record effective for the period 1952–1962, taken together with crop patterns for each land type as recorded for the sub-tehsil geographical tract surrounding Shahidpur, with similar soils and water supply situations, as recorded in the *Statements Relating to the Assessment Report of Rupar Tehsil* for 1962 (Caprihan 1962b).

erally misrepresented. The only necessary corrections, which will be noted in the text, pertain to some local practices stemming from the atypically high proportion of irrigated land in Shahidpur, attributable to its greater age than is usual in the area.

Table 1 shows the proportion of each category of land devoted to each kharif crop, and the proportion of total acreage devoted to each crop. The calculations were based on four hundred acres as an average amount of land cultivated.

The amounts and distributions of crops reflect multiple considerations, and clearly illustrate the way seemingly determinate and invariant biological relationships give rise to a structure that meets the definition of a high entropy message source. The biological needs of each type of plant can be met in a range of ways, depending on human ingenuity, often with a variety of outcomes. Conversely, the products of each plant can be utilized in a range of ways, depending on the farmer's other resources and needs. In the end, biological law provides parameters along which alternative choices are differentiated, but not the differentiations themselves.

Maize

Maize is an excellent example of the relationship between biological regularity and high information value. The variety grown in the village is a stable race (not a hybrid) similar to American field corn, hardy and drought resistant. Its grains dry without shriveling, and are hard enough to pop when heated in hot sand (a winter treat sold in towns and at fairs). Each year, farmers select their biggest and best ears for seed for the next year's crop.

Flour made of maize is preferred over wheat for breads eaten in the winter. Dried cobs are stored whole until needed, and then are shucked and ground in small batches. The stalks and leaves are a major source of fodder, high in sugar and easy to store for use in the winter when the wheat crop—the source of the dried fodder most used in summer—is still growing. No part of the plant is wasted—even the roots are used for fuel. The market price for maize is often much higher than that for wheat.

While this maize responds well to variations in inputs of fertilizers and water, the yields in grain vary more widely than the yield in stems and leaves. Conditions that would increase roughage by 50 percent increase grain by much more, while conditions that would reduce roughage somewhat would reduce seed more than proportionally. On the average, villagers expect one ear of grain for every three plants standing in the field. Under better conditions, this would be expected easily to go up to one per plant, but without a corresponding trebling of the total outrun. Under bad conditions, grain yield would be expected to drop to one ear in six plants. All these characteristics of the plant affect the way it is cropped.

Given the utility of both fodder and grain, the properties of the plant present a continuum of possible cropping strategies between two extremes. On the one hand, by dense planting and minimized inputs of labor and fertilizer, a reliable high-yielding fodder crop can be produced that also provides a "bonus" of edible grain with good storage properties, in at least some amount, and possibly in a fairly high amount. On the other hand, by more open planting and more intensive inputs of labor, water, and fertilizer, a valuable grain crop can be produced, although the fodder component is more costly.

Whether a farmer chooses one extreme strategy or the other, or some compromise, depends on both his needs and his resources. If he has cattle to feed, and is short of labor or of cash for fertilizer, he will obviously choose the fodder-producing strategy, either deliberately or by default. If his fodder needs are otherwise met or nearly met, and he has cash or labor on hand, he can make the choice that will turn a very likely profit in the market. And if his needs and resources are somewhere between, he might compromise at a level of input he can afford, in terms of cash or fertilizer or water or the particular piece of land on which maize is planted. (In a few cases, farmers who have elected the high-cost grain-raising policy have changed from local seed to newer varieties, purchased outside, that respond somewhat more to the increased inputs.)

The high proportion of the total land devoted to maize, 21.3 percent, indicates the importance of all of its products, its hardiness, and its ability to be used in multiple ecological strategies. Its distribution over all types of land also indicates, to some extent, the utilization of the full range of cropping possibilities that it presents. Rainfall land is always used for production primarily oriented toward fodder. The other categories of land produce fodder or grain, depending primarily on water and fertilizer inputs. The farmer who used the new varieties in pursuing an intensive grain-yielding strategy, for example, used well land. Others reportedly pursued similar policies, but most land, including most or all canal land, was apparently devoted to compromise strategies.

Whatever the strategy, the cultivation itself has certain general features. Since the plant is not as sensitive to deficiencies of moisture as most other kharif crops, sowing is spaced out over much of the early summer months. The most critical time in the growth cycle of maize is at the time of tasseling. This is its period of greatest vegetative growth, when good supplies of water are essential. Once the crop is mature, harvesting, like sowing, is leisurely. The usual practice is to tie groups of standing stalks in bundles and let them dry in the fields while other crops are being harvested, then to take them in as time permits, using family help as much as possible to avoid the higher costs of labor hired at day rates.

Finally, the variability of the yield in grain has an effect on the growth and use of wheat. Because of it, farmers plan the wheat crop so that an entire year's supply can be set aside for their household at the time of harvest. This is held, whatever else may be sold, until the maize is completely harvested. Only then (and depending of course on prices) will farmers release the amount of wheat equal to the amount of maize obtained. The various strategies and practices pertaining to maize are now so highly interrelated with other systemic considerations that it is difficult for many farmers to believe that it is an import from the New World and not an indigenous Indian crop.

Similar interactions, similarly based on the botanical characteristics of the plants in the village setting, affect other crops.

Mung (*Phaseolus mungo L.*) and mash (*Phaseolus radiatus*), pulses, are small beans similar in size and shape to lentils. The beans are eaten in the form of a thick soup called *dal* (*dāl*), while the greens provide a high-protein element in fodder. The nitrogen-fixing ability of these and other legumes is recognized in the pattern of rotation, which frequently sees them planted before wheat or other grains on good quality land. Mung is also quite drought resistant. All these properties apparently are reflected in the rather even distribution over the different categories of land.

Sugarcane

Sugarcane is an unusual crop in several respects: it is a perennial; it produces no appreciable amount of fodder; it requires an unusual amount of labor per unit of land; it requires large amounts of fertilizer and water; it is not harvested at the usual time or in a usual manner; it is subject to direct government control; and, since November 1964, it is by far the most profitable crop. Cane seed is sown early in the hot season, before the spring harvest is completed. The plants grow rapidly in the hot summer months, and become dormant when the weather cools with the onset of the winter monsoon. All during the winter cane is cut and its stalks are processed or taken to market. One field is generally cut back three times before the roots are pulled out and a new field reseeded on new land. Because of this pattern, there is no need to plant sugarcane on the canal land, whose advantage is felt in the drier winter months. But because it produces no appreciable fodder, its energy requirement must be "paid" for by planting intensive fodder crops alongside it. Maize is one such crop, and various sorghums and green fodder are the others. The great cash value of the cane, along with cotton, provides the rationale for using more costly canal irrigated land for the seemingly "unprofitable" fodder than for any other crop, as shown in table 1. Cane also provides two essential elements of human diet, sugar and iron, neither of which is obtained in appreciable amounts by any other means. Raw sugar in various forms is eaten in large quantities. Cane leaves are used as fiber in making coarse ropes, and the squeezed-out stems are stacked for use as fuel in boiling down the following year's green crop.

Government involvement in sugar production, as part of its effort to develop more favorable patterns of international trade, is interesting and relevant because it led to one of the few clear instances during the period of study wherein villagers' ecological and economic interests were directly challenged.

The state government has the power to designate a specific area around a sugar mill as an official "mill area." All farmers within such an area can be compelled to sell cane only to that mill instead of following their usual practice of refining it to one of several forms and selling it on the open market. The government also sets the price that the mill will pay. In the beginning of the cutting season of 1964, the government cane price was far below the amount that would have been returned, per acre, if the cane were sold at market prices. Since farmers had no alternative use for the labor they would normally apply to processing cane, the price was unacceptable. A "strike" was therefore organized in the mill area that Shahidpur belongs to, the purpose of which was to boycott the mill. (A description of the strike is given on p. 117.) The upshot of the action was a new price so high that it spurred acquisition of land for cane growing and increased the demand for fertilizer and for all classes of land in order to accommodate the resulting squeeze on fodder and foodstuffs.

Chilis, like maize, are so integral to the modern Indian culinary tradition that it is difficult (particularly for many who grow them) to believe that they are imports from the New World. Although villagers say that chilis are only for "flavor," they provide the chief source of vitamins A and C in the diet, and have a high mineral content, all of great importance in the context of a near absence of fresh fruits and of the avoidance of raw vegetables. One hundred grams of dried red chilis contains, in part, 77,000 USP units of vitamin A, 154 mg of vitamin C, 240 mg of phosphorus, and 1,201 mg of potassium (Watt and Merrill, U.S.D.A. 1963, p. 44). The recommended adult minimum daily intakes of vitamins A and C are 4,000 units and 30 mg, respectively. The distribution over land types in the table reflects the general practice of growing them along with onions and potatoes and other condiments, in rich garden plots generally near wells.

"Fodder" in the summer array consists primarily in sorghum millet. As indicated in the table, it is often grown intensively on canal land because well irrigated land is used by valuable crops that do not pay their own way in terms of feed for the animals that provide the draft power and the milk supply of farm families. And since it is drought resistant, it can also be reliably grown on rainfall land.

Cotton

Cotton is the principal light-fiber crop and a major source of cash income. Although nearly all the clothing used in the village is now made of commercial cloth, many other products are still made almost exclusively of local cotton, including strings, nets, beds, the stuffing of quilts, cloaks and blankets, ropes, and many small items. A spinning wheel is part of every dowry, and using it is a common spare-time occupation. I never walked through the village, as I recall, without seeing at least one woman, in a doorway or a courtyard, making thread or twine. Farmers pick the best bolls in the quantities they need, principally for seed for the next crop, and have them ginned locally, keeping the fiber as well as seed. The dry stalks of the plant are occasionally used in gardening, but their main use is for fuel for cooking, along with the roots that are picked out of the soil when it is plowed in preparation for the winter crop. The largest part of the crop is now sold for cash, although it is not marketed through the *mandi* in the usual way. It is sold in boll form, without ginning, to itinerant jobbers that visit the village each fall.

Cotton, like cane, produces no fodder and has to be supported with intensive fodder crops. Cotton is a demanding crop that requires fertile soil and attentive care. It is unusually sensitive to heat and to improper timing and amounts of water, particularly to rain when the bolls are beginning to dry and open (Tharp, U.S.D.A. 1965). Since these factors are to a large extent beyond human control, two varieties are grown, in about equal areas, as the table indicates. Each flourishes under conditions that harm the other, so at least one crop is assured. The native, or desi, cotton grown on well and well-canal land, succeeds in drier weather and matures faster; the "American" cotton, grown on well and canal land, flourishes with more water and matures later. In a heavy monsoon, the American cotton benefits, while the desi may be destroyed by rains that continue while the bolls open. Conversely, the desi cotton does better in a light monsoon, which terminates sooner.

The ecological relevance of the "other" crops is self-evident, since they all serve special local needs. They include hemp, grown for coarse fiber processed locally, as well as garden crops already alluded to, such as onions, garlic, carrots, and a few table vegetables. Some native tobacco is also grown, and some special-purpose medical or fodder plants, such as a special pulse with a very small seed that is said to be essential for camels.

The rabi crop pattern (table 2) is basically similar to the kharif pattern in its primary orientation toward local needs, and in the thoroughness with which its different components are utilized.

Table 2
RABI CROP PATTERN BY LAND TYPE

Crop	Well	Canal	Well-canal	Rainfall	Total all types
			Land Types		
Wheat	38.2	32.3	41.5	9.4	31.4
Barley	0.1	2.5	—	0.8	0.9
Gram (chick-pea)	1.4	10.2	—	32.7	8.1
Wheat and gram	33.5	43.5	48.8	41.5	36.8
Barley and gram	0.8	0.9	—	2.8	1.2
Oilseeds	2.5	—	2.4	3.3	2.4
Fodder	20.3	9.3	4.8	.6	15.1
Lentils	0.4	0.4	—	2.0	0.7
Other	2.5	—	—	2.0	2.1
Failed	0.3	0.9	2.4	4.9	1.3
	100.0	100.0	100.0	100.0	100.0
Area of each land type as percentage of total area sown	61.8	11.8	4.4	22.0	100.00

SOURCE: Same as for table 1.
NOTE: The total area sown in kharif crops is less than the amount sown in rabi crops by the proportion of total crop land sown in cane, which is perennial.

Wheat

The relationship between wheat and wheat mixed with gram (chick-peas) in the table does not apply exactly to the practices in Shahidpur. Wheat in the village is now almost never mixed with gram, probably because of the dense planting permitted by the assured water supply and intensive fertilization. Harvesting would be much more difficult with a mixture of crops. Since young wheat plants can be killed by soil that hardens after being wetted, sowing is done as early as possible, well before the rains. Ground preparation for the crop begins long before all the rabi crops are harvested. The crop can be sown densely, and responds well to intensive watering and fertilizer action.

Wheat is the principal grain in the human diet, a major market crop, and the main source of dry fodder used over the time that the rabi crop is growing. The total acreage devoted to it is about one-half the available winter land—about two hundred acres. It is eaten as a soft, pan-baked, unleavened bread called a *roti*, which is like a tortilla. It is one of the few grains with well-defined significance in religious rituals.

Barley is fairly drought-resistant and is grown mainly as a fodder. As the table indicates, it is most commonly grown in drier fields and is mixed with gram. The rationale for this practice involves both the ideas of drought insurance in the cotton strategy and the ideas in crop rotation. Gram is more drought resistant than barley, and will survive even if the barley will not. If, on the other hand, there is adequate water, the barley will benefit. On the second point, two very good farmers both insisted that barley grown with gram did not do less well than barley or gram alone, despite occasional government efforts to discourage the practice. Their view is supported by recent controlled experiments comparing wheat and gram grown singly and together under rainfall conditions. A five-year study showed a significantly higher return to the mixed crop (Dayal, Singh, and Sharma 1967). In contrast with wheat, barley is planted openly enough so that intercropping with gram does not increase the difficulty of harvest.

Gram (called *chōle* locally) was not grown as extensively in Shahidpur as the table indicates, at least during my visit, and lentils were grown more extensively. Gram is marketed and is a major item of diet, both as a *dal* and as a flour, but it was a distant second to mung, mash, and lentils in the many meals I saw in the village. It is nitrogen fixing and is rotated with grains and fibers. The beans are high in protein. They contain 20.5 grams of protein per 100 grams of dry weight, as compared, for example, with 34.1/100 gms for soybeans and 14.8/100 for beef, according to studies of the United States Department of Agriculture (Watt and Merrill 1963).

Oilseeds involve two crops: mustard and sesamum. In both cases, oil is just one of the products obtained. Mustard is the more important crop and provides a principal dietary staple in the winter season. Women pick the young leaves of the growing crop each day or so as needed. At the end of the growing season the plants are cut up and pressed for oil. The oil is used for cooking and as medicine and is sold on the market. The plant residues are used as fodder. These oils are the principal source of fat, along with milk products and commercially available hydrolyzed vegetable oils. Sesamum is treated much the same way, except that the separated seeds are used for the preparation of a number of confections and form an item of commerce in their own right. Mustard is often intercropped with a low-growing clover called *barsheen* (*barshīn*), which continues to grow after the mustard is cut off.

Lentils, as noted above, are an important *dal* crop eaten in both seasons. With 24.7 grams per hundred of protein, lentils are the most concentrated available protein source, slightly richer than mung (24.2 grams per hundred). With mung and mash, they are the principal source of protein in the diet. In Shahidpur, in apparent contrast with the general practice in the tract (probably because of the greater fertility of the land), lentils are commonly grown on good quality well or canal irrigated land, and are rotated with cane or cotton.

The crops of each array interact with crops in the other through the pattern of rotation, and they interact with those in their own (and the other) array in the way they meet complementary human, animal, and other needs. All the parts of every crop are useful, and at least one part of every crop is essential. Each one supplies a product— sometimes several—that would have to be brought in from outside if it were not produced locally.

But while the properties of each part of the food crops grown correspond in kind to local human and animal needs, their relative amounts do not correspond equally to the intensities of those needs. This is an essential element in the structure of the message source as one of high entropy and low organization. To pretend that all elements in the ecology are equally essential to the system as a whole would be to overstate its integration and to mistake the amount of calculated human intervention perpetually required to maintain it. An important version of such an overstructured view of the ecology has already appeared, implicitly, in anthropological views of the practice of trade within the framework of a larger society that is a more or less constant feature of peasant productive systems. In Shahidpur, as elsewhere, some grains, cotton, and sugar are regularly marketed outside the village, and must therefore be presumed to be not essential for maintenance of the local ecology. Such marketable portions of crops have often been viewed as a "surplus," an additional increment to production induced or extracted by outside pressures (Wolf, 1966, p. 17). This suggests that without such intervention the village ecology would be entirely self-regulating and self-contained, and this, in turn, fails to recognize the full array of choices the system presents, as well as the strong possibility that outside "forces"— urban-based powers—are as much a product of village "surpluses" as the reverse. In fact, the mechanism that leads to a large part of the export of products from Shahidpur is internal to the village ecology. It can best be seen by noting more carefully the relationship between crops and cattle, and human populations.

Village Cattle

Except for dogs, which are generally not cared for systematically, all the animals of the village come under the meaning of the Punjabi term *dangar*, translated as "cattle." Their kinds and numbers as recorded in a house-to-house census are summarized in table 3. The profile of the population indicates a "cultivation" of cattle comparable to that of the village crops. Table 4 shows the ratios of cattle per capita for each caste group in the village and indicates thereby some major aspects of the cattle distribution in relation to patterns of action. (In these tables a "caste" is a group of individuals who claim to be related and to have real occupational features in common, but who are not necessarily "castes" in the sense of groups that conform to the established stereotypes that are related in chapter 7.) Since the terminology, as well as the animals, may be unfamiliar, it is best to proceed again item by item, beginning with what are called bullocks.

The term *bullock* translates the Punjabi term *bāld*, and specifically designates a castrated male of the same species of large white ox whose female is the "sacred cow" of India. There are no uncastrated males in the village. Bullocks are specifically draft animals. Bulls are used only for stud. The practice is for an occasional farmer who has a male calf that is prevented from working because of injury (generally a broken leg) to release him to wander freely, presumably to eat and cover cows proportionally as he moves from area to area, wherever he is not driven off.

The distribution of bullock ownership follows the distribution of land. Farmers (81 bullocks, .21 per capita) are the principal land-

Table 3
COMPLETE CATTLE CENSUS BY CASTE OF HOUSEHOLD

	Br	Fa	Ma	Go	Ba	Po	Wa	Co	Ha	Sw	Sa	
Total Cattle	4	260	11	4	3	52	1	12	69	29	13	458
Bullocks	—	81	—	—	—	—	—	—	—	—	6	87
Cows	—	10	1	—	—	4	—	—	2	1	—	18
Ox-calves	—	9	1	—	—	—	—	1	1	—	—	12
Cow-calves	—	2	1	—	—	1	—	—	1	—	—	5
Cow buffaloes	2	96	5	—	2	9	—	—	35	1	4	154
Male buffalo calves	—	2	2	—	—	1	—	—	1	—	—	6
Cow buffalo calves	1	31	1	—	—	5	—	—	13	4	2	57
Rams	1	—	—	—	—	—	—	1	—	—	—	2
Goats	—	7	—	2	1	4	1	10	10	10	—	45
Kids	—	7	—	2	—	1	—	—	5	—	—	15
Mules	—	—	—	—	—	25	—	—	—	—	—	25
Donkeys	—	—	—	—	—	2	—	—	1	—	—	3
Camels	—	15	—	—	—	—	—	—	—	—	1	16
Pigs	—	—	—	—	—	—	—	—	—	13	—	13

Table 4
MAJOR CATTLE PER CAPITA IN EACH CASTE

	Br	Fa	Ma	Go	Ba	Po	Wa	Co	Ha	Sw	Sa
Total Cattle Per Capita	.25	.7	.26	.25	.38	.67	.5	1.2	.28	.61	1.3
Bullocks	—	.208	—	—	—	—	—	—	—	—	.6
Cows	—	.02	.02	—	—	.05	—	—	.08	.02	—
Cow buffaloes	.8	.25	.16	—	.25	.11	—	—	.14	.02	.4
Camels	—	.04	—	—	—	—	—	—	—	—	.1

NOTE:
Br = Brahmin
Fa = Farmer
Ma = Mason
Go = Goldsmith
Ba = Barber
Po = Potter
Wa = Water-carrier
Co = Cotton-ginner
Ha = Harijan
Sw = Sweeper
Sa = Sadhu

owning caste, and own all the large farms. Sadhus (6 bullocks, .6 per capita) are one family associated with a village guest house, or dharmsala (*dharmsālā*). It is operated for the benefit of an order of mendicants, and holds lands donated to it by the villagers—nearly 24 acres. The overall ratio of teams of bullocks, or "plows," to land is about one to 10 acres—very near the average of one team per 9.57 acres for central Punjab as a whole (Punjab Pub. no. 72, 1961, p. 11). The ratio of teams to households is .83 each. There is, among farming households, a Pearson's linear correlation of +.47 between amounts of crop income of families and the number of bullocks they own (and a correlation of +.55 between number of plow animals and the amount of income from well irrigated land alone). It is hard to consider this number excessive in relation to need.

The table shows that cows are much rarer in the village than male oxen. This is prima facie evidence of selection by farmers, since it is a genetic certainty that male and female cattle are, in the long run, born in approximately equal numbers. (All farmers questioned said their own bullocks and cows were obtained locally, and that this was the general practice.) The distribution of cow ownership also differs from the distribution of oxen. Eight of the eighteen cows of the village are owned by families with no bullocks at all. The ten owned by farmers are all in families that keep bullocks. This distribution reflects the relative unpopularity of cows as milk animals. Farmers keep them primarily as a source of more plow bullocks, while a few nonfarmers have them because, unlike cow buffaloes or goats, they can be had for very little money, even for nothing at all. Cows, but not bullocks, are occasionally turned loose by farmers who hesitate to sell them, whether for religious or economic reasons. Such cows occasionally form small groups that wander from village to village, or rather that are driven secretly at night from village to village by farmers who outwardly respect the convention that they be allowed to wander.

The differential proportions of the ox calves, male and female, respond to the same situations as that of the adult oxen. Among nonfarmers, interested only in keeping the adult cows for their milk, both male and female calves are disposed of. At least some of the male calves disposed of by nonfarmers are given or sold to farmers. To my direct knowledge there are at least two cases of such acquisition reflected in the tables.

The large number of cow buffaloes, more than an average of one per family, reflects both their greater desirability as a source of milk and the extreme dietary importance of milk itself. Milk is the principal source of calcium and of animal fats. It is the only significant bridge between mother's milk for babies and the hardy adult fare that is eaten with only slight modification by children. Buffalo milk has a much higher butterfat content than cow's milk and is more abundant. Buffaloes are also easier to milk. Cows were stated to yield four to five seers of milk per day in Shahidpur, while buffaloes yielded about seven seers (one seer equals 988.1 grams). In addition, the buffalo's period of lactation is said to be nine months, against seven for a cow. Taken all together, and allowing for the fodder consumption of a buffalo in lactation being twice that of a cow, buffaloes would be a cheaper source of butterfat on an annual basis. Unfortunately, it was not possible to check these reports by systematic measurement in the village. It is true, however, that statistical analysis of household ecological positions showed a +.605 correlation between total number of cattle (milk and plow) and family size. This was the highest correlation of any factor with cattle, and much higher than the next highest correlation of +.47 between the number of plow animals alone and family size. It suggests a calculated choice of these animals to fill human dietary needs.

Male buffaloes are not used regularly in agriculture and are generally sold while young, and this is reflected in the small proportion of male calves. (Females, of course, are kept either for milk or for later sale, because of their greater value.) Accordingly, as with "sacred" bulls, no adult male buffaloes were found in the village, although one does wander in the area. Additional stud service is provided by a government artificial-insemination program with an office at Dinpur.

The even distribution of goats throughout the village groups reflects their use as food rather than as a power source. Rams are used for meat—by far the most important meat animal. Females provide milk and kids. While milk goats generally cannot be acquired for nothing, they are far cheaper than buffaloes. What is more important for many families, goats eat little and are clean enough to be kept in a courtyard or house by those who lack a barn.

Mules and donkeys are owned exclusively by potters. They are used for carrying fairly heavy but compact loads, like new clay, pots, and bricks, that do not require carts. They work both for the potters themselves and for others on hire. When mules and donkeys are hired, their owners serve as teamsters.

Camels are becoming more popular as draft animals. They are twice as costly as bullocks, and although one eats as much as a full team, one can also do the work of a team. In addition, camels can be used for several tasks more easily than bullocks. They will tolerate a blindfold and work without constant guidance, which makes them preferable to oxen for the tedious operation of drawing water with a Persian wheel. Since bullocks do not tolerate a blindfold, they can see when the farmer is not present, whereupon they cease work until prodded to it again.

Pigs are kept by sweepers, as table 3 shows. Sweepers are the group most like the "traditional" caste represented in the literature describing the jajmani system (cf. Kolenda 1963). They divide the families of the village into twelve groups, one for each of their own twelve families. They sweep houses—principally the barns—on a contractual basis, taking payment in kind according to the animals in the families. In addition, the sweepers sweep certain public areas, such as the village gate. The pigs come into the balance at this point, for they are fed whatever they can eat in the village rubbish—such otherwise useless items as mango seeds, for example. They are also driven from village to village in the winter and fed the skimmings from sugar-boiling pans. The sweepers retain the proceeds from the sale of the pigs and of bristles.

No one has an animal without apparent use for him. Nonlanded people have no draft animals, and even among landed families draft animals are not found in every house. The critical importance of milk as an item of diet—in bringing calcium, butterfat, vitamins, and some animal protein into a diet otherwise dominated by carbohydrates, vegetable oils, and vegetable protein—is obvious, particularly in relation to children. There is an almost total lack in the native diet of an equivalent to Western processed infant food to fill the gap between dependence on mother's milk and competence in dealing with the challenging adult fare. The overall pattern of food animals per capita also suggests that they are in somewhat short supply. Although all castes that have large families in them have at least some milk animals, the proportion of buffaloes per capita and of buffaloes to cow oxen is substantially higher in the wealthier landed groups.

Milk and ghee (*ghī*, clarified butter) themselves fetch a high price. Ghee is sold in the village for Rs. 4.50 a kilo, equal to ninety-five cents American at the legal exchange rate at the time. By comparison, twenty cigarettes cost Rs. 0.36 in the village, wheat flour costs Rs. 0.50 a kilo, and a shirt, village style, costs approximately

Rs. 1.50 for tailoring and Rs. 4.00 for cloth, depending somewhat
on taste and the size of the buyer. In addition, ghee is in fact only
rarely offered for sale, reportedly because people are seldom able to
produce more than they require for immediate consumption.

The importance and scarcity of cattle in the village ecology is
a critical element in its structure as a message source of alternative
significant behaviors. It reflects and is in fact structured by an underlying scarcity of fodder, which in turn structures options throughout
the system.

It is possible to show the fodder scarcity only indirectly, by
describing the way it is conceptualized and dealt with. The standard
unit for estimating fodder requirements is the *jorī*, or "pair." Two
oxen make one *jori*, as does one buffalo, one camel, two mules, or
four donkeys (see table 5). The consumption of a working *jori* is
reckoned at 54 quintals (metric), or 150 bundles of fodder a year.
An average fodder outrun for wheat is stated to be about 25 bundles
an acre, each season. Assuming that the higher yield of maize fodders
and sorghum in the summer cycle will compensate for the loss of
fodder due to the planting of cotton, the total fodder outrun of the
village for a year would equal the amount of acreage under all fodder-
producing crops times 25. Estimating five hundred acres (total of
two seasons) under such crops, the average village outrun of fodder
would be 175,000 bundles. At the stated rate of 150 bundles per
jori, this outrun would support 84 working *joris*. By count, there are
245 *joris*. One arrives at a similarly high actual count if one takes the
established estimates of acreage necessary for fodder. This rate is
stated to be 2 acres of dry fodder and 2/5 acre of green fodder, or
2.4 acres per *jori*. At this rate, there should be 145 *joris* in the village.
The meaning of these and other similar figures is not that the farmers
do not know how much their animals eat, or that they do not pay
attention to their own estimates. But it is perhaps partly that they
understated their yields of fodder to me, but mainly that they consciously maintain the animals on what are conceptualized as short
rations. The quoted average annual consumption figures out to be one
bundle per *jori* every 2.4 days. The readily stated rule-of-thumb rate
rounds this out to three days per bundle. It was also readily stated on
further questioning that one bundle actually is used to feed one
animal for ten days, which equals one *jori* for five days. This is less

than half the rule-of-thumb rate. But it is almost exactly in line with the figures given for yields and consumption, and with visible practices. When I sought an explanation for the lower figure, I was always told that the specific animal or animals in question would not be working. If it was an ox, it was not being used in the fields. If it was a buffalo, it was not lactating. One specific cow I observed being fed a small amount of poor fodder (about a kilo) happened to be sick to the point that its survival was in doubt. When I asked if it would help to increase its ration, the farmer agreed that it would, but said that the working animals needed all that was available. In sum, fodder is regarded as a fuel, to be fed to the animals according to their present uses. The higher figures are allowances for animals as work units, while the lower figures are for animals individually, taking non-working time with working time on an annual average basis.

Table 5
PRICE, CONSUMPTION, AND YIELD OF MAJOR CATTLE

Animal	Life span	Prime price	Annual consumption	Yield
Bullock	10–12 years	Rs. 500	27 quintals (metric)	One pair can pull 25 maunds in a cart, or operate a plow or Persian wheel
Camel	12–15 years	Rs. 1,000	54 quintals	One can carry 8–10 maunds or replace two oxen
Buffalo cow	6–10 years	Rs. 800	54 quintals	One will give about seven seers of milk per day (c. 7 quarts)
Mule	20 years	Rs. 3,000	27 quintals	One can carry a 5-maund pack
Donkey	12 years	Rs. 200	13½ quintals	One can carry a 2½ maund pack

The methods of feeding are appropriate to the selective use of consistently "short" rations. Twice daily, morning and evening, each animal is staked down or tied to a part of a trough. Its food is chopped, mixed, and brought to it individually in the correct amount, more and better if it is working, less and poorer if not. Of course, if the animal is ill and valuable, some richer grains may be added if they are available. But conversely, if the situation warrants, it may receive only dry chopped maize or wheat straw, a few kilos a day.

This method of feeding hedges against the expected but random effects of disease, accident, and natural unproductive periods, just as the planting policies followed for cotton and barley and gram hedge against expected crop losses.

When I was new in the village, and before I took a census of village households, I was told that everyone took care of whatever cattle were born in the village, and never sold them. As an "ideal" behavior toward cattle, this is consistent with both the religious and the kinship conceptions described in chapters 6 and 7. But later, when advised of the results of the actual count of cattle in the village, no villager explained that the normal patterns of births—about half male and half female—did not hold in the village. Instead, the pattern of concrete management was frankly acknowledged and then explained as one forced upon villagers against their wishes by "necessity"—a point of view that fits nicely with the practices of calculating rations.

While it would be difficult to prove that the present number and distribution of cattle in the village was "optimal" in some sense, it seems obvious that it responds more to the villagers' calculated needs for food and power than to any other factor, and that the bases for these calculations lie within the ecology itself. Larger numbers of cattle could be supported only by cutting back on the nonfodder crops—such as cotton and cane, or by replacing grain acreage with fodder acreage. The unwillingness of villagers to do this reflects a judgment that present numbers of cattle are more useful than the grains within the ecology, while lesser numbers would not be.

The needs of cattle set an upper limit on the amount of land that can be devoted to nonfodder crops, within a range structured by the opportunities for increased intensification of labor, water, and fertilizer. But within the portion that must reflect the needs of cattle, the fodder grown can take many forms, and these include, as was noted, maize, wheat, barley, pulses, and chick-peas, as well as the leguminous fodder crops of sorghum millet and *barsheen*. Each of these, however, has a slightly different set of "by-products" that, because of the nature of the plants, are produced in direct ratio with the fodder itself. From the perspective of the fodder supply, for example, grains are a by-product of maize roughage and wheat straw. The beans, which are essential for human diet, are a by-product of high-protein fodder, as is the nitrogen they fix in the soil. All of these side products and effects of fodder plants constitute an area of ecological "free choice" that is maintained continually and deliberately at each sowing.

The choices among different crops that can meet fodder requirements are to some extent self-structuring, in that the differences between the grains and the legumes as classes lead naturally to the development of sets of crops for supplementation and rotation, rather than concentration on just one crop or another. But additional considerations also enter to further narrow the selections of possible alternative combinations of seeds and times of sowing. One important set of such considerations is naturally based on the work capacities and dietary needs of the human population of the village.

Human Population

In describing humans in the ecology it is useful to speak in terms of a difference between the "microecologies" and the "macroecology" of the village. A microecological perspective takes the village as a setting for each individual. A macroecological perspective takes the village as a setting for the entire human population as a unit.

From the perspective of microecology, the human population exclusive of the individual as its focus looms large as an effective part of the village setting as a whole, what is "given" and has to be manipulated and responded to along with the other animal populations and the adapted crops. The individual villager as the focus of his microecology has little freedom to reject the means he can use to maintain himself and satisfy his needs, and little freedom to reject the felt needs he seeks to satisfy.

It has been recognized in the long history of anthropological concerns with "needs" and prerequisites for society that the situation is much different from the perspective of macroecology. For the human population as a whole, very little appears to be "given," particularly in the long run. The only clear "need" or condition is that the community perpetuate itself and make some provision for subsistence and reproduction—and this itself is more a condition of analysis, a logical prerequisite, than an empirical condition representing a "natural law" of some sort. The possible limits on different ways of remaining a community are set by the total surrounding region. The dilemma, or frustration, of development analysis is that people often cannot find a way to bridge the gap between what is possible for them as individuals and what is possible if they could, somehow, act only as part of a larger collectivity.

To see the human population as an element in an ecology as a message source is to see it from the perspective of microecology only. But even with this clarifying restriction, it still has properties that are complex and elusive. Each villager who responds to the human component of the information source, choosing an element to act on, is also in an important sense chosen by that element (or elements) who is at the same time acting in his own right as an active communicating individual. Furthermore, the way this reciprocal or reflexive action among villagers takes place is to a great extent structured by several factors that are not in themselves ecological. Since these factors form the subject matter of succeeding chapters, I will describe here only some of the broader features of the human population that affect all interactions between it and individuals more or less equally.

Table 6 presents the results of a census of the village taken in May 1965. The figures are collated by sex, age, and marital status, and by caste (occupational group). Although several important aspects of the overall census tabulation are more germane to other information systems to be described, presenting them here will indicate the general division of the population between agricultural production and support activities, provide some insight into the conditions encouraging population growth, and permit us to estimate the impact of human needs in the overall set of ecological balances that lead to production of an agricultural "surplus."

Reading across, the table indicates the relative size of the different groups. The Farmers, by far the most numerous, are engaged almost entirely in agriculture as well-capitalized private farmers. The second largest group, the Harijans, also engage in agriculture, to only a slightly lesser extent, and more often as laborers, partners, or tenants without land of their own. Together, the 637 people of these two groups make up 73 percent of the total village population. Since they preponderate in the use of agricultural land, their immediate

Table 6
Reported Population by Caste, Showing Residence, Sex, Age, and Marital Status

	Caste											Totals
	Br	Fa	Ma	Go	Ba	Po	Wa	Co	Sa	Ha	Sw	
Totals												
Residents returned	24	380	43	16	8	79	2	10	10	251	48	871
Persons returned	24	395	43	16	10	79	2	10	10	251	48	888
Sex, age, marital status												
Resident males*	12	210	23	11	5	45	1	4	7	138	24	480
Boys 0–15 years	6	75	7	6	1	23	—	—	4	61	11	194
Bachelors over 15	—	49	7	2	2	6	1	1	1	18	1	88
Husbands and widowers	6	86	9	3	2	16	—	3	2	58	12	197
Daughters' husbands	—	—	—	—	—	—	—	—	—	1	—	1
Resident females	12	170	20	5	3	34	1	6	3	113	24	391
Girls 0–15 years	6	57	9	3	1	14	—	3	1	54	10	158
Maidens	—	16	1	—	—	5	—	—	—	7	1	30
Wives	6	77	9	2	2	15	—	3	2	51	12	179
Widows	—	14	1	—	—	—	1	—	—	1	1	18
Resident married daughters	—	5	—	—	—	—	—	—	—	—	—	5
Nonresident females†	—	15	—	—	2	—	—	—	—	—	—	17
Second domiciles*	—	31	2	—	4	1	—	—	—	12	1	51

NOTE: Br = Brahmin   Go = Goldsmith   Wa = Water-carrier   Ha = Harijan
Fa = Farmer   Ba = Barber   Co = Cotton-ginner   Sw = Sweeper
Ma = Mason   Po = Potter   Sa = Sadhu

* Some resident males maintain second domiciles outside Shahidpur
† Returned as outmarried daughters or sisters by Shahidpur households

needs and abilities are the principal determinants of the scope and content of agricultural activity.

The remaining differentiated caste groups each consist of far fewer people and families. The overall pattern is of a relatively uniform wealthy group and a poorer group of many households who work the fields, supported by a much smaller set of more or less technical specialists in groups of one or a few households.

Reading down, table 6 indicates that the demographic structures of the different caste groups do not vary significantly. There are no groups where females predominate, or where the age relations differ sharply from the overall pattern. Rather, there is a uniform manifestation of two general tendencies. First, men outnumber women; second, there is clear preponderance of those who are either too young to be married, who are married, or who have been married. Eligible but unmarried men and women are scarce. These trends reflect an underlying interest in marriage and family growth that is directly related to the importance of milk cattle and should be understood in its proper context.

It should always be borne in mind that villagers depend for survival on their own local resources. There is no government social security program for them, and bank savings are unreliable. Investments in land or local agriculture cannot alone support an old and weak man, who lacks the power to sanction collection of interest or rents due him. In the end, the old must count on the strength and cooperation of the young. Given the ecological importance of human labor and skill in the context of the conditions imposed by the other information systems (principally those described in chapters 4 and 7), the most dependable young people are generally one's own sons, since other young people are more beholden to other elders. The importance of marriage reflected in the census tables follows directly from this. A person would be foolish not to take the opportunity of creating a family of his own, except in the related and not uncommon case where he deliberately gives up his opportunity for another very close relation (generally a brother) and then depends on him and his children and lives with them throughout his life.

Given the desirability of children, the strategy of conceiving as many as possible follows from the high rates of child mortality. The average age of all males reported in response to my census was 28.8

years. For all females it was 27.5. But for only those ten years old or over, the average of all reported ages for men was 51 years, and for women 33.2. (The seemingly disproportionate lowness of this latter figure reflects an apparent tendency for women to report themselves as being between twenty and forty at a greater rate than one would expect on statistical grounds alone. Despite the general preponderance of men over women in all other age categories, there was both an absolute and a relative preponderance of women over men in this age range.) The great difference between overall averages and averages for those over ten indicates an exceptionally high mortality rate in the youngest age group. The dangers to children are well known to villagers, of course, even though they do not express them numerically. They know how many funerals occur, and they know the ages and many more intimate details of those who die. A man who has a good healthy family, a few sons and perhaps a few daughters, and who loses none throughout his life is considered fortunate indeed.

There is an obvious connection between the ecological importance of cattle, the importance of children, and the general diet. The gap between nursing and adult fare has been noted. Some idea of what that adult fare consists of will be useful, both because it is conceivable that this gap or difference between adult food and child food itself affects the mortality curve and because an appreciation of the diet bears directly on the question of a marketable "surplus."

The basic diet in Shahidpur rests on a small number of standardized dishes. There are basic summer and winter menus that are seldom departed from during their respective seasons. The "habitual" summer meal consists generally of two to five wheat *roti*, about a cup of the preparation of lentils or other pulses as *dal*, and one or more tumblers of tea or some other drink. The "habitual" or "favorite" winter adult meal consists of two or three maize *roti*, a cup or more of a preparation called *sag* (*sāg*), and hot tea. *Dal* and *sag* are prepared in similar ways. First, sliced or chopped garlic and onion is fried in a substantial quantity of butter or ghee until brown, with some chilis, generally some cloves, black pepper, and sometimes ginger. Then mustard or other greens are added, fried, and boiled to make *sag*, or the pulses are added (soaked dried, or fresh) to make *dal*. With water added as necessary, the vegetables are cooked until tender, often for several hours. They are served in small bowls, generally with an additional pat of butter or ghee and perhaps some raw sugar added. Each person takes his food on a tray and sits on a stool or the ground, a tumbler of tea or water to one side. The method of eating is to scoop up some of the *dal* or *sag* with a bit of *roti* held in one hand. The tea is made with a large proportion of milk, preferably half the total, and the equivalent of from two to four teaspoons of raw sugar per tumbler. The person eating is generally served by a woman of the house or a younger man (women's arrangements are less formal), while fresh *roti* are prepared as needed. The general sense in the serial order of eating is that each person is free to eat what he wishes, without having to feel that he is competing with or taking anything from others.

The food as served is compact and "rich"—not well suited for infants. Nor are there many intermediate phases such as yeast-raised breads or simpler preparations of vegetables, to say nothing of the blended baby foods now available in wealthier countries. Since in most cases milk and sugar alone soften the diet for the very young, the absence of milk has serious effects on a child's growth.

The foods of these staple meals appear also as leftovers or as snacks, including breakfast. Leftover *roti*, for example, are generally eaten cold or fried in a bit of ghee for a man starting to the fields on a cold winter morning, with the usual few glasses of tea. Cane, radishes, fresh chick-peas, and other similar products are eaten as fresh snacks in the fields, while *shakkar* (brown sugar in powder form) and *rotis* are commonly eaten by people working in the houses as a late morning or afternoon supplement to tea.

Farm households use various methods to keep count of the quantities of foodstuffs they consume. For example, special vessels are set aside for milled wheat. The amount they hold is known, so all that is needed for the household record is for the women to remember how many times they filled it from the household store. Similar systems are used for other products, so that there is general consensus on the amount of major foods that an average adult family member would eat. After arriving at my own estimates, I discussed the matter with a group of women for confirmation and clarification. They stated that the daily allowance for a working man includes about ¾ pound of *roti* (the major part of the weight is flour), about ½ pound of sugar in various forms, ⅔ pound of *sag* or *dal*, and about a quart of milk in tea and other forms. Consumption levels are generally higher in winter. Meat, generally goat, is said to be eaten only at weddings, and the annual amount consumed is too small to average on a daily basis. Fish, chicken, and eggs are rarely eaten.

The diet is by no means inadequate. The stated allowance for a working man represents a daily consumption of approximately $\frac{3}{4}$ pound of wheat, $\frac{1}{6}$ pound of fats, $\frac{1}{4}$ pound of mustard greens, $\frac{1}{4}$ pound of lentils, 1 pound of milk, and $\frac{1}{2}$ pound of brown sugar. As these products have been analyzed by the United States Department of Agriculture in comparable forms as they are purchased in the United States, the amounts represent a total of approximately 3,141 calories per day. In terms of its components, it contains 81 grams of protein, 85 grams of fat, and 562 grams of carbohydrates. Prominent among minerals and vitamins are 1,390 mg of calcium, 3,085 mg of phosphorus, 30.7 mg of iron, 3,400 mg of potassium, and 22,500 international units of vitamin A. Even though these figures are only rough approximations, they must approach both what is desired and what is eaten. It is not a bad diet, one with glaring deficiencies, incapable of sustaining a population as a stable part of the ecological system. On the contrary, it appears that one can live rather well, gastronomically speaking, as a part of the village ecology.

The Problem of a "Surplus"

The dietary allowances permit a projection of the total land necessary to meet the needs of the human population of the village, which can be compared with the actual acreage under locally consumable food crops. The difference between what is needed and what is grown estimates the village "surplus," and its place in the total system indicates the real basis for its presence.

Even though the dietary allowances are for the heaviest eaters in the village, the total land that would be required to produce the same level of diet for all who are not infants would be far less than that actually farmed. For example, if eight hundred villagers ate $\frac{3}{4}$ pound of wheat a day, their total annual consumption would be about 219,000 pounds, or 2,675 maunds (1 maund is 82 2/7 pounds). The stated grain yield of average wheat land is 5 maunds per bigha (1 bigha is 5/24 acre) or 24 maunds per acre. At this rate, about 110 acres would supply the needs of the village, yet the total wheat area is almost double this, and it is clear that nowhere near this amount of food is really consumed. In short, there is more than enough to meet the highest level of human dietary needs.

A comparison of village food production and needs with fodder production and needs clearly indicates that the "surplus" is not absolute and imposed by an extraction of labor from outside, but rather is relative and structured by the biological laws that structure relationships within the system. The "surplus" of grains can be directly attributed to the shortage of fodder, which is in turn related to the crucial importance of cattle as a direct means of maintaining the numbers (replacement) of the human population, as well as of providing a source of motive power. The cattle generate fodder needs, while cropping and human dietary considerations require that some of the fodder be provided by grain and legumes that humans can also eat. But beyond this point, the farmer is faced only with a question of how much fodder is to come from grains and edible legumes, and how much from other sources that do not provide grain. Under these circumstances, the question of why produce a marketable surplus becomes more like Why not do so? That is, why not grow crops that provide marketable grain in addition to fodder, rather than fodder alone? The cattle, interacting with the nature of the different available crops and other ecological factors, produce an area of choice within which market considerations can operate. The total structure of the ecological message source includes both the determinate relationship, where internal supplies closely match needs, and the regularly structured areas of relatively free choice, where goods can be traded out of the system or transformed into nonbiological products.

This is not to say that villagers do not depend heavily on productive goods obtained from outside by selling their internally generated "surpluses." High interest rates reflect these dependencies, along with many other actions and practices. Bicycles, cane crushers, tools of all sorts, radios, books, storage utensils, and many other items ranging from combs to motor cars are acquired and used whenever possible. Ancient equipment that an American might throw away is carefully tended and in fact fetches high prices—for example, a 1942 Pontiac station wagon that was recently purchased by a villager nearby for Rs. 2,000, or $400 at the legal exchange rate. Moreover, money obtained from outside is now used to defray the costs of what is generally called "fixed" property—cattle, houses, land, wells, and their accouterments, whose importance is described in the following chapter. These capital goods are really direct and extensive modifications of the effective environment of people in the village.

The internal ecological basis of the "surplus" of grains does not mean that the village system is autonomous. On the contrary, it indicates most clearly the integral relation between the local systems and the economic organization of the region. When one sits in a farmer's house and observes the careful order of feeding, the conservation of leftovers, and the strict self-discipline exercised by those who could ask for food, one realizes that all this reflects a constant awareness, springing from local circumstances, that food can be sent out and transformed into other crucial forms of capital—not that it is liable to be extracted by a powerful suzerain.

Summary: System Stability and Change

Land, water, sunlight, and human care produce crops. These produce food, fiber, fodder, and in the end, money as well. Fodder is used to raise animals that provide manure and human food, and these in turn provide both organic matter for the soil and energy for cultivation and care. Various crops are interdependent. Some provide nutrients that others remove. One crop provides physical shelter or economic support for others, and so on. Humans and animals provide support for crops that crops do not get from each other. The bulk of goods involved in these and other related cycles originates in the village, and is consumed, at each stage, in the village.

As the following chapters should make clear, the village is not an economic or demographic isolate in the same way that it is an ecological isolate. The consequences of choices of ecological acts are felt locally, and are structured primarily by local requirements. But other kinds of choices are made which are structured by elements more widely distributed and which affect a wider field. The commodity and labor prices and markets in the village are part of the regional pattern of price adjustment and allocation. The division of labor likewise reflects the pattern of capital use and control around the village, the public laws, and the regional supply of skills and goods. In fact, the ecological isolation of the village—the localized character and integrity of its ecological message source—is itself protected by decisions undertaken in response to the regionally and nationally determined cost of transportation of commodities for sale, and the factors that lie behind it. The ecological isolation of the village goes hand in hand with the fact that economic information which affects choice in the village is not itself local or isolated from the economic structure of prices and markets in general.

As constituted, each part of the overall system has a value in itself, and also in what it permits or maintains. While fodder does not provide a possibility of exchangeable cash "profit" as does cane or cotton, it permits the farmer to maintain the animals to pull up the water which both these valuable crops depend on. Conversely, these seemingly profitable crops, in the ecological system, have "hidden" costs in their inability to pay their own way by balancing water needs with fodder production like other crops. The interrelations of the various crops should explain some apparent "reluctance" to adopt improvements, as well as the pattern of innovations that do take place. To the agricultural adviser, who often thinks in economic terms but ignores the ecological interrelationships of objects and actions, it might seem evidence of a "traditional" or backward mentality to see farmers fail to adopt a new variety of wheat that will grow more grain with a shorter stalk and less chaff. But given the ecological system as the farmer sees it, the reason is obvious. The system already has plenty of grain, but is short of fodder. And fodder, when it is in short supply in the village, simply cannot be gotten anywhere else at an acceptable outlay of energy and goods. It is physically too difficult to handle. Village farmers said they would adopt short wheat if it would not produce less fodder per acre (for example, if it could be grown more densely), or if it were possible to put in compensatory high-yield fodder crops, cut back on wheat acreage by the same amount, and still come out ahead.

As a high-entropy (low-organization) message source, the village ecology structures multiple alternative solutions to particular problems. But while farmers know this, they also find calculations of the various possibilities difficult to make and compare—this too is because the system is not highly organized. Given the costs of failure, the strategy of most villagers in response to possible innovations is to wait and see, to let a few who can afford it bear the cost of establishing the necessary new information in the system through an experiment. Just one or a few farmers try first; then others follow. Failure to understand that villagers see themselves as part of an ecological system that provides a challenging array of possibilities, and yet is based on firm and inexorable laws of cause and effect, has led many Western observers to be surprised that in the adoption of new techniques the usual pattern is for the wealthier farmers to be more "progressive," and for the poorer, smaller farmers to be more "conservative" or "traditional." The truth is that the small farmers cannot afford the uncertainties of new unknowns, new manifestations of the sanctions hidden behind the complicated pattern of ecological objects, knowledge, and practices they use and respond to in gaining their livelihood.

Chapter IV

The Division of Labor

While the ecological message source provides the basic material for human subsistence, it does not provide assurance that any individual who acts on ecological information will be secure in the products of his action. Nor does it provide for a division of responsibility wherein one individual can be associated with a small enough part of the total array for him to become expert in its operations. Both these latter needs are met simultaneously in a second self-sustaining message source of high entropy that is best called by the name it was given by those seventeenth and eighteenth century social philosophers who saw it as the basis of all civic order—the division of labor, or the division of rights.

The division of labor breaks the ecological populations into subpopulations, not on the basis of ecological relations but on the basis of managerial efficiency. It establishes subgroups of people whose welfare is attached to specific subgroups of plants and animals. The people in each group depend on the crops and animals they maintain, and this dependency leads them to assume a competitive stance toward other groups—in competition for new ecological resources as well as for the fruits of their own past actions.

Traditionally the division of labor has been treated as a system of "rights," moral or juridical linkages between persons and property (a method of analysis that has carried over into some social structural studies), but this does not present the entire picture. Nor is the picture completed by adding, as Hobbes did, elements of central arbitrary power to enforce rights. Conceptual "rights" (or rather their Punjabi counterparts) and enforcement sanctions are both present, of course, but there is an important material element that is intertwined with them—a system of conventional objects mixed with these more abstract conventional entities just in the way conventional words and other symbols were mixed with "real" ecological objects. These consist of the tools that are designed specifically for use by the groups that the division of rights creates. Important among these tools are the physical houses that shelter each complex of people with goods. The relationship between houses and behavior fades off into the relationship between the less material conventions of "rights" and patterns of legal and personal enforcement of them, and behavior. Rights, personal enforcement, the passive security of walls, and the functional utility of houses as tools all form one system of relevances that is distinct in nature and form from the system of relevances called the ecology, as well as from the other systems yet to be discussed. A change in one element of the division of labor has necessary repercussions on other elements in the system, but does not necessarily affect the ecology. Conversely, changes in ecological elements have necessary effects on the balance of the ecological system but not on the division of labor.

The special importance of houses has two aspects. First, they are the largest items of capital most people use and want, and one of the principal artifacts of past human efforts in the village. Second, the human groups they shelter, contain, and thereby help define are the basic elements of the division of labor, containing the basic managerial subunits of the ecology. The human group in a household is called a *parivar* (*parivār*), a term that was expressly defined on repeated occasions by villagers as "the people who cooperate in some (one) property." The cattle, tools, land, and crops in storage of one household are almost always exclusively its own, divided off from the goods of others to dispose of as it wishes. But within a household there are no such clear and exclusive divisions of rights, even though such divisions can exist potentially or in theory for certain kinds of goods, particularly land. This is what makes households, rather than individuals or larger groups, the competing groups in the village. By the same token, households are the village groups that effect the principal internal efficiencies.

The dynamics of household organization are examined in the

first section of this chapter, but certain questions left for the second section should be anticipated. These concern the role of putative rights-holding groups other than households in the overall message source.

While households compete, they are not entirely independent. And although they have, at any point in time, definite properties that they "control" or "own," this control depends in part on the tacit cooperation of other households and on the ability of each household to promise general rewards to others in return for this cooperation. Further, those goods of each household that are ecological entities are changing at all times. As people age, their ability to aid others and to enforce their claims change, as do their needs. As cattle age, both their needs and their value change. As crops grow and mature, are harvested and stored, their needs and value change also. Patterns of birth and death change the configurations of affection and affinity; changing household populations change household needs and cap-abilities. These factors all interact to ensure that the limits on the property of each household, and hence the overall division of right and labor, are not fixed and immutable but fluid and dynamic.

This fluidity of the division poses a problem in notation for those within the system—the problem of developing a stable way of speaking about a changing phenomenon. A rigid structure of con-ceptualized rights detailed enough to account for all the differences a person might want to be aware of to organize cooperation with any other villager could not resolve the problem, because the more its detail was developed to cover the situation, the less fluid it would be. Conversely, a fixed but general taxonomy could not cover the de-tailed differences between the units of the system. A changing tax-onomy might seem plausible, but this could be effectively developed only where a small group was classifying a large set of entities. A peculiar feature of the division of labor is that one of its principal elements, people, talk back. There are as many classifiers as people classified, and this is too many to convene for decision on a change in terminology every time an element of the system changes. The solution, then, must involve a system that is simple and rigid enough to be promulgated widely once and for all, yet detailed and fluid enough to encompass all the significant adjustments to the pattern of control that constantly occur and affect the consideration of each householder seeking help from or competing with others.

The need for flexibility combined with wide and uniform currency is met by employing a system of terms that are vacuous as a general frame that can be modified by the use of other general terms and descriptive qualifications. The particular terms used in the context of Shahidpur's division of labor are defined with the necessary low-information value (vacuity) in three formal systems, each as independent of the division of labor as the fundamentals of the real-number system are from the practices of engineering. These are the low information message sources described in chapters 6, 7, and 8 and called conscious sociological models. The rigid, even tautological character of these systems, together with aspects of their putative content, permit terms from them to be selected and employed as vacuous class names to delineate and group features of the division of labor. The low-information concepts of caste, faction, kin, and religious community, used in this way, appear to their users to designate broad realities that underlie the specific units of the division of labor, and that explain the demands one villager can make on another.

Similar systems of nomenclature used in other societies have apparently led social analysts to confuse the low-information systems of social concepts with the division of labor itself. Most natives do not make this confusion in practice, and sophisticated natives can explicitly point out the differences between the two systems. On several occasions, for example, different villagers provided me with a full description of the village in terms of caste, each with the definitionally appropriate traditional occupation, exchange relationships, dues, and duties (some of which will be noted later), and then proceeded directly to redescribe the people who represented the different castes in terms of their actual occupations, mutual relationships, and so forth. Even when asked directly, they did not see any significant discrepancy in this—anything that could or should be remedied. The implication was that there was no reason for concern if the Carpenter caste, Mason caste, and Blacksmith caste, each with its separate status and ritual positions, all turned out to be represented by the same families. There was no reason to think of changing either the caste concepts or peoples' behaviors so long as one was confident that someone could be found to do the work of a black-smith, mason, or carpenter when needed. When I attempted to insist that there was a discrepancy, there was a definite show of irritation and impatience.

Since the definitions of the social concepts and terms used in the division of labor are standardized in other systems, there are wide differences in the ways they are used within this system to describe the effective groups and the bases of control and interest of parti-cular individuals. Some villagers describe the division of labor with emphasis on caste identification, others, on religion. One or two spoke of a traditional religious "panchayat," and some said factions were most basic and important. These differing views cannot be reconciled, because of the inherent low-information content of all of the terms used. But very few villagers held one position exclusively, and those who did were men on the fringes of village social affairs. As men were closer to the center of village life, they took a progres-sively wider and more flexible view of the "real" basis of village groups. Those who were most widely acknowledged as the principal leaders and "resourceful men" of the village took the widest possible view, and the view that will be used here. They did not insist on any one scheme of their own and described the village as much as possible in the terms of the conceptual preferences of others. The scheme presented in the second section of this chapter is the one these men seemed to agree on. It takes caste groups as a general framework, and then describes the general social outlooks of the prominent men of the various households.

The purpose of a villager in constructing a description of the division of labor is not merely to represent it but also to influence it. The idea is to develop categories that will be convincing not only to the describer but to those described as well, as a means of eliciting cooperation or avoiding impositions. This is the basis of the superior efficacy of the scheme that takes most account of the orientations of others, and it also reinforces the theoretical point that description is itself one of the elements of the division of labor rather than some conceptual parallel to it. In fact, the individual elements of house-hold structure to be described first are conceptualized as thoroughly as the wider groups used in public descriptions. But the functions of the two conceptualizations, for the members of any given household, differ in such a way as to complement each other and contribute to the maintenance of the division of labor as a whole.

Household Organization

Housing Structures

The Punjabi term *pinD*, normally translated as "village," refers to all the lands of a village, as well as the houses and house area. The houses themselves, when centrally clustered as they are in Shahidpur, are specifically designated as the *abadi* (*abādī*, from *abād*, "population"). Land in the *abadi* has a special legal status, and is not subject either to land tax or to the tax records that constitute the comprehensive system of titles to agricultural land on which all legal claims must be based.

As shown in figure 2, the *abadi* of Shahidpur is enclosed by four lanes arranged in a square, which is called the *phirmī*. Roughly in the center of the *phirmi* is a raised mound, partially natural and partially built of earth taken from the surrounding ponds, or tanks, used for building structures in the past. A comparison of the water level in the well on the mound with levels in wells in the fields indicates that the height of the mound is approximately twenty feet above the level of the fields at that point. The height indicates, in part, the age of the village. But more important, the height of the mound raises houses above the level of possible flooding during the monsoon season and contributes substantially thereby to their value as storage areas.

All but two houses of the *abadi* are made of fired brick. The houses are seldom built to stand free of one another. They are generally grouped with their doorways toward inside lanes, rather than out toward open spaces or toward the fields surrounding the *abadi*.

The *abadi* is divided into two sides, each with its own distinct system of interconnecting lanes. The principal side, covering all the raised mound, is called variously the Farmer side or the Durwaza side. It contains the houses of all castes but Harijan and Sweeper. Farmers are most prominent by far. The Durwaza (*durwāzā*) is the village gate, a substantial brick construction that marks the formal entrance to the principal street on the side, and is the site of several rituals "for" the village. Within this side, houses of different castes

65

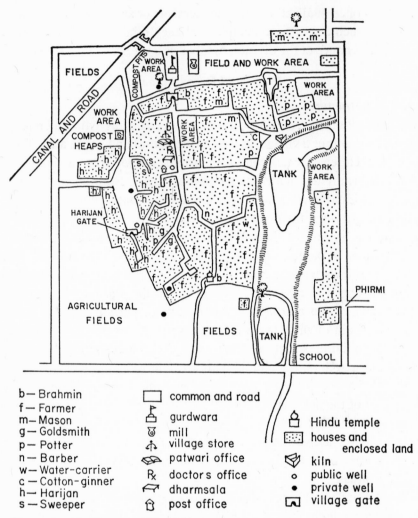

Figure 2. Abadi map of Shahidpur.

are intermixed without distinction. There is no segregation by either street or cluster, although there are several instances where related families share adjoining buildings.

The Harijan side has no formal gate, but it has its own entrance distinct from that of the Durwaza side. As the map indicates, its entrances open onto a wide central street, almost a plaza. In contrast to the Durwaza side, houses on this side are clustered by caste, and in one lane, by clan.

The houses of the Sweepers are concentrated around one lane

66

The Division of Labor

and adjoining portions of the front entrance of the area. Harijans live behind them. One lane extending beyond the central street has a gate of its own, indicated on the map, and contains only houses of Harijans of one clan—the largest on this side (although all the houses of this clan are not in this lane).

Because of the complex pattern of building, and several other practical difficulties, it was not possible to measure houses in the village systematically. But table 7, which summarizes the reported number of discrete units of construction per household, can provide a useful indirect estimate of their size and function. Although such units ranged in size from that of a small single room to a large building with several rooms and a barn, the variation was regular. The houses with more units tended consistently to have the larger units.

Table 7

UNITS OF HOUSING REPORTED PER HOUSEHOLD CENSUSED, BY CASTE AND SIDE

	Single	Double	Triple	Total houses	Total units	Average units per house
Durwaza side						
Brahmin	2	—	1	3	5	1.7
Farmer	14	28	4	46	82	1.9
Mason	6	—	1	7	9	1.3
Goldsmith	4	—	—	4	4	1.0
Barber	—	2	—	2	4	2.0
Potter	5	3	—	8	11	1.4
Water-carrier	1	—	—	1	1	1.0
Cotton-ginner	1	—	—	1	1	1.0
Sadhu	1	—	—	1	1	1.0
Totals	34	33	6	73	118	1.6
Harijan side						
Harijan	36	3	2	41	48	1.2
Sweeper	8	1	—	9	10	1.1
Totals	44	4	2	50	58	1.2
Totals	78	37	8	123	176	1.4

The subtotals indicate the general differences between the two sides of the village, while the individual caste collations indicate the pattern's occupational significance. The Harijan side has mostly single-unit houses. On the Durwaza side, slightly over half of the housing units are part of multi-unit establishments. The Farmer caste, most of whose members do operate farms, shows a clear preponderance of multi-unit houses.

Generally, the single-unit houses of the resident Harijan side, and those of similarly occupied residents of the Durwaza side, are specialized as living areas and storage facilities for personal goods only, except for three households that have additional units for looms. The larger, multi-unit establishments of the Farmers contain living and similar storage areas as well, but they include in addition large areas for barns and agricultural storage, and work areas. Most commonly one of the two or more units of the typical Farmer's house is primarily a living and storage area, the other a barn and work area. Additional units generally provide more barn space, although they may also be used to store goods, like oxcarts, that do not need constant attention.

In size, the discernible housing units of the Harijan side generally resemble small cottages—one to three rooms with a usual floor space of about four hundred square feet. The Farmers' house units are generally two to four times as large, which means that their total establishments average four to eight times the size of those of Harijans. One Farmer with an average-size family (ten members) and an average amount of land (about eight acres) had a principal unit consisting of one large and two small storerooms, a covered veranda and an open inner courtyard, and a small sitting room and storeroom in the entrance way. The total floor space was about nine hundred square feet. In addition, he had a second walled courtyard somewhat larger, with an attached storeroom and, on its second floor, a sitting room. He also had a third, partially walled plot within the *abadi* of about a quarter of an acre. Most of the non-Farmers on the side live in similar dwellings—generally old farm houses, but without the additional units. The principal exceptions to this rule are the Brahmin "doctor," who lives in a residentially specialized unit similar to those on the Harijan side, several Potter households, and the Cotton-ginners, whose small establishments are similar. The Masons live in small houses too, with large courtyards that provide work areas. Finally, the village shopkeeper lives partially in his shop and partially in the upper room of the barn of the Farmer just mentioned.

In all cases, the rooms within the housing units are differentiated for occupational functions rather than in relation to social or familial activities as such. There are no "bedrooms," "kitchens," "dining rooms," or even, strictly speaking, "sitting rooms." During the day, bedding is stored in tin trunks or hung from the ceilings, while beds are stacked against a convenient wall along with other goods not then in use. Meals, because of the heat and smoke of cooking fires, are generally prepared in the courtyards, but they may be served or eaten anywhere. And at night, beds and bedding are placed almost anywhere—inside rooms, on the roof, or even in the street, depending on the season and circumstances. Barns have fixed functions that are obviously ecological and managerial, as do work areas that have fodder-cutters and similar devices permanently installed. Other areas, while not permanently set aside to one type of work or another, are available for each type of work a member of the household engages in, from sorting cotton to making pots.

Two knowledgeable Farmers on different occasions indicated that in general opinion the overall value of all houses and equipment of a working Farmer was about ten times that of the establishment of an average Harijan. Whatever the exact ratios, they exist not because the Farmers are wealthier, but rather because they cannot farm without the additional goods and space. Large houses are part of the Farmers' capital, not a net gain after all of their expenditures. The number of beds and amount of bedding, number of suits of clothes and pieces of brassware, and other such small personal items per capita are more or less constant throughout the village. The Harijan houses are small because Harijan families are small and the houses hold only these items, a stock of foodstuffs, and the few hand tools required by the usual work they obtain. The Farmers' houses are bigger to accommodate the goods of the larger families together with the additional goods, over and above personal items, that make them farmers.

Many of the functions of housing in the village may seem trivial in the abstract, yet taken together in practice they make the major part of the difference between some 850 people camped on a plain and a full-fledged village. Although land is easy to rent, and equipment only a little difficult to hire, land and equipment alone would do little good without an adequate shelter to store harvested produce and provide work space.

The danger of theft of useful or consumable goods is considered to be constant and real, and the sturdy gates—generally made of iron—on the Farmer houses provide a major measure of security, particularly in the absence of local policemen. But even apart from this, houses provide protection against climate and pests that can spell the difference between a successful and an unsuccessful production unit. One recurrent climatic danger is from flooding. In the monsoon pattern of concentrated and heavy rainfall, a sturdy ceiling and walls and the raised elevation of the *abadi* mound are of great importance. The rains would soak through a light structure, and the fields and other low areas are often, reportedly, completely flooded. (My visit occurred during two years of exceedingly weak monsoon, and there was no such flooding.) There is then no safe place for storage but the barns in the *abadi*.

Rats pose another and substantial danger to stored farm commodities. The animals live in the fields during most of the year, but are forced into the *abadi* by flooding and during the harvest and sowing seasons, when all but a few of the fields are completely cleared and plowed. Because of the intensive use of direct human labor in all field operations, and because of the danger to cattle and to children who move about freely and frequently accompany their parents in the fields, rats cannot be poisoned. There is some trapping, but the principal measures taken are defensive and center directly on the houses. Doors are sealed as tightly as possible with frames and sills, and walls of storage rooms where grain is kept are regularly repaired. Recently farmers have adopted the practice of building a concrete floor in a high area within the house as a place to stack sacks of grains so that they cannot be burrowed through from beneath. Other bulk consumables, such as brown sugar, are stored in galvanized drums within the house. Small items like rope, string, and bedding are stored in lockers or in nets suspended from the rafters. Without such measures, which all depend directly or indirectly on a house of good construction, losses would be expected to amount to from 10 to 20 percent of the stored goods each year. With them, damage is effectively limited to standing crops in the fields, before harvest.

Examples can be multiplied indefinitely, but perhaps the best way to make the point is to restate the obvious. With the exception of a post office and an unused patwari (revenue clerk) office, there are no toolsheds, barns, workrooms, potter's shops, smithies, or other productive establishments in the village except those that are parts of houses. And it is as accurate to say that the villagers sleep in their barns and shops as it is to say that they work in their houses.

Family Composition and Size

From the point of view of the villagers of Shahidpur, the most important component of a household is, of course, the domestic group itself. Humans, in the absence of the engines and devices familiar in the more industrialized countries, not only are a principal means of utilizing and maintaining a house and its goods, but also are a major resource that those goods and the house itself help to exploit. The large houses of the Farmers permit development of their large families, which will be described. But is is also true that a large family permits one to make use of a large house.

Domestic groups range in size from 1 to 25 members and average about 7. Farm families are generally large, averaging just under 8.5 persons each, while Harijan families average only 6 members. Different domestic group sizes impose different restraints on the individuals within them. Because of the importance of human labor in all aspects of productive activity, no major decision can be implemented without the direct and full cooperation of those who share immediate control of one's resources. And because of the dependence of people on others for their long-term security, no decisions can be formulated without due regard for the needs and reactions of others in one's own living group. Even with consensus, the material of each household and the size of its group interact to limit the range of decisions that any one of its members can act on. Farmers are in a better position to diversify occupations than are weavers, for example. During much of the year, a farming family can spare one or two men to go to school or to fight in courts because the work has seasonal peaks and slack periods. A working weaver, who would typically be the only adult male and the principal worker in his household, cannot take time out for similar unremunerative periods even if the long-range rewards are known to be high.

The pattern of domestic group size and organization is summarized in table 8. Each group is organized around a hierarchically organized group of men related by direct descent, so that family size is directly related to the number of generations in the group. Families expand vertically, but they do not combine horizontally. Nor do they stay together if two full-fledged families develop within one in the course of time. A minimal family group centers on a single father and his children. If those children include more than one son, and they reach adulthood, the entire family will still stay together as one domestic group if it is not forced to divide for economic reasons. But if these two or more sons marry and in turn have sons, the family will invariably split. One or more of the sons with sons will leave, so that the overall pattern of a single lineal hierarchy will be preserved. In my census of the village, I found no family, regardless of size, with two sons who in turn had sons, all living together in one household.

The table shows the percentage of family groups of one, two, three, or four generations in each caste, and the percentage of people of each caste in each type of family group.

The majority of the people in the village (55.2 percent) live in households of three generations. The variation from caste to caste is obvious in the percentage comparisons. Of the Farmer households, 55.3 percent are of three generations, and these same households make up 69 percent of the Farmers of the village. By contrast, 68.3 percent of the Harijan (Weavers and Leatherworkers) families have two generations, and they contain 56.2 percent of that population, with 42.6 percent in three generation households. For the Sweepers, who are numerous enough for the percentages to have some comparable meaning, the contrast with the Farmers is even more marked. Of the Sweepers 66.7 percent live in two-generation houses, and only 33.3 percent in three-generation houses—less than half the proportion of Farmers who are comparably organized. The force that structural differences of this magnitude have on the thoughts and actions of the people is considerable. Each person in a large family has greater resources to draw on directly, but by the

Table 8
HOUSEHOLD SIZE AND STRUCTURE, BY CASTE

Caste	Households					Persons				
	Total number	Types by generations (in percentage)				Total number	Types by generations (in percentage)			
		1–	2–	3–	4–		1–	2–	3–	4–
Brahmin	3	0.0	66.7	33.3	0.0	24	0.0	45.8	54.2	0.0
Farmer	46	4.3	38.3	55.3	2.1	380	0.5	27.9	69.0	2.5
Mason	7	0.0	71.5	28.5	0.0	43	0.0	69.8	30.2	0.0
Goldsmith	4	25.0	75.0	0.0	0.0	16	6.3	93.75	0.0	0.0
Barber	2	50.0	50.0	0.0	0.0	8	25.0	0.0	75.0	0.0
Potter	8	0.0	50.0	50.0	0.0	79	0.0	39.3	60.7	0.0
Water-carrier	1	0.0	100.0	0.0	0.0	2	0.0	100.0	0.0	0.0
Cotton-ginner	1	0.0	0.0	100.0	0.0	10	0.0	0.0	100.0	0.0
Sadhu	1	0.0	0.0	100.0	0.0	10	0.0	0.0	100.0	0.0
Harijan	41	4.9	68.3	26.8	0.0	251	1.2	56.2	42.6	0.0
Sweeper	9	0.0	66.7	33.3	0.0	48	0.0	66.7	33.3	0.0
Totals	123	4.84	54.9	39.5	0.805	871	0.9	41.7	55.2	1.1

same token they must always coordinate more of their activities with many more other people. The general trends are common knowledge in the village, although of course the exact statistics are not.

The pattern of household organization is articulated with a pattern of legal and traditional rights. Indian law recognizes a fundamental distinction between property that is "ancestral" and that which is "self-acquired." Self-acquired property is that which one obtains by one's own resources. "Ancestral" property is that which has to be inherited or obtained by rights of inheritance from others, or property which has been obtained on the basis of "ancestral" resources. In the absence of evidence to the contrary, there is a presumption in law that caste property and, more generally, whatever major good a family depends on, is inherited property in this technical sense. In the case of village Farmers, this legal presumption naturally extends to land.

Self-acquired property is analogous to personal property as it is conceived of in the United States and Europe. It can be sold at will by the owner, or transferred in any other way. If it is not sold by him and is inherited by those who share his ancestral property, it falls under the heading of ancestral property from then on. Ancestral property is quite different. Rights in ancestral property are obtained not by inheritance upon the death of a former owner—except in the special case of property formerly self-acquired—but rather by birth of the new owner. A son, from birth, is an owner on equal status with his father and any brothers of the property that was originally his father's share, as will be described in chapter 7. The holder of a right in ancestral property cannot sell or transfer any part of it without the approval of those who share equal rights with him. In the event he should do so—even if he should sell only an amount equal to his own share or less, they have what in law is called rights of preemption. That is, they can preempt the sale and reclaim the property, only paying the purchaser the exact purchase price. Formerly, rights of preemption extended more widely than they do now —even to anyone in the owner's village. At present they extend only to his sons, brothers, and brother's sons. Those who hold rights of preemption are in law the first sharers of the owner's property, either from birth, as in the case of his sons, or upon his death, as in the case of brothers and more distant kin. Beyond those who hold rights of preemption, there still are kin with residual rights of ownership. Who they are exactly, and in what order of remoteness, varies from region to region, but in every case they are people whom each individual knows to have an interest in the management of his ancestral property. Effectively, this all means that all the men in a household in the village are co-owners of the major property of the household, and that their rights and interests are often shared with the members of related households as well. The needs for consultation and cooperation within households reflect these relationships.

Cattle

Of the 123 households identified by villagers in the census, 108 reported the possession of cattle of one kind or another. The general distribution of cattle among these households has been described in chapter 3.

To think of the management of village cattle in the analogy of beef ranching in the Western United States or Latin America would be to underestimate the importance of the barn facilities provided by the village houses. A more appropriate analogy is that of an American or European dairy, whose proportionally more delicate and expensive animals, like those in Shahidpur, are fed carefully prepared mixtures of roughage and enriched matter. Like dairy barns, the village structures permit the animals to be staked separately and fed and cared for in accordance with their individual needs, following the general policies noted in the previous chapter. Most important, the village structures, like dairy barns, permit the village animals to be milked. In short, the barns—whether they are large-roofed structures with built-in troughs and fodder-storage areas, or open spaces with stakes driven into the ground—are an essential component of the pattern of intensive exploitation of cattle through intensive but selective application of human labor to individual animals. The care, feeding, milking, washing, moving, and guarding of cattle in this context all takes about one day of human labor for three major head.

Land

The principal and probably the single most valuable productive good divided among households is land. Indian land-tenure systems are frequently said to be extremely complex. A more important observation is that they are integral to the overall division of labor, and therefore have to be understood in that context. When allowances are made for the principles of the overall system, the pattern of landholding can be seen to be orderly and efficient, and the choices it structures and that maintain it can be readily understood.

In both courtroom law and village tradition the "property" of a person, whether ancestral or self-acquired, is seen to consist primarily in rights vis-à-vis other persons, specifically in the right to the production of major goods, rather than in those major goods themselves. A person is not, for example, so much the absolute owner of a certain plot of land as the owner of a right to a certain size of a share in the total village land. The actual land used by him to realize his share may be changed by village legal action, as well as by the action of higher agencies.

The rights that any villager inherits, buys, or sells in land can be thought of as existing along a continuum from those most secure and most difficult to transfer, to those least secure and easiest to alter. The most secure require the most money for transference, and also require the fullest documentation. The least secure, conversely, require the least money to transfer and the least amount of documentation.

The most secure right is that of outright ownership, which may be single or joint. Ownership is recorded in the revenue record and several subsidiary documents compiled and maintained by the state revenue officials. A sale of land can be effected only by buyers and sellers appearing together with witnesses before the tehsildar (head revenue official for the tehsil, headquarters at Rupar), physically transferring the money, duly counted out, in his presence, and then signing all the appropriate documents, with witnesses, and paying the requisite legal fees.

Every unit of land in the village has at least one owner. In the case of public lands, including roads and schools, the village cemetery and village gate, the owner of record is the village panchayat, and the rights are nontransferable. The owners of agricultural lands are specific villagers, or more commonly groups of related villagers. Because ownership rights are difficult to change, a larger number of them come under the heading of ancestral rights, and are enforced as such by the revenue officials.

The laws enforced by the court officials and the police are not directly part of the division of labor in the village, in the sense that official understandings of them differ from the presumptions acted on by villagers. But the laws stand behind the system, just as the general climatic regularities and the laws of biological growth and interaction stand behind the ecology. The configuration of legal rights is manifested in the village not by public knowledge of the record, or by the courts or police as such, but rather principally by the annual tax assessment announced to each owner by the patwari (revenue clerk) of the area, and by the way villagers manipulate the courts and officials in their appearances before them. On application and payment of fees, villagers can obtain transcripts of those records that pertain directly to their holdings, but they cannot obtain records of the holdings of others. In fact, they seldom do either, partly because, they say, the technical language is difficult to learn.

Since they appreciate the difficulty of changing the record of ownership, most villagers accept the patwari's word for the portions they own and for the fact that they do not own anything else. It is always possible, however, to argue a point of ownership directly in the courts, since identification of any given person with a person named in the record has to be made with the help of local witnesses. But such identifications, and other points of the record, are not often directly disputed.

The most common way that villagers attempt to change the record of ownership while escaping the requirements of the law is to argue that one of the lesser forms of rights was misrecorded. It is argued most commonly that the arrangement called "mortgage" was in fact an arrangement of sale of rights. At the time of the study, there were two cases wherein this was alleged to have occurred, and which were the focus of a good deal of hard feeling. In a mortgage arrangement, a temporary transfer of use of land is effected by paying the owner about one-half of its sale value. The payer then uses the land as his own until the owner makes a repayment, whereupon the person who advanced the money—and who is in fact a lender—has to return the land (taking whatever crops are growing, at their

harvest). Alternatively, if the borrower decides to sell out completely, the person who advanced the money has first option to buy the
land. To obtain ownership, a person who has advanced money in
this arrangement can argue before the court that the amount transferred was the full value of the land, and that the transaction was
therefore a sale.

Barring improprieties, mortgage arrangements cost half of
ownership arrangements, but they are less than half as secure a
means of obtaining land. The other principal arrangements are
various forms of tenancy. They are much cheaper than mortgaging,
and generally are for one year only. They are recorded for the village
when the overall revenue record is changed every eight years, but
villagers seem not to be greatly concerned to keep the record up to
date on interim arrangements. Almost always, however, they officially shift their tenants often enough to preclude the possibility of a renter's argument that his tenancy rights themselves were ancestral, which
would bring in all the apparatus of preemption to give him security
of tenure and freedom from raises in rates. Tenancy arrangements
are based on share-cropping for about one-half of the gain over costs,
as is described in detail in the following chapter. As a practical matter, and since no tenancies are ancestral, these arrangements are enforced by mutual needs and, therefore, mutual ability of owner (or
mortgage-holder) and renter to exploit the land and each other.
These needs reflect an overall strategy of exploiting the shorter-term
rights to make progressively finer adjustments between the amounts
and type of land held and other household resources and needs.

By combining the data of my village census with that of the
revenue record current for the time of the study, it was possible to
develop household profiles of internal population, cattle and land
use, and social relations. Statistical analysis of these profiles with the
help of the Statistical Package for the Social Sciences program (Nie,
Bent, and Hull 1970), utilizing the IBM 360/75 computer facility
at the University of California, Los Angeles, provides precise general
information on overall averages and correlational tendencies among
different parameters in these profiles.

The revenue record refers all rights to a "field map." The fields
in that map are not themselves owned or farmed units. They are
rather subdivisions of owned units made for convenience in survey-

ing. The fields form a grid for the identification of the holdings and managed units of specific persons, as well as for the separation of agricultural land from other types of land, such as roads, well sites, and *abadi*.

For analysis, the 123 village households were subsequently divided into 126 effectively discrete economic units, which included both the gurdwara (temple) and the single villager who lived in the village gate, neither of whom had been censused. (I lived in the gurdwara myself, and overlooked it through a combination of familiarity and confusion, for it had an attendant with a family, recently moved in from another village, who have not been included in the data here, but who would, because of their peculiar role, not add greatly to any of the general trends reported.) To these, 45 nonresident families named in the revenue record were added, along with the names of 23 persons whose whereabouts could not be definitely determined. With the addition of the panchayat and the canal department, this made a total population of all village households and all households mentioned in the record of 196 households. Of these, 142 were actively exercising rights in some portion of the village lands. (The rest were either those who were censused but lacked land or those who were mentioned in the record but who had sold out or otherwise vacated their rights.)

Analysis showed each of the 142 right-holding groups to be involved in from one to forty-two of the fields set out in the revenue map. The average number of fields per group was just over ten. The fields each group owned were generally redivided by them into several interpersonal arrangements of transfer or exercise of rights, ranging from one to twenty-six and averaging four. The total amount of land involved in all arrangements made by each right-holding family ranged from 1 to 242 bighas, or from 1/5 acre to 50 acres, and averaged 36.12 bighas.

Not all of the 142 right-holders are owners. There are 99 holders of rights in ownership out of the total, and these involve 62 of the resident groups in the village, 25 nonresidents, and 12 of those groups whose location could not be determined. The average amount of land owned was 18.73 bighas, and ranged from .02 to 103.35. Of 99 owners, however, 23 of the residents own land amounting to less than one bigha, and the land was in almost all cases agricultural land in name only. That is, it was purchased for house-sites on the edge of the *abadi* and would be carried as agricultural land only until the current record was revised. Of the nonresident owners, only 21 had rights in units of land large enough to farm. These pieces were often quite small, generally about one acre. There was one piece, by far the largest, of five acres and three of about three acres. Finally, of the groups that could not be located, 7 had units of land of less than one bigha, leaving 5 with significant holdings. Thus the largest group of owners, who hold by far the most land, are 39 families resident in the village.

Although a large amount of the land held on ownership rights is farmed by its owners, this is by no means always the case. Many farmers find it expedient to mortgage off or to rent some of their land, or to acquire additional land by either or both of these means. Table 9 summarizes the numbers of groups involved in each of the five main types of rights, together with the average size of land held in each case and two measures of the distribution of land among such arrangements. Some measure of the extent to which each group enters into multiple arrangements can be obtained by comparing the sum of the cases of each such arrangement with the total number (126) of groups who obtain income from land. Since the total number of groups involved in all statuses comes to 206, it is clear that on the average each family must participate in at least two types of arrangements.

The arrangements are often more complicated. Fourteen in-

Table 9
DISTRIBUTION OF RIGHTS IN RELATION TO INCOME

Right	No. of groups	Range of holding size	Mean size of holding	Standard deviation
Full ownership	33	.15– 73.00	16.32	20.68
Part ownership	64	.02– 42.13	3.91	9.10
Mortgage	25	.10– 24.53	4.69	5.75
Tenancy	77	.10– 65.72	11.59	14.07
Partner of owner	7	.35– 8.53	4.63	3.03
Total households deriving income from land on any combination of rights	126	.02–111.36	14.78	21.64

dividual men in the village farm land on various bases but own none outright. Fourteen other men who are owners let out some land on various tenancies and farm the remainder. Fifteen other owners both let out some land and take in other land on tenancy. Another eight own and farm some, let out some, and farm some held on mortgage, and also hold some on tenancy. Seven hold all they own but take additional land on rent, mortgage, or both, while eight others let out all the land they own and use other land that they hold on rent (four) or mortgage (four). Only two resident owners do not farm at all. Since there are often several men to a household, household arrangements can be still more complex than these. In general, the larger farms show the more complicated arrangements.

The overall pattern is one of interchange of resources within an occupational class, rather than, for example, a two-class system wherein a group of owners is clearly distinct from a group of landless renters. Land is readily moved about among households wherever considerations of mutual advantage seem to require it. The nonresident owners, consisting of fifty-eight individuals, represent an extension of the same pattern. Since they own in total just fifty acres of land, their average holdings are somewhat smaller than those of resident owners.

There are two principal reasons for people to manipulate their rights of ownership into the broader and more complex pattern shown by table 9, both of which reflect the importance of houses in the division of labor. First, almost all of the absentee owners mortgage or rent their land to residents, since they find it physically impossible to farm it and since, in many instances, their intention is to obtain capital to reinvest in agriculture in less well developed areas where labor and land prices are lower. Second, there is the interchange of land among villagers to obtain better balances in relation to household needs and resources.

While it is almost a truism that absentees cannot farm because they lack adequate village facilities, the relationship between landholding adjustments and household needs may not be so obvious. It appears quite readily, however, in a correlational analysis comparing household population, cattle, amounts of land owned, and amounts of land actually used to obtain income. The basic relationships are shown in table 10.

Table 10
HOUSEHOLD RESOURCES AND RIGHTS IN LAND:
GENERAL CORRELATIONS

	Family size	Cattle (all types)	Plow cattle	Total land owned	Total land from which income is obtained
Family size		.605	.466	.327	.421
Cattle (all types)	.605		.862	.384	.457
Plow cattle	.466	.862		.417	.490
Total land owned	.327	.384	.417		.564
Total land from which income is obtained	.421	.457	.490	.564	

NOTE: N = 142. Correlations are Pearson's coefficients calculated with SPSS subprogram PEARSON CORR with option 1, inclusion of omitted data (O values).

Family size is most closely correlated with the total number of cattle, then with total number of plow cattle, a result to be expected in the light of the critical importance of milk products for food, particularly for the very young. In addition, the correlations show the amount of land actually farmed to be more responsive to population of households than the amount of land owned (.421 compared with .327), while at the same time land owned and land used are both more responsive to the number of plow animals than to the total number of cattle. Finally, the high correlation of total land owned with total income (.564) shows landownership to be primarily a means of obtaining income. These are the relationships that most clearly demonstrate that progressively less permanent land rights are exchanged in order to bring about progressively finer adjustments of land to other resources and needs of household groups.

Of course, all types of land do not meet the same needs, since they are not equally well adapted to the same crops and techniques. Nor do all people start from the same point in respect to the land they own. Acquisitions that might best exploit the labor of a large number of adults will tend not to be the same as the acquisitions necessary to provide additional fodder for a buffalo that is needed to feed young children. Land that can offset fodder needs created by a decision to grow cotton may be different from land on which cotton itself is grown.

Table 11 describes the interplay of types of land actually used by working farms, and table 12 conveys some sense of the different ways long-term rights are traded off for short-term rights to obtain this land.

Table 11
STRATEGY OF USE OF IRRIGATION TYPES AS
SOURCES OF CROP-SHARE INCOME

	Well	Well-canal	Canal	Rain
Well		.061	.348	.649
Well-canal	.061		.019	.043
Canal	.348	.019		−.035
Rain	.649	.043	−.035	

NOTE: See note for table 10.

Table 11 shows the correlations, among all household holdings, of the amount of each type of land from which income is obtained with the amount of each other type of land from which income is obtained. Reading across the first row, the correlation coefficients obtained by analysis show that there is no particular connection between holding well-irrigated land and holding well-canal land, but that there is a fairly strong correlation (.348) between using well irrigated land and using canal land (the pattern of supplementing grains with intensive fodder), and a very strong tendency (.649) for those who use well irrigated land to offset it with proportional amounts of rainfall land (probably supplementing labor intensive crops with labor extensive fodder crops). By contrast with the pattern for well irrigated land the second row of correlations indicates that those who tend to farm larger amounts of well-canal land do so without offsetting it with other types (probably reflecting the internal efficiencies of this land which permits pacing in the use of draft animals).

Table 12 summarizes the general tendencies for families with differing amounts of owned land of each ecological type to use it themselves or trade it off through short-term arrangements for other types of land (or differing amounts of land as against cash or kind of income) in order to obtain the desired balances.

Table 12
LAND-SHARE IRRIGATION TYPES CORRELATED
WITH CROP-SHARE IRRIGATION

Type of land providing household income	Type of land owned			
	Well	Well-canal	Canal	Rain
Well	.626	.021	.163	.374
Well-canal	−.003	.607	−.056	.040
Canal	.165	−.021	.473	−.057
Rain	.437	.058	−.054	.411

NOTE: See note for table 10.

The diagonal shows the tendency for land of each type to be retained and used by its owners. The numbers to the side show the tendency for each type of land used to provide income to be associated with ownership of land of other types. While land in general tends to be retained for use by its owners, well irrigated land tends to be retained more often than canal land (.626 compared with .473), which is itself retained more often than rainfall land (.411). In addition, household income derived from well irrigated land tends to be slightly associated (.163) with ownership of canal land and more strongly associated (.374) with ownership of rainfall land. Conversely, those whose incomes derive from rainfall land tend more strongly (.437) to be owners of proportional amounts of well irrigated land, reflecting the pattern of interdependence noted in table 9. By contrast, households which derive income from well-canal irrigated land (considered the best and most productive of all types) tend only slightly to own additional rainfall land and tend slightly to avoid ownership of other types of land.

Reading down, the table shows the uses of ownership that correspond to the strategies for deriving income. Those who own well irrigated land derive income mainly from it (.626), secondarily from proportional amounts of rainfall watered land (.437), and third from canal land (.165). They tend, very slightly, to avoid obtaining income from well-canal land (−.003). Those who own well-canal tend to derive their income mainly from it (.607) and slightly from rainfall land (.058), while tending slightly to avoid utilizing canal land (−.021). Those who own canal land tend to use it and well land, and tend not to use other types. Finally, those who own rainfall land tend somewhat strongly (.411) to derive income from it and from well irrigated land (.374). In addition to these tendencies it can be inferred from the table (and explained by villagers) that there is also a general tendency for those who own canal land not to use it for direct income. Most of the owners of this type of land are not now resident in the village. It is a preferred form of investment, probably because its value is least dependent on integration in a local household that provides labor and fertilizer inputs. Owners of rainfall land also tend not to use it directly for income, though on a different basis. They apparently trade it more freely for other types of land within the village system—particularly well land, as indicated by the table (.374).

These patterns indicate the processes by which ecological relationships become part of configurations of households and, in return, the way households continue to maintain and modify the ecology by competition and cooperation.

The shorter-term adjustments of rights in land that each household makes to bring its holdings closer to its needs are carried into their even shorter term adjustments of crops on the land they acquire. The well land is divided in accordance with the farmers' estimates and given over to grains, legumes, and market crops; the rainfall land is divided among fodder, fiber, grains, drought-resistant legumes, and so forth. Each season, the farmer demarcates the subunits of his fields, raises furrows for flooding if the land is irrigated, cleans his channels, puts up thorn fences, and does whatever else is necessary to prepare the land to yield its final product in the desired proportions. Shares in wells and some other equipment are also traded, rented, sold, or mortgaged, as part of this pattern where necessary.

The system is constantly changing, and constantly requires adjustments—this is part of what is meant by saying it is a system of low information. But the locus of the sanctions—those things that can be lost or damaged by improper responses—is not the ecological objects per se but the household establishments, centering on the physical houses and those who keep their possessions within them. Perfectly healthy crops, which in no way damage the overall ecology, may be inappropriate to the labor supply of a household or to its food needs or, more likely, fodder needs, and the household will suffer thereby. Conversely, failure to properly manipulate the public consensus required to activate legal rights, or to obtain the fruits of more informal short-term arrangements, can also damage a household's position without having ecological effect. The system is integrated, and an action in one part affects others, but linkages that transmit the effects between these parts are different in form and substance from linkages that transmit effects from one ecological object to another.

Tools

In addition to cattle and land, many houses contain and are adapted to movable or semimovable tools that represent major investments, either in time or savings, and that cannot profitably be possessed by all of those who occasionally require their use. These major goods are listed in table 13.

While these tools are not ecological goods per se, they interact with houses and other household goods as do cattle and crops. Further, these particular tools, since they enable some houses to serve others and to maintain necessary internal economies, have an important general bearing on the overall division of labor. For example, the diesel engine of the masons, and the courtyard they keep it in, provides internal reasons for them to run a mechanical cornhusker, centrifuges for refining crystal sugar, and more recently a device for threshing wheat. They can profitably take up trades which someone without the engine, or a place to run it, or the necessary paraphernalia could not, and these trades serve the village widely and affect the internal structure of other households thereby. Similarly, the potters' goods and wheels, as well as their need to haul raw clay, makes it reasonable for them to keep donkeys and mules, so they alone are in the natural position to become the village teamsters for work which does not require an oxcart. Other houses rely on them both for pots and for this type of drayage. The village miller, who is also a Mason, needs a scale for milling, so it was more reasonable for him than for anyone else to get a large scale and do the village weighing for such transactions as the sale of cotton to itinerant jobbers and for packing grain to be sold by the farmers in the nearby markets.

Weavers' looms, particularly the *kumbal*, require a particular

Table 13
MAJOR MOVABLE EQUIPMENT OF VILLAGE

Number	Item and description	Owning group
1	Medical office	Doctor (Brahmin)
25*	Crushing presses for extracting juice from cane, complete with pans and beam for boiling juice down and turning press, using draft animals	Farmers
10	Geared beam for operating fodder-cutters with draft animals	Farmers
60*	Hand-operated water pumps	45, Durwaza side 15, Harijan side
80*	Cutting-wheels for making fodder	Generally on Durwaza side; one is in Shamlat
1	One-cylinder diesel engine, portable	Mason
3	Centrifuges for making sugar	Masons
1	Diesel-powered grain mill, in a brick house	Mason
1	Corn husker	Mason
2	Sets of carpenter's tools	Masons
2	Small forges	Masons
2	Potter's wheels	Potters
2	Kilns	Potters
4	Gins and *taRas* (bows used to fluff out cotton for quilts)	Cotton-ginners
19	Looms, generally in pairs of one *khadi* and one *kumbal*	Weavers (Harijan)
1	Anvil for shoemaking and repairing	Leatherworker (Harijan)
1	Bagpipe, used for wedding music	Sweeper

* Indicates approximate number.

type of house and a particular set of resources. The *kumbal* is a long, frameless, horizontal loom, essentially a hole in a floor where a weaver sits to open and close the warp in a random pattern, by means of foot pedals attached to the threads, while throwing a shuttle through it by hand. The warp is strung between short posts about eleven feet apart and near to the floor. Simple as this is, possession of it makes it easier for a person to go on to acquire and use the *khadi* (*khādī*), a wooden frame loom that can make a continuous roll of cloth. A working *kumbal* entails the possession of a moderate-sized house, specialized spindles, combs, customers, some supplies, and of course practice. These make a *khadi* a safer and less costly investment than would otherwise be the case. People generally begin with the *kumbal* and then acquire the *khadi*.

The poorer one is, the more significant are items of small cost. A simple loom is much cheaper and requires lower supporting arrangements than a useable piece of farmland, but it is perhaps as difficult for an agricultural laborer to acquire a loom on the basis of his sickles and trowel as it is for a mason to acquire land. If nothing else, the loom takes time to learn about and build, as well as a bit of wood and wire and a long room. But the closer one comes to a day-to-day subsistence living, the more difficult it is to acquire the surplus food that would provide the time, the money for wire and wood, and perhaps the extra house space. The more closely income approaches only what one needs to subsist on, the more difficult it becomes to divert production to the accumulation of new productive resources.

Every village house is connected with and contains the equipment that unifies a segment of ecology, bringing it into form as a unit capable of being managed. Each house thereby commits those who live in it to a certain limited range of actions, a certain range of reasonable responses to the overall situation. Given his house and other capital, the mason can buy or invent another machine to be run by his diesel in his courtyard, as he did during the time of my visit. But he cannot reasonably buy a large amount of land and go into farming, without selling out the entire mason establishment. Conversely, a farmer could not reasonably buy such a machine, since it would be less helpful to his overall pattern of work and capital than other alternative investments.

Supra-household Organization

The organization and the properties of each household create certain natural "interests" for its members—certain natural alliances it should form and certain types of opposition it should avoid. Among farming families arrangements of tenancy and mortgage are one form such alliances take. Groups fighting court cases are another. Households of laborers often have cows that produce manure but need fodder, so they form links with one or two appropriate farmer-houses and trade the former for the latter. Households such as the village miller's or the tailor's deal with different types and numbers of other households, on still different bases. Potters deal with all occupations, but no one potter can serve the whole village, while the blacksmith deals only or mainly with farmers and serves all families in this occupational category.

Each person in the village, to the limit of his abilities, argues for a particular picture of the village and of himself that meets his needs. He argues that he "is" bound to those he may wish or need to be bound to, and that his connection to them is of mutual utility and force. When he finds it necessary or useful, he says he "is" cut off from those who are not of use to him, or who may be harmful. A description of the overall pattern of such arguments is the "best" description of the division of labor, used by the most sophisticated, and respected, village leaders. It also best reflects the division of labor as a message source maintained by the choices of individual householders.

The use of ideas is most conveniently described in the way villagers themselves speak of them. Instead of saying what is literally true—that a group of people apply the ideas of caste to themselves, say they are more important than other ideas, and give them a certain sense—we will follow conventional village usage and say that the people in question are "in" or "of" (the word in consistent use translates best into "of") a certain caste, are not in other groups, and follow the caste occupation to some certain extent. Similarly, those who utilize the ideas of conflicting factions (or parties) will be described as being "in" the faction conflicts. And to say that a person is widely respected in one or another capacity is to say that many people support his conception of himself in the terms he uses. It should always be borne in mind, however, that what one is "in" can and does change from situation to situation and as one's position in the division of labor changes from time to time. That is, such "groups" are no more "real" than ways of talking in order to obtain the needed cooperation of others.

There are ten groups in the village that are recognized as containing families whose members consider themselves to be of "the same" caste (*jātī* or *jāt*) in some broad sense. They have general occupational interests in common, recognize themselves as "related" in some general way, and often are of one clan. These may be called caste groups without confusion, although, as was noted earlier, there are two conspicuous cases whose members assume more than one specific caste name from time to time. It is convenient to use these ten groups as the basis of discussion, and to describe the uses their constituent families make of the common ideas on social organization. The order of description is an order of rank derived from interviews with twenty-odd villagers.

Brahmins

The Brahmins are three small households, each of a different clan and economic occupation. Only one is a traditional village Brahmin whose family is "ancestrally" connected to Shahidpur. He owns the village temple and says that he prays in it each morning "for the welfare of the village." He is the Brahmin who farms, and is also the village postmaster and a retired schoolteacher on pension. His livelihood comes primarily from these latter positions. Apparently in connection with his farming, he participates in faction alignments, but does so freely and independently with a view to his own needs and ambitions. Recently, for example, it was said that he withdrew support from the dominant party when he did not obtain chairmanship of the village cooperative loan association. His son is presently a teacher. The land he and his son have is in a few well-irrigated plots near the *abadi*.

The village "doctor" (whose father is reported to have once held a certification to engage in minor practice in another state), head of the second family, is a relative newcomer to the village. He owns a small new house, his office is in a small building owned by the panchayat, and his income apparently derives from his profession alone. Mainly he dispenses first aid for cuts and small injuries, removes warts, and so on. But he is not recognized as being particularly effective. He participates in factional politics on the side of the group that dominates the panchayat, apparently in exchange for this office space. His role and manner is dependent, and he is not generally held in high repute.

The third Brahmin family is that of the village shopkeeper, who is widely respected in the village for a number of reasons, including remarkable personal humility and honesty. Such is his reputation that on certain holidays some people of the village give to him what is due the village Brahmin, sometimes instead of and sometimes in addition to what they give the "actual" Brahmin (the postmaster). This contrasts sharply with the way people deal with the doctor. The shopkeeper's income is from his shop, but his expenses are offset by friendly considerations. For example, it is reported that he was recently "given" a piece of land for a house site by a farmer who refused to sell the same piece to the doctor. He serves the whole village, and carefully avoids involvement in factional matters. His own way of putting it was that he did not "know about" any factions in the village.

Farmers

The Farmer (*jat*) caste contains forty-five families of one clan. There is in addition one Farmer family of a second clan in the village, who are not considered "permanent." They own no land, but are connected as long-term partners of one of the largest landholders, who is aligned with the dominant faction. All village Farmers report that their name includes "Singh," and that they are Sikh. In fact, they give their caste name, in Punjabi, as "Jat Sikh." The major clan group is internally divided into six *pattis* (*pattīs*), which means simply "divisions." The number of houses in each *patti* ranges from three to thirteen. Large numbers of members of the smaller *pattis* are reported to have migrated out—generally first to areas now in Pakistan, and thence, after Independence in 1947, to nearby parts of Punjab, Uttar Pradesh, and Rajasthan (many of these are the absentee owners previously described). *Pattis* are considered by most farmers to be crosscut by faction, more politely and commonly referred to locally as party (*pārtī*) affairs. Factional divisions in fact cut not only into *pattis*, but even between brothers and, in at least one case, between sons and father—though such cleavages are seldom made much of when they occur within one household group. Thirty-eight of the forty-six Farmer households have at least one member who actively and publicly asserts himself in these conflicts. No household has only members who are clearly and universally recognized by other villagers as not supporting one side more than the other. Eighteen of the active households are associated in the weaker party group. These households generally show high average landholdings per capita (4.72 bighas). Twenty households are associated with the dominant faction, and these generally have low average per capita landholdings (2.53 bighas). These ratios (discussed in more detail in chapter 8) reflect very different ecological conditions within the households, which structure conflicting strategies for the acquisition of new resources. Each party in its own way is competing for the help of others, in a general framework that encompasses many specific forms. Those with no land who ally with landowners supply labor and political support, and obtain regular employment, fodder, and other considerations in exchange. Farmers in each party help each other by informally exchanging labor, carts, major tools, and animals—which are not all possessed by all farming households. More formal support is provided by members of households who support the legal cases of their friends by witnessing in court, generally in matters pertaining to landholding.

The apparent reason for the pervasive factionalism among the Farmers is that there is no real need for solidary action across the whole group to countervail against the forces for division within it. The help needed by any one household can be provided by a few other households, and a large number of friends is, in a sense, less useful than a few friends and a few exploitable enemies. A friend can supply help, but enemies might "supply" land—both of which are in perpetual and related demand. Farmers' active interests in education and salaried work reflect the factional strategies, since education and cash are both helpful in acquiring land and in wider political activity. Young men, and women, in Farmer households are thus in an unusually good position to take advantage of new opportunities that should lead to increasing rates of gain in the future.

The only point on which Farmers have described Farmers as acting as a unit is in enforcing a ban on the sale of manure outside the village. The reason given for the ban is that the manure comes from the soil and must go back to it to maintain the village—a recognition of the ecological cycle and its overriding influence on all action. But in fact, as the next chapter will show, the "ban" does not imply the existence of real collective action by Farmers, since its "enforcement" can be attributed entirely to economic conditions that operate at the level of the individual.

The overall strength and importance of the Farmers create pressure on other groups in the village to define themselves in relation to the Farmers' interests and groups. The way they do this depends in good part on their own numbers and resources, as the description of the Brahmins has already suggested.

Masons

The Masons are the fifth largest caste-group in the village. They are one clan divided into seven families, and all adhere to the Sikh religion, report Sikh names, and dress as Sikhs should. They all avoid taking part in the party alignments of the village, generally following the pattern of the shopkeeper and claiming not to know about the local party groups. There seem to be two principal reasons for this, similar to the reasons of the Brahmin shopkeeper. As matters stand, they grind the grain, repair tools and implements, shell the maize, separate sugar, and do masonry, smithy, and carpentry for the entire village—both parties and all castes. Each of the seven Mason families is somewhat specialized, according to its specific properties. Four families earn almost all their income outside the village, and obviously have nothing to gain from factional activities. The other three families earn from half to nearly all of their income within the village. One does carpentry and owns the diesel engine and related devices. His brother, living with him in one large compound, mainly does the smithy work. The second household head specializes more in masonry, but can work with the first two when needed. The last household head runs the grain mill, which is owned by one of the four family heads who work outside. This arrangement obviously reduces internal competition to a minimum, and with it internal pressure to split into party groups. Masons emphasize that they all are not only clan members but also known kin to one another. They form, in fact, the largest group of actual kin in the village, although not the biggest household group or undivided family (which is a Farmer family of twenty-five members). In addition to their internal specialization, their specialized capitalization, and their avoidance of village politics is the fact that they do not work as laborers in the fields. They are few enough in number, and resourceful enough, so that they all earn their separate livings as specialists, skilled laborers of one sort or another. They are the only large group for which this is wholly true. It would probably not be true if they had not taken over the work of three traditional separate castes: Carpenter, Mason, and Blacksmith. (They say they receive no traditional dues, though some Farmers, without conviction, said they paid dues to them.)

Goldsmiths

The four Goldsmith (*sonār*) houses are all of one clan. They do not now report owning any equipment for goldsmithing. One family, consisting of one person alone, earns his living by transporting eggs to nearby towns (generally Samrala) and selling them. He has an egg crate mounted on a bicycle for the purpose. The other three small families earn part of their incomes from agricultural labor and part from tailoring. They own sewing machines for the latter trade. These have not been listed as capital goods in the same sense as the carpenter's tools because, first, they are relatively cheap, and can be purchased complete, whereas the Mason's engine and tools are more expensive, and require more esoteric information to operate. But more important, sewing machines are now so common a household item that ownership alone cannot be regarded as the exclusive mark of a tailor. Several knowledgeable informants estimated that there were about seventy sewing machines in the village during the last eight years, when the machines have become a customary part of a bridal endowment. The Goldsmiths do not take part in village politics, and from time to time leave the village to find employment elsewhere. Collectively, they are not numerous or wealthy enough by themselves to be a force in the village, and their occupations give them nothing to gain from alliances. Most members of the caste appear to have little social intercourse with other groups. Their religious affiliation is said to be Hindu, and they use the Hindu last name "Das" and wear no stereotyped Sikh symbols.

Barbers

Of the two Barber families reported to belong to the caste, only one presently resides in the village. The head of the second has been absent for many years, though he still owns a single, rather poor house, which stands locked and unoccupied. The present Barber in residence has a moderate-sized family in the village, and a son with his own family, who is employed outside the village. The house is quite commodious, in the center of the Durwaza side.

The Barber is sometimes described as being in "both" parties.

He talks politics but is not clearly allied, unlike the Brahmin and Masons who consistently claim not to know about factional matters. Barbering itself is not his major vocation, if he practices it at all. Shahidpur is a predominantly Sikh village, and he himself is Sikh. The rules of the religion specifically forbid the cutting of one's hair or beard. Instead, aside from what his son provides, he earns his living as the general director of marriage ceremonies on the Durwaza side of the village, and from some field labor. His wife serves as the midwife on the same side. Everyone queried listed him as their *lagi* (*lāgī*), a receiver of traditional dues, *lag* (lāg) paid in kind. In fact, however, most people don't provide such dues most of the time. If they did, his income would be far higher than it is. His due is stated to be one maund (about 82 pounds) of wheat and one of corn a year, each in its season, beside what is given to him by people he summons to weddings. Traditionally, each person he summons gives one rupee, some cloth, and a meal. He might summon up to twenty people for a wedding, but at least two. If each person who names him as his *lagi* gave him the dues, he would have 61 maunds of wheat, and 61 of corn each year—or a total of 10,004 pounds of grain a year. This would feed over thirty-six people. Its monetary value would be Rs. 2,806, which is obviously much more than the Barber makes or consumes. It is in fact much higher than the average income in the village, and would probably rate as high among the better-off landowning farmers. It is equal to the total outrun of about eight average acres.

If only those who actually have marriages in any year were inclined to give the Barber an approximation of his traditional dues, the total annual amount would be about four to six maunds of wheat and an equal amount of corn as well as some cash. The total grain would be about 840 pounds, which with the cash and wages from labor and from his wife's work would give him an income consistent with what is visible. Some did report this payment of "dues," and it is most probably what is uniformly done in actuality. In this context, the Barber would have little to gain by serving either party alone.

Potters

The Potters of the village are also all of one clan, and all are Sikh. As implied by the kiln noted in the inventory of equipment (table 13), they actually manufacture pots for the village. This is done on a contract basis. Each of the six houses of Potters serves a number of the houses of the villagers, in proportions and on bases that they decide among themselves, at least in theory. (Two of the houses seem to do most of the work in fact.) They take payment in kind, again called *lag*, from these houses, for each year. In the course of that year they supply the household needs for pots. (Here, as below, *lag* is clearly understood as an actual contractual payment based on market condition, not a ritual due or "traditional payment" in the sense of a gift that is not contingent upon the performance of specific services.) A Potter also has a traditional role in marriages as they occur, which is in fact carried out. The annual amount of *lag* reported is ten kilos of wheat and ten of corn, each in its season. There is a corresponding understanding of "normal" amounts of pots of different types that a family requires, above which its contract might be renegotiated. At current market rates for both grain and pots, this is a reasonable "price" for the goods. Since different people report different Potters, and personal observation confirms that pots are manufactured and distributed without immediate tallying or charging, it is reasonable to suppose that the system is more or less as described.

The Potters' incomes from contractual payment in kind are supplemented by agricultural labor on a per diem basis, and by more diffuse exchanges with Farmers and others on the basis of personal friendships. The two houses who predominate in potting also receive income as village teamsters, and this has become even more important as their work as local brickmakers has been ended by outside competition. They haul small quantities of bricks from a large brick-kiln near Morinda.

Two other Potter households are involved in the rivalries of party, and support the dominant group. One of these has a small amount of farmland on rental. This involvement is consistent both with their basic professional positions and with reliance on agricultural labor, as well as with the lack of an internal division of labor among Potters comparable to that of the Masons. At the same time, however, their clan connections to other Potter families seem strong. Each household lists the others as their main "friends" and supporters on ceremonial occasions. This is very likely connected with their

collective low ranking in the village, and with certain internal problems that appear to make them collectively sensitive to exploitation
by some Farmers. Judging by rumors, there is a disproportionate
amount of involvement of Potter girls and wives in the clandestine
romantic affairs of the village, which can in part be related directly
to the economic and demographic constitution of the households.

While all Potters, when asked directly, say they are Sikhs, they
do not all consistently use "Singh" as part of their name, or adopt all
the other outward marks worn by the Farmers, Masons, Barbers, and
others.

Water-carriers

The Water-carrier (*mehira*) caste of the village is represented
by one woman and her son. They live together in a small room in
the compound of a large old farming house, shared by a few other
poorer families and an older bachelor, in rather uncomfortable circumstances. The woman's husband died in 1963, but he was still
generally returned as a *lagi* by other villagers in 1965 (which indicates that the formal caste relationship is seldom if ever invoked in
practical day-to-day matters). The small income apparent from her
circumstance seems to come in part from the *lag* that she collects
from those who are having weddings, in which, like the Barber, she
has a traditional place. The Water-carrier can act for the Barber in
his absence, and several people reported giving her token gifts—
more out of sympathy than because of a response to tradition alone.
The reported due of the Water-carrier is a half maund of wheat and
of corn in their seasons, plus perhaps a bundle of each for fodder at
the same time. Although it is conceivable that the Water-carriers
might be provided for at their apparent standard by carrying water
for the few houses without pumps on the Durwaza side, I saw many
people hauling their own water. But I never saw her carry any large
amounts. The son works as an agricultural laborer, and I saw the
mother working in the fields too, although no one would acknowledge
that a woman in her circumstance was in their employ or in the employ of anyone they knew. (To do so would appear to condone lack
of charitability.) Since at the stated rate of dues, seven or eight
families—which is just a bit more than the normal number who have
weddings each year—would provide the income she appeared to have

if it were supplemented by the son's field work and possibly her own, it seems most likely that her income derives principally from these sources and not from carrying water. They are unambiguously Sikh.

Cotton-ginners

The Cotton-ginners are one family, the only Muslims in the village. They have been established in the village since before Independence, and were apparently not disturbed during the violence attendant upon Partition. In addition to the work their equipment shows they do, for which they are paid piece rates, they take agricultural day labor. As ginners they serve a number of nearby villages. The family has a second residence in one of them—and is in fact segmented into three subfamilies: one of the father and one of each of two sons. The sons move from place to place according to their work. The family comes together in Shahidpur only at the peak work seasons. Just after the summer harvest, farmers bring them cotton to gin for the fiber they will use for their own houses and for the seed for the next crop. The stated rate of pay at this time is an equal weight in wheat for the weight of cotton they process. If nothing else, their small numbers, specializations, and mobility keep them from being involved in the village politics. They, like the Brahmin shopkeeper, the Barber, and the Masons, stand only to lose from such involvement.

Sadhu

The Sadhu "caste" is represented by a religious sadhu and the family of his brother. The sadhu is an Udasi, a particular order of sadhus associated with Sikhism. As the name of such an order, whose members are celibate, it is not properly either a caste or a clan name. Locally, the "clan" of the one family of this group is therefore said to be of *sād* caste, a term translated, sometimes mirthfully, as "beggar." The actual head of the dharmsala, *mahant* (priest) Mahanand is said to be celibate, in accordance with the tradition of his order. But his brother obviously is not celibate. The family group manages the lands of the village dharmsala with one permanent partner.

The family is held in rather low esteem in the village for various reasons, mainly respecting the moral character of several members.

Partly in token of this, their religion is generally said to be Hindu rather than Sikh, and their "true" final name is said to be Das. This is in the face of the fact that the son of the old mahant's brother styles himself with a regular Sikh name and the outward marks of a Sikh. The agricultural lands they farm were given to the dharmsala for the life of the mahant. They are supposed to use it to maintain the dharmsala, which is a considerable structure just into the village from the village gate. Its resources are intended for the comfort of guests of the village, particularly other Udasi sadhus. The son mentioned makes an effort to become involved in village politics, but his help is not used. It is doubtful, in fact, that he could be useful or dependable, since his status as a landowner is legally unclear. There is consistent though speculative talk among Farmers of resuming the lands or displacing this family perhaps when the mahant dies. But it appears from the revenue records that similar dissatisfaction has existed for about one hundred years without any such village action. The brother's family is described as the principal current source of embarrassment, however, and not the mahant or the Udasis as such. This family is not considered to be permanent. They were invited to come to the village only about seventeen years ago and they could be forced out of the village without any change in the legal status of the dharmsala. As it stands, the dharmsala as an institution with one hundred bighas of land (about twenty acres) is the largest landholder in the village. As a "house" it is also one of the village's most impressive structures.

Harijans

On the Harijan side of the *abadi*, the Harijans group themselves into four clans, two large and two small. As was already indicated, Harijans are intensely involved in agriculture, generally as agricultural laborers. Their ideal relationship to Farmers was illustrated by a short folk-story told to me by a Farmer in a discussion of this same topic. It describes the beginning of the world, when God had all the castes before him and was giving to each his special property. He first asked who would take the land. None would. He offered it to the Potter, and the Potter refused. He offered it to the Harijan (*Camār*, or Leatherworker), and the Harijan refused, as did all other castes

99

in turn. Finally, God offered it to the Farmer, and the Farmer also refused. Then the Harijan said to the Farmer, "I will help you," and the Farmer accepted the land.

Strictly speaking, "Harijan" is not a caste term. The word was popularized by Gandhi to remove the stigma of the English term "untouchable," and literally means "born of God." Unfortunately, in the opinion of villagers this carries implications of illegitimacy— that one born of God is not born of man—and the term is not considered appropriate to use in direct address. It is reported to be used only in reference because of a peculiar condition within the group it names. It commonly happens in Shahidpur that two people who acknowledge membership in this one caste group or even in one clan (in one case, two brothers), often report the names of their castes differently. A man who reports his caste as Weaver not infrequently has a brother who reports his as Leatherworker—both names of traditional callings and both suitable for use in address. The logical paradox of attributing two castes to one group of kin is freely acknowledged, but when they are confronted with it most members of the group simply "decide" that they are Weavers, which traditionally has a higher status. Yet it is also true that even those who have looms refer to themselves and their occupation as Leatherworker (which has more of the sense of "general laborer") when they hire out for agricultural work. (As was noted, the actual profession of leatherworker, or cobbler, is almost nonexistent.) Weaving itself is always done on a piece-work basis, and the title is used only in that context. There is, of course, no way to decide on an "objective" basis what the "real" caste is, and no point in doing so. "Harijan" is a convenient cover term. The more specific caste terms are utilized for address depending on the purpose and the preferences of the speakers in specific situations.

The largest Harijan clan comprises twenty-four houses and includes among its members the elected head of the panchayat, the *sarpanch* (*sarpānch*), of the village. Most of its members live in the lane with its own small gate that can be closed at night. Other lanes similarly tend to be dominated by one clan or the other. The second largest clan has fifteen families and includes the one Leatherworker with the complete shoe-repair bench, a retired army cobbler. The remaining two clans comprise two families each. The owners of looms are all in the larger clans, seven out of the first and eight out of the second. Of these, only three families have full-fledged *khadis*. The others own *kumbals*. The *kumbal* can only make a piece of cloth of fixed width and length—also called *kumbal*; two are stitched together lengthwise to make a blanket and general wrap. One *kumbal* takes two days to make and sells in the village for about sixteen rupees. Since these looms are most of the time not in use, it must be considered that the only really "professional" weavers are the owners of the *khadis*, and that the *kumbal* owners weave to supplement their incomes. This means that the vast bulk of the income of the Harijans comes from day labor, as was regularly reported and observed.

All villagers, Harijan and others, who were asked directly said the Harijans were all Sikh by religion. But in my own census, several returned their names with "Das" or other such Hindu markers in place of "Singh." The official revenue record showed that even some who told me they were "Singh" had reported Hindu names officially. The traditional marks of Sikh men were also less consciously employed in this group, and still less among Sweepers, than among Farmers.

Next to the Farmers, Harijans are the group most intensely involved in the village factional politics. Four of the forty-one Harijan households actively support the weaker faction, while five support the dominant faction. Most of the supporters of the dominant party are from the clan of the *sarpanch*, with one house from the other large clan. The weaker party is supported by three houses from the second clan, and one from the *sarpanch*'s clan (who lives outside the closed lane). The basis of factional activity among Harijans can be seen in their numbers, lack of internal specialization, and reliance on agricultural employment by Farmers. This is particularly true for those who have no looms. Since Harijans are dependent on the Farmers, they are naturally in competition with each other, just as Farmers are. They align themselves internally into groups connected with the alignments within the Farmers. Their ties follow ties of friendship and economic cooperation between individual men and families, and add an element of security which would not otherwise exist. The *sarpanch* himself farms over ten acres of land held on rental and mortgage, while several other Harijans hold at least some land on a similar basis. The two households that support the weaker faction, however, hold no land on any basis—as one would expect from the complementary differences between the Farmer groups themselves. The weaker faction of land-rich employers needs employees, the dominant faction of small owners needs help from other small owners. One can see the Harijans' political activity as an attempt to capitalize their physical strength, which it undoubtedly does, over and above the value of their performance of agricultural labor alone. Since the Harijan houses are similar to each other in not being occupationally specialized, each household is to some extent in competition with the others. Under such conditions at least some families have more to gain by conflict with other Harijans, joining with Farmers in party alliances, than they would gain by supporting the idea of caste solidarity and avoiding party conflicts.

In their capacity of Leatherworkers, the Harijans are said to receive dues from the Farmers, in exchange for which they provide shoes for the families of the Farmers at the rate of two pairs per person per year. Some add that they provide two days of free labor a year, and, in addition, work in the field. The pay for this is differently reported, from one-fortieth of the yield of the farmer to a flat (and fancifully high) four "bundles" of wheat and corn (at about seventy-four pounds each), plus forty-one pounds of gur, and "whatever else" the Harijan would ask for, worth a minimum of ninety-three rupees. In this case, all this was paid out, supposedly, for ten pairs of shoes a year, worth about five rupees a pair. As with the Barber, the verifiable accounts are those which minimize the dues. Setting aside the fact that, with the one exception noted, Leatherworkers cannot make shoes, the higher figures are both too high for what is said to be done and too low to provide an income adequate to sustain life, given that there are on the average only between one and two Farmer houses per Harijan house. Actual perquisites are only meals at the weddings of families the Harijans are on friendly terms with and work regularly for, and some understanding of basic casual work over a period for a basic consideration in kind. The bulk of Harijan income, even from people who give them *lag*, certainly comes from direct payments for prearranged daily work. This income is supplemented by weaving wherever possible, by working for the Masons in unskilled capacities at the same rate as for the Farmer, by military service, by teaching, by sweeping out houses, by working in the sugar mill, and so on. A few old men of Leatherworker caste have to supplement their income by simply begging, appealing to the obligation to care for those of one's village which some, at least, of the Farmers feel. If wedding expenses may be held as an index, spendable incomes of Harijan households are a tenth or less than those of the Farmers—the difference between hiring a bus to go for one's new bride, or going on bicycle and on foot.

Sweepers

Finally, the Sweepers are the poorest in the village, and the lowest in rank. They are in fact the only group in the village about whose position on the rank scale, which must exist by the definition of a caste, there is unanimity. They are also the only group whose caste term is considered to be humiliating and is not used in their presence. When they are within hearing, the members of the group are politely referred to as Balmik, or "of" Balmik. The name Balmik refers to the author of the Ramayana, a pious sadhu of Sweeper caste. He is considered to have been one of India's greatest literary and religious teachers.

The Sweepers are of one clan, and nine families. One of them keeps the only pigs of the village, whose reported number—thirteen —is a little misleading. At the time of my census there was just one adult pig, a sow, and her litter of twelve piglets. Thus the more normal population of pigs is the sow alone. Apart from the pig, and of course the houses, the only notable moveable capital owned by the Sweepers is a set of bagpipes owned by one family head. He is part of a band composed of his brother, a son, and brother's sons, who play at weddings in the area. Another Sweeper supplements his income by making for most of the villagers winnowing fans for wheat out of reeds and gut. Two houses farm fair amounts of land they hold on mortgage—about five acres in one case and an acre and a half in the other. The rest apparently subsist on agricultural labor and sweeping.

There are twelve working men among the Sweepers. They divide the houses of the villagers theoretically among themselves and then contract with the individual owners to keep the barns of their respective houses clean. (As with the Potters, there is no sense that the division of work must be in equal units.) For this they are paid according to the heads of cattle owned by each family. Rates quoted by Farmers vary. The one that seems most trustworthy grades the rate according to cattle, in a way that accords roughly with the mess they make: ten kilos of grain per buffalo, five per ox, five per camel, and two per goat; this is given once every six months. The actual dung of the first two animals remains the property of the house. In addition to sweeping barns, the Sweepers rotate the duty of sweeping the *durwaza* once a day, along with other such public areas not near the houses. If only adult animals in the village are counted, the income of the Sweepers would be about 3,500 kilos a year of grain, or about 3/8 pound of dry flour per person per day. In the context of their action as laborers and the supplementary activities noted, this is a believable figure that conforms with their visible means and actions. The owners of houses are responsible for seeing that those who sweep their barns also sweep the lanes by their houses. In addition, the Sweepers have to rotate the duty of sweeping the *durwaza*, both of which duties are in fact regularly performed.

It should again be noted that the *lag* is stated as a rate rather than a fixed due. It is not a formal obligatory payment based solely on inherited relationship.

Although both landholding Sweepers support the dominant party, Sweepers are not generally described in the village as important politically. In the recent consolidation operations, land was parceled out to Harijans in order to provide each household with a work area. Despite Gandhi's intention, "Harijan" in this case meant precisely what it means in the village and in this account. Sweepers received no land.

The social isolation of Sweepers on the Harijan side has no precise parallel on the Farmer side of the village. In part, it may be related to occupational convenience, since the Sweepers apparently maintain compost pits for their Farmer employers in the area between their houses and the *phirmi*. (I neglected to enquire specifically into the way these were managed, through an oversight.) But it also seems related to the difference in numbers between Sweepers and Harijans. Because the former are few, they can expect a basic living out of their "traditional" calling. Because the Harijans are many, they must depend on agricultural labor, which is both more competitive and more subject to market conditions. The work also naturally encourages "bargaining" over political influence and favors. All Harijans could not pursue their traditional calling even if they wanted to. In these circumstances, Harijans have more to gain than to lose by trying to isolate the Sweepers and thereby to circumscribe the political importance any individual could gain.

The overall pattern in the descriptions of these village "castes" reflects the dominating importance of agriculture as the focus of concern of most households. Villagers are described in terms of their involvement in agricultural work. The description recognizes a first commitment to farm work by the Farmers. It then indicates a second rank of people who because of numbers and lack of capital are specialized farm laborers, the Harijans. Beyond them are the marginal workers of the village, who have nonagricultural trades and who work occasionally in agriculture: Potters, Watercarriers, Cotton-ginners, Goldsmiths, and Sweepers. Actual weavers, though not a caste in themselves, should be placed in this category. Last are the groups almost never drawn into the agricultural labor market: Brahmins and Masons. They are few in number and highly capitalized. The intensity of party activity follows roughly along with the dependence on agriculture, being mitigated by religious differences or small numbers in cases noted. Whether a caste as a whole fulfills its "traditional calling" depends on the necessity for the calling, the numbers of persons and workers in the caste, and their equipment in the general context of the system and demand in the village. Such fulfillment is not of great importance to the authors of this description of the system, because it is not germane to the function of the description. The fulfillment or nonfulfillment of a traditional calling does not affect the service any household can perform in aiding another to meet its managerial needs.

Summary

Perhaps because of its force on practical actions, there is more temptation to speculate and theorize on the various "needs" that the division of labor fills, or the evolutionary forces that underlie or shape it, than there is to see it as a system of information.

But for all its apparent solidity, the division of labor cannot be consistently or properly construed as some sort of objective reality rather than a set of symbolic keys for differentiating behavior. There are, of course, some odd bits of truly "hard" phenomena, like houses, cows, and goods in general. But other equally crucial elements in the pattern, the boundaries of the controlling groups, seem on in-spection to evaporate into a matter of people's beliefs about people's beliefs. The village census, for example, would have been meaning-less if it relied on a physical record of the human beings actually in the houses when they were visited. Instead, it is (in part) a record of answers to the question "Who lives here?" The person answering gives the proper names of people he or she believes to live there, and who, in their view, would themselves claim to live there. In some cases there was disagreement. Some individuals were reported in several houses, others in none. In each case, the confusion arose when dif-ferent people made different evaluations of either the intention of the census or the probable report of the persons accounted for, or both. Since the questionnaire for the census deliberately included not only the question "Who lives in this house?" but also, for each person, the further questions "Where does ——— sleep?" and "Where does ——— eat?" there can be no question of ambiguity. Even these latter questions, in the opinion of the villagers, involved guessing at the loyalties, not the actual place of sleeping or resting, of the person in question. Actual physical places of eating are not worth remembering. They are not part of the message source we have called the division of labor; they do not themselves constrain the formation of significant actions in relation to control and man-agement of productive goods. With matters such as caste member-ship and party affiliation, it is obvious that what is being reported is a combination of the informant's own views with those he thinks the person described would acknowledge.

Although the fact is obscured by the distance between the vil-lagers and those who will read this description, and by the conven-tion of not using proper names in ethnographic accounts, the division of labor is the one system of information that is directly organized around the living individuals of the village. The villagers use it to enable them to act properly in respect to named individuals just as they use their ecological knowledge to enable them to produce the greatest biological product with the crops and animals resources at hand.

The form of the division of labor reflects its function, as in other systems. Even though we can find no clear "referents" for statements about the group membership of any given villager, the effort to find out about his membership will lead us precisely to those people who influence him most, and to those material circumstances that enable us to predict his cooperative and competitive interests. We would go to the person, to his family, and to those he claims as associates, to those who claim him as associate, and to his properties (or the properties he claimed and those that people said were his). The form of the message source resides precisely in this pattern of action, of association of relevant elements, and not in the seeming "referents" as such. The same pattern of associations, as applied in arranging action, in turn maintains the system.

This procedure for obtaining and using information on the division of labor, for tracing the form of this message by responding to its cues, should seem very natural and normal to us. We do it in our own societies, if we are wise, with respect to people whose actions might affect us. But familiarity and naturalness should not obscure the fact that this specific procedure involves different patterns and modes of action from those followed in obtaining and using ecological information, or information of other systems yet to be described. This is why information from the ecological source cannot guide manipulations of controlling groups, and vice versa.

It is important to observe that, as with the ecology, the high entropy of the division of labor as a message source is an aspect of its form. It is the direct result of the number of elements that make it up and their degree and kind of integration with one another. Although the term "entropy" can be construed as meaning "randomness," the high-entropy source is not *simply* random, in the sense of disorganized or chaotic. It is not irregular or disorganized in the sense that it is not a system. Rather, it is a specific type of system that presents a large number of choices to any individual who uses it. These choices are socially and conventionally structured. But they are structured in specific ways that permit both systems to fulfill the formal requirements of the definition of a high-information message source. They are structured so that the choice of one element—action on the basis of one element—does not determine action that must or can be taken in relation to a relatively large portion of the remaining elements. In the ecology, areas of free choice are structured by the interaction between biological patterns of growth and dependence and human and animal needs, and by the overlap among needs and uses of each object in the system. In the division of labor, similar areas of free choice are structured by the interaction of requirements for a uniform mode of communication of common needs with the inherent irreducibility of the position of one communicator to that of another. Each villager knows his needs with respect to his management strategies (principally household strategies), and has some general appreciation of the needs of others. He also knows the common means of describing the broad overall pattern, the caste groups and their characteristics and inclinations. In practice, each person combines these two principal elements—his sense of strategy and of loyalty and interests—to decide on his relations to any other villager. But at the same time, each person who is identified with others by means of the common problems and concepts cannot by that fact ever be fully equated with them, even if they describe themselves in similar terms. Each person is and is known to be irremediably locked within the resources he shares with those he lives with and who depend on him. It is because of this that the social group terms are only metaphoric. Also because of this, each person can only use the commonly employed low-information concepts in his own way, a way that is systematic from his perspective and with respect to his needs, but which cannot be fully equated with the usages of any others. Each such individually formulated system of concepts and resources, together with the pattern of strategies of those of each person's household, makes up one of the basic elements of the division of labor, analogous to each biological population and its needs and effects in the ecology.

Since no person can occupy the position of another, a person using the system not only has the option of adapting his usages toward that of any other person, or any other selection of persons, but he must do so, with a considerable range of freedom in the modes or methods or combinations he can use. Because he is inherently unique, each person in the system has (and cannot avoid) the freedom to choose any current way of defining perspectives, or any combination of them, so long as he can retain some appearance of consistency. And he has, unavoidably, the freedom to apply these manipulations to any needs he may have or construct. He does not have the option, however, of developing a wholly new perspective, of forcing others to completely accept his, or of using concrete resources not available within the system. These requirements spring from basic conditions that make him seek cooperation and help others. They cannot be violated without the violator ceasing to function as a part of the village system. Once a person accepts these prerequisites, each action he takes imposes its own conditions that further limit his freedom. Each person he cooperates with imposes his own demands in return for help. Even though these demands can be changed, or minimized, they are nevertheless quite forceful when they operate. Frequently, as can be inferred from the foregoing description of loyalties and alliances, commitment to support one other person's perspective within the village confines one to the avoidance of other conflicting perspectives for fear of diffuse or specific sanctions that may be imposed in the context of interpersonal and inter-household competition. Loyalty of one Farmer to a Harijan in times of slack work, when the Harijan is in need, precludes the Harijan's cooperation with some other Farmer at the times of harvest, when farm labor is generally scarce. Adherence to one faction is expected by those in both factions to entail certain obligations to some and antipathies to others. Avoidance of factional disputes precludes seeking certain kinds of considerations, again under threat of diffuse or perhaps, in some cases, particular sanctions. (During the 1955 conflict between Pakistan and India it was necessary for me to be absent from the village for several months. During this time certain shifts of loyalties among those I had been working with put me in the position of having all of my active helpers in one faction. Thereupon members of the other group took me as a factional participant as well, rather than a neutral. Later when I was out of the village again, they went to the village gurdwara, where I stayed, with the intent to destroy the goods I had left in my room there. Their idea was that the gurdwara was common property of all villagers, and that its use by one faction was a threat or affront to them. Fortunately the village granthi, an acknowledged neutral, spoke up in my behalf and prevented their entering the building for this purpose.)

A final aspect of both the division of labor and the ecology— and to a certain extent, of the economy, to be described next—is that because of their size and complexity there is no possibility that one person can use the system as a whole to guide his daily actions. A user of either message source must specialize. He must confine himself to only a small part of it in order to master the detailed responses called for. No one can learn or enact all the agricultural or supporting skills, or know how to raise all the animals involved in the system as a whole. Nor can he exploit what he does produce in all possible ways. No one, in the division of labor, can cooperate with all other households or individuals, or exploit all possible strategies with those he does work with.

The high entropy of the division of labor, as of the ecology, is the overall product of the relationships between the different options it directs and the total number of possible options it presents in relation to those that any person can utilize. High entropy in this sense is a result of very definite organizational structures, and of highly systematic actions that maintain those structures. It is not mere absence of order, and most particularly it is not the absence of organizational modes that affect behavior and that are susceptible to precise description and analysis.

Chapter V

The Economy

*O*nce the ecology and division of labor have been analyzed out, the economy of the village can be seen to consist strictly of a self-adjusting system for quantitative monetary evaluation. It includes both the practices of measuring and marketing that provide the operational framework for the system, and of the practices of currency exchange and use.

A system of quantitative evaluation in the present sense is something much more specific than a system using "money" in the sense recently discussed by Helen Codere (1968). Working in terms of a continuing debate in anthropology and economics, Codere spoke of money as a "symbol of . . . exchangeable goods" (p. 559). Codere recognized that systems of such "symbols" are not necessarily quantitative, although they may be coupled with quantitative concepts and devices for applying them (pp. 561 ff.). Nor, in the nature of the case, are such symbols "standards of evaluation"—bases for comparing one good with another, rather than with "money" itself. Codere speaks readily of money that is only exchangeable for one or a few other goods. Since it is neither quantitative nor an evaluative standard, "money" in Codere's sense cannot be the basis of a self-adjusting system for the evaluation and selection of alternative courses of action, though what it *is* is not clear, since the boundary to be drawn between it and "goods" themselves is not encompassed in the definition provided. Any good capable of being exchanged must be regarded as a "symbol" of its capabilities, as something meaningful in terms of expectations about it. But if this is so, in the last analysis any exchangeable good is "money" in Codere's sense.

In the present case, "money" is legal money as defined in India, neither more nor less. The monetary system of evaluation in Shahidpur is laid upon the ecology and the division of labor, in the sense that the monetary prices are prices of items in the ecology and division of labor. Economic markets are the means by which the monetary values are applied to these desired objects, and the markets also serve the purpose of transfer of rights to them, either directly for other objects or for currency. Villagers turn very little money to other than productive ends—that is, very little money is used to obtain ownership of items that have no ecological significance.

As with the ecology and division of labor, there is no point in distinguishing the economy in some "real" sense from the economy as known to and acted upon by the dominant segments of the community. "Standard economic theory" cannot be presumed to be an applicable description of what is "real" (as against information that natives operate with), for three principal reasons. The first is an ethnographically unrealistic notion of "price."

Economists commonly consider that a good has, at any given time, one definite price. While there can be no objection to this practice in a general form, the further common understanding that a price is "definite" only when it is written, say "$120" or Rs. 23.47," not "between Rs. 23 and Rs. 33," places unreasonable strictures in the way of accurate description. The position that a price is definite only when it is written a certain way makes prices into something other than decision-making devices that must be seen in the context of the decisions to be made. Village prices are subject to an annual fluctuation because of the pattern of production and the facilities for storage of agricultural commodities. Many prices, even prices actually paid, have an indeterminate character because of the importance of "good will," the possibility of nonmonetary rewards over a long period of time, the changing practical value of money itself, and the "value" of nonmonetary accouterments to cash transactions, all of which naturally arise in a community which is both small and ecologically self-contained.

Two other current assumptions in economic analysis that do not readily apply to Shahidpur have recently been summarized by James Duesenberry (1967) in relation to his own reassessment of their general utility. These are (1) that every individual's consumption behavior is independent of every other individual, and (2) that consumption relations are reversible in time (p. 1). These two assumptions are implicit in the common strategy of economic analysis whereby a decision is analyzed only in terms of the price of the good in relation to other goods, productivity of the good in relation to other goods, and ability of the buyer to pay for the good. Whenever these quantitative variables arrange themselves in a certain way, a transaction should occur. The temporal position of this occurrence in a sequence of events is not itself a factor in the scheme. To conform with these assumptions the monetary evaluation that analysts place upon options can depart radically from the evaluation placed on them by the actual persons making the decisions. This is because the economists' evaluations must include all the "hidden" or "economic" costs, and even "social costs," that arise from the various possible actions. Certain empirical difficulties that this approach creates in analyzing peasant behavior will be discussed below. But first it is important to recognize that it also has very broad implications for the overall structure of any analysis of the present sort.

The practice of assigning arbitrary "economic" prices to conform with the "standard" theoretical postulates corresponds to the practice of assigning arbitrary cultural "norms" to conform with the idea that such norms govern all action. Each practice tends to inflate the scope of its theory and thereby precludes recognition of the influence of factors covered by the other. "Price," like "norm," becomes a rubric to explain in retrospect *all* action, all decisions. When thus magnified, as it was in the famous Knight-Herskovitz controversy (Herskovitz 1952) the scope of economics comes into conflict with that of anthropology, and a balanced combination of insights from each is precluded. In the present context, such a view of economics (or of culture) could obscure the contribution of the village economic system as one message source among several, each with its own assignable but distinct relationship to individual action.

In this connection, it is useful to point out that Duesenberry attacked these assumptions (within an economic framework) precisely by deflating them—by arguing that the predictive value of economic analysis could be improved by seeing economic decisions in the context of such things as the *relative* socioeconomic positions of those who make them (pp. 24–26, 111) and by seeing economic decisions as interrelated because they are based on shared "learning and habit formation," including emulation, rather than simply on individualistic "rational planning" (p. 24).

By saying that economic behavior is influenced by social and psychological factors, Duesenberry is saying that the traditional economic parameters of these choices, prices and values, need not be stretched to encompass such factors within their numerical quantities.

Economic considerations occur in a context of other considerations. Although the content of these "other considerations" in America and Shahidpur are very different, the basic relation of prices and economic choice to some larger noneconomic context seems to me to be the same. In the West, many economic choices involve nonproductive goods, and those that involve productive goods involve productive means of a technological, mechanical, or chemical nature. The behavior of prices naturally reflects the behavior of these objects. In Shahidpur most choices involve productive goods, and most such productive goods are ecological. In this context, economic descriptions in terms of prices, rates of depreciation, rents, and the like naturally reflect the different properties of these evaluated goods.

When the economy is understood as a system of conventional usages designed to store and transmit information about the overall desirability of certain aspects of different ecological options, the difficult notion of the "rationality" of the economy, which has been of interest to anthropologists at least since Herskovitz explicitly made it an empirical issue (1952), can be seen in a manageable perspective. With respect to the uses of the economic system, "rationality" must reflect productive efficiency of the choices it guides. The "best" option in terms of monetary returns should actually lead to the best result for the productive system, or as a minimum condition, the viable monetary options should be sustainable in the long run. Economic rationality (that is, still, rationality of the economy) should also imply that the system of evaluations is internally consistent, so that we may arrive at the same policy no matter which one of a group of related options we begin our considerations with.

With respect to individual behavior, "economic rationality" must mean that the rational actor selects the aspects of the system relevant to whatever problem he is considering, and that he then acts on the information the system provides. That is, action structured by the message source should feed back into the source with a minimum of "noise" or confusion. Such action will naturally reinforce parts of the overall system, not only of the economic message source but of the ecology and other systems as well, and the cycle will be ready to be repeated in an orderly dynamic progression.

The particular form of Shahidpur's economy is tied to the specific kinds of significant options that are evaluated and the specific conditions (such as simple educational backgrounds in mathematics) under which the evaluations are constructed and used. While any person in the village is free to offer any price for a "good" defined in any way he chooses, almost all transactions that occur follow one well-established conventional pattern or another. Each pattern includes a classification of objects by kind and a scheme for measuring them quantitatively, together with a set of conventions on the application of monetary quantities to the measured units. These conventions that define a set of goods for quantitative measurement and comparison, and attach monetary values to them, may be regarded as village "markets." Within each market, one product can be evaluated against a range of others and, in effect, sometimes "transformed" into another at will, without the intervention of biological or other physical processes. One crop can be transformed into another. One type of land can be transformed into another, meeting short-term adjustments or arrangements of mutual benefit. More than this, the inherent generalizing power of money permits evaluations in one market—one group of similar goods that are related "naturally" in some sense—to be equated with and transformed into physically dissimilar goods in other markets. The equations come about automatically, by the mechanisms made familiar by economic analysts: the adjustment of prices with respect to no other criterion than the effective demand for each good among all others against which it might be chosen.

The four major markets within the village are those in land, cattle, crops, and labor, both skilled and unskilled. These encompass most of the goods or the money exchanged in the village (with the single major exception of building materials). Although there are significant numbers of additional goods brought in from outside on a more or less casual basis, using money obtained in exchange for village products, these four markets can indicate the general relationships between and within the components of the economic system of information.

The Market in Land

Not a few anthropologists and some economists interested in economic systems regard markets as places where transactions take place and goods are exchanged (Belshaw 1956, pp. 79 ff.; Nash 1966). Although this definition has sometimes been described as lacking the theoretical power of the standard economists' definitions of a market as a configuration of projected supply and demand rates for a good in different combinations of price and quantity, there is a serious purpose behind it. Anthropologists have always attempted to see economic transactions in their social context, and they have generally felt that the economists' definitions did not accomplish this. By considering a market as if it were a physical place one can say, in effect, "Look at what else goes on here, apart from the interaction of supply and demand for goods," or "See how this interaction fits in with other relationships."

The definition of a market in land that is consistent with the general concept of a message source includes not only the land that is evaluated but also the configuration of all other major factors directly affecting the choice of prices of land, or directly affecting action on the basis of those prices as they would actually be paid or referred to. This configuration of elements that are integrated with land as the object of economic action involves the various capital goods that land requires and those which can provide alternative uses of resources for the same ends. We need to know what must be considered in buying land, and how the transaction would be carried out.

Land prices are directly related to the cost and ecological importance of wells, houses, agricultural tools, and, of course, crop values. Conversely, because of the central importance of land among productive goods, the cost of money reflects the return to it. Land has both a purchase price and a rental price, a price for long-term possession and a price for its short-term use. Both are tied to productivity and by the same token to a set of related costs involved in controlling productivity, principally the costs of water and fertilizer.

As has already been noted, land with well or canal water is more expensive than rainfall land. In addition, some land in each irrigation category is considered "stronger" than the rest and fetches a slightly higher price. "Stronger" land includes more carefully fertilized land and land nearer the *abadi*.

One farmer was attempting to sell a piece of land at Rs. 5,000 an acre late in the fall of 1965. But even though this was the price generally quoted for such land at the time, there was some doubt of his being able to find a buyer. Previous sales whose records I had seen were for lower prices, one of the last being about Rs. 4,465 an acre, in 1961. (Later records were under legal review and not available to me.) This was well irrigated land including a share in the well itself. Ten years before, according to the farmers, the same parcel of land that the farmer was trying to sell for Rs. 5,000 would have sold for half that amount. The reasoning behind the price being sought, as it was presented by several farmers in a discussion, illustrates the relationship between productivity and land price, and will also be relevant to a later discussion of cropping economies.

During the cane-cutting season of 1964–1965 the government set a price to be paid for sugarcane in the mill areas and ruled that the farmers had to sell all their cane to the mill at that price. They were not permitted to make gur to sell on their own. The gur price was very high then, yielding a return per acre greater than most other crops. The legal cane price was so low that it yielded a poorer return per unit of land than most marketed crops, and much less than gur. As a result the farmers had a strike. Throughout the area, with no enforcement or organization other than common assessment of the situation, no cane was moved to market. The farmers made gur, and with the village centrifuges, they made white sugar from a solution of gur in water, which had been allowed to crystalize. The government sent police to the villages, including Shahidpur, to issue citations and to seal the centrifuges by tying them with ribbon and sealing the knot with wax. Within a few days, the wax of the seals was broken as a result of the knots having been opened and retied. The centrifuges and other equipment were still in use. The police returned and physically removed from the village all the centrifuges they could find. The remaining centrifuges, which had been hidden or otherwise saved from confiscation, were then made mobile: their owners hired them out, and carried them from village to village at night. The manufacture of sugar without the government mill went on. Finally, the government raised the rate, and the cane went to market. It was then that cane became the most profitable crop.

In the subsequent season, gur prices were down somewhat. But the new cane prices were so high that the effect on land management was considered to be the same. It was then that the rise in the price of land was predicted, and this is what the farmer sought to take advantage of. The reasoning was that the profit from cane was so high the people would buy new land to grow it. One bigha of land (5/24 acre) would yield between one hundred and two hundred quintals (metric) of cane or four to eight quintals of gur, whose values were Rs. 5.36 a quintal and Rs. 80 a quintal, respectively. Even figuring with the lower (gur) price, the farmer could buy a bigha of land, incur the expected expenses of Rs. 133 a year (including interest but ignoring transportation costs), and still earn Rs. 500 a year, thus paying for the land in two years even if it cost Rs. 1,000 (equal to about Rs. 5,000 per acre). The normal expectation for recovering the cost of land would be three to four years, which is related to present levels of return on other crops. The difference would force land prices up as land was purchased for conversion to the now more profitable cane. The reasoning out of all possible consequences is not complete as it stands, and no good farmer would think it was. But it does demonstrate the way land price reflects the value of land as an investment in an economic and ecological context. It should be noticed that the calculation of land's return assumes that the farm was a going concern. The land is evaluated in the context of the farming situation, not as some sort of isolated abstract entity.

Since wells have been built outward starting from the *abadi*, there is an overall correspondence between age, capitalization, and fertility within the village. Land nearest was in most cases also "best," and estimated at Rs. 7,200 an acre, middle land was "average" at Rs. 4,200, and land farthest was the "poorest" rainfall land and priced at Rs. 3,600 an acre in 1965.

Comparison of land prices in Shahidpur with prices in the immediate area shows the same covariance between productivity and price. In the neighboring villages prices are substantially lower. The estimates of farmers in Shahidpur, and the official revenue estimate for the tehsil as a whole, both place the price of average land at about Rs. 2,000 an acre. This average land in these generally younger villages, unlike the average land in Shahidpur, is not supplied with well irrigation. Irrigated clay loam of Shahidpur's grade in another village would fetch the same price as in Shahidpur.

It is commonly said that the price paid for land also reflects the village of the buyer and seller. Land is sold more dearly to a person in one's own village. A stereotypic reason given for this is that a farmer is "ashamed" to see another person on his land, and his shame is more acute if it is someone he has known. Hence it takes a higher price to make him sell to a fellow villager. However, this price difference would also follow from the evident fact that land is generally sold in small portions to farmers with going capital establishments. The most recent sales for which I saw official registration records were one parcel of .86 acre sold in two shares, one unit of .68 acre, and one unit of 3.23 acres. As the cane-price calculations assume, land is usually bought to produce better overall return to storage facilities, wells, and other resources. That is, it is bought in the context of the household strategies of the division of labor, and not to set up a whole new enterprise. Land in the village where one has the rest of one's holdings would thus be cheaper to use than land in another village. It could, therefore, command a higher price.

In Shahidpur, the average ratio of irrigated land per well is 12.15 acres each, or conversely, one twelfth of a well per acre. The cost of a well is now Rs. 2,000, compared with Rs. 3,000 before the canals went into operation. A Persian wheel to lift the water costs an additional Rs. 500. Therefore, cost per acre for such a well now comes to about Rs. 200, an expenditure that can make the difference between poor and average land, whose price difference is Rs. 600 an acre. This probably indicates why so little land was sold during the eighteen-month period of study (only one sale seems to have been completed), and at the same time the construction of the unusually large number of three new wells was undertaken, one with a diesel pumping set. Sixteen well shafts were recorded in the official field map of 1952. Nineteen, an increase of three, were demarcated in the field map of 1962, and the newest three were begun between 1962 and 1965. The difference in gain between buying land or investing in wells was further increased by the availability of low interest government loans for the latter (through the Block Development Office in Chamkaur) but not the former during the same period.

New wells both permit and require more intensive cropping, and a concomitant shift to more irrigation crops. These crops in turn require more fertilizer and of course more labor. The ratio of return to capital—profit—is reported to go up slightly under such circumstances, but only slightly. The amount of actual income does increase, of course: more goods are produced and handled, and higher levels of reinvestment are maintained, which means more personal security for the owner and his family. But at the same time, the labor rates in the village are being forced upward by increased demand, and there is added need for supporting capital: bicycles for bringing fertilizer and seeing officials, storage facilities, better carts, fertilizer, and related small items. The pressure to continue to do better is unremitting.

The principal alternative to meeting the pressure is to move out, as was noted. Fifty of the fifty-eight individuals who made up the forty-seven nonresident "households" in 1964–1965 were recorded as resident owners at the time of the initiation of current official land records in 1955–1956. Those who move out usually first "mortgage" their land. In most cases, they then take the money and go to areas where land and labor are cheaper, principally to three villages in neighboring regions. There they buy a mortgage or rent land. If they judge the venture to be a success after a few years, they sell out completely in Shahidpur, usually to the mortgage holder, and move over permanently. If not, they either move back and reclaim their land, or try again elsewhere. This behavior can be seen as a means of testing the return of capital to the farmer in alternative employment.

Rental rates and practices reflect the same relation to productivity as sale and mortgage. The calculations that villagers make in deciding to rent out land or take land on rent, in the context of their strategies of household management, are generally phrased in monetary terms, rather than in qualitative benefits as such. Even when the rental is not itself to be used for cash crops, rental rates can be evaluated in terms of the money value of other crops that rental may permit on other classes of land. Finally, in those cases where economic trade-offs for cash crops are not involved, renters have to calculate rental costs against other ways of meeting their needs—such as buying milk or fodder, or trading land use for manure or labor.

Rent takes three standard forms, three modes of payment. The most basic and most common form is called *batai* (*batāi*). In this arrangement, the owner and the tenant each supplies one-half of the fertilizer, and each takes one-half of the grain or fiber at the harvest. In the second form, *panj-do-banjī* (literally "five-two arrangement"), the owner gets two-fifths of the crop and the tenant takes three-fifths, each again supplying proportionate amounts of the fertilizer. In *jab-ti* (*jab-tī*), the final form, the tenant tills the land at an agreed-upon money rent, about Rs. 30 per bigha per year for most land at the time of the study. He then takes the entire crop and puts in all the fertilizer. In the case of one crop, cane, *batai* is consistently one-third for the farmer and two-thirds for the tenant, because of the relatively higher labor requirement, which falls upon the tenant. In each of these arrangements the tenant supplies the cattle and takes the entire fodder production. If the land has a well, his animals work it, and he does not pay the farmer for the water.

In the long run the cash rental, *jab-ti*, rate is the same as *batai*, and demonstrates again the contextual relevance of the ecology and division of labor. For example, the wheat yield of average land is around 5 maunds per bigha. One maund (82 2/7 pounds) sells for 20–22 rupees (midwinter 1964–1965). Therefore five maunds yield 100–110 rupees, half of which is the owner's share, 50–55 rupees. This is paid only when the crop is successful. In loss years, the owner takes the loss along with the farmer. Two or three years in ten are reckoned as loss years, when *batai* would not be paid though rent would be. Rent for land with these yields would reportedly be Rs. 40 a year. Multiplying out a projection, we can see that seven to eight years of *batai* shares are worth about Rs. 350–440, against Rs. 400 for ten years' cash rent, an effective equality. The farmers say that this equality *should* hold, which is to say that *batai* is, by convention, taken as the basis of cash rent.

In the context of the ecology and division of labor, the rental conventions assure the farmers that rent represents a true portion of a gain, not consumption of capital. Since fertilizer is used in small quantities in specific relationship to each crop planned, it does not accumulate as expensive "capital" in the soil for an extractive renter to waste or consume. Its depletion is not a loss to the owner. Similarly, the cost of cattle to the tenant is offset by the gain in fodder, so that there is no extra or "hidden" expenditure for fuel or draft power to either tenant or owner. Thus real capital "expenditures" are narrowed by the system of practices to meeting the costs of wear and tear on the tenant's equipment and on the owner's wells. A well is reckoned to last fifty years, thus costing an average of a hundred rupees a year. It needs minor repairs every two or three years, at a cost of perhaps another ten or twenty rupees a year. One seventieth of this annual cost would be the owner's capital expenditure share for one bigha a year, since a well serves about seventy bighas. A smaller amount would be the cost of wear and tear on the agricultural equipment of the tenant—his barn, house, plow, and hand tools. There is thus no possibility that this destruction of productive goods approaches what could be replaced with the rent paid.

Land rent has figured in several related attacks on the rationality and coherence of Indian village economic systems. These arguments have had wide currency, both in the West and in India, and are worth reviewing together in the present context. One argument has centered on the seemingly small amount of rent in relation to the cost of land. Such a small rent by itself seemed to imply either that the system was unproductive or that people were renting out land when they had much better economic options open to them, such as selling the land and lending out money at the interest rates that have long been considered to be extremely high. If this were so, it would indicate that the natives were ignoring the dictates of the economic system, and were responding instead to "tradition" or to social pressures of various kinds. A second, closely related argument pertained to the profitability of farming such land. This consisted in showing that the tenant paid rent for the privilege of losing money through hard work—that he realized either no gain or a negative gain from his effort. But since he persisted in his work, he was seen as operating from other than economic considerations—and tradition and superstition have been indicated as the alternative bases of action. A final point concerns high interest rates themselves, which have been named repeatedly as a cause of a backbreaking burden of rural debt, a burden which the peasant was often felt to assume out of fear and lack of sophistication in the face of the moneylender—

who in Shahidpur would presumably be the person I have named as his jobber, or *arthier*. Each of these views embodies difficulties that arise from lack of appreciation of the close fit between the ecology, the division of labor, and the economy. Exposing the difficulties can provide a glimmering of an answer to an important underlying question: why does the economy reflect the ecology and division of labor, and how is it adjusted to continue doing so?

The appearance of irrationality in renting out land disappears when one considers the other relevant economic factors: the interest rates and the rate of appreciation in land valuation. There is no significant advantage in lending one's capital rather than buying land and holding it by renting it. At least this is true of the purchase prices and the rents reported for land of all three levels of quality in Shahidpur ten years ago and now. The rates are given in table 14.

Table 14
REPORTED RENTS AND BUYING COSTS FOR LAND
1954–1955 AND 1964–1965
(rupees per bigha)

	Price			Rent		
	A	B	C	A	B	C
1954–1955	700	400	250	20	15	8
1964–1965	1,500	800	600	40	30	25

Take the price of average land, grade B, as an example. The farmer who let it out to rent in 1955 would have collected a total rent of Rs. 224.85 up to 1965, based on an average increase in purchase prices of Rs. 44.4 a year and a constant rental rate at the 3.6 percent that was reported for both the beginning and the end of the period. He would also, at the end of the period, hold land worth Rs. 800, for a total return of Rs. 1,024.85. If he had sold the same amount of land at the beginning of the period and had lent the Rs. 400 at the stated usual rate for "safe" loans of 12 percent, compounded annually, he would have had Rs. 1,110.55 at the end of the same period of time. This is admittedly greater than renting, but hardly so great as to make renting irrational. The person who rents the land has it to hold and to fall back on, and does not take the lender's risk of a defaulting borrower. Nor does he have to purchase food at retail rates. In addition, it would be difficult in practice for a lender to keep all his money in circulation all the time. On the other hand, the lender is free to shed the expenses of maintaining a farm household. The difference is more a matter of taste and talent than of economic return.

The apparent negative return to labor devoted to farming disappears when farm labor is seen in its proper context of related significant actions and objects. The problem arose years ago, in the early days of the "marginal revolution" in economics and the first attempts to apply it in gathering reliable economic data on peasants in India. Such agencies as the Punjab Board of Economic Inquiry developed accounting techniques and conducted in-depth studies of villages, and of detailed household and farm accounts, including several types of tenants as well as owners. Over and over again the results showed that the accounts were so nearly balanced in matters of income and expenditure to the household or farm that when any reasonable amount was added as a return to the farmer's own labor, or as a price for his labor that should appear as a "profit," a net gain over the year, the household or farm appeared to be operating at a deficit. For example, a household budget survey for 1939–1949 shows income averages for thirteen cultivating families in three economic classes to be Rs. 1,090.55, Rs. 452.63, and Rs. 559.14. Expenses for the same groups averaged Rs. 1,338.61, Rs. 515.07, and Rs. 296.40, respectively (Punjab Pub. no. 86, 1962, pp. 1, 2). Oddly enough, the only group to show a "profit" on this basis are tenant farmers. Again, a 1951–1952 survey (Punjab Pub. no. 23, 1953) of eleven cultivating families shows nine out of the eleven with a deficit in household accounts at the end of the year. The deficit ranged from Rs. 82.99 to Rs. 2,765.62, and averaged Rs. 253.51 (p. 32). Similarly, a 1955–1956 survey of thirty-five holdings of various types in all different sections of the Punjab showed a net loss per acre of between Rs. 18.69 and Rs. 110.85 for all but three out of ten classes of land: irrigated land in the southwestern portions of the state (Punjab Pub. no. 45, 1957, pp. 28–30). Of these, the highest net gain was Rs. 29.47 an acre. All these figures were arrived at by the long-standardized technique of assigning evaluations of "costs" as if they were "expenditure for a businessman who takes land on rent, employs hired labor and borrows capital" (p. 28). Negative net gains obtained on this basis imply that a farmer would be better off selling or lending his capital and hiring himself out as a laborer. The farmer who does his own work is seemingly taking hidden losses. Such figures can be taken to imply that the whole economy is "irrational" or contains "disguised unemployment," in the sense that there is a negative marginal return to labor (Bennett, 1967; Epstein 1967).

The figures show that if a person paid himself what he would pay a laborer, he would go broke. This is taken to imply that he earns less than a laborer and that, therefore, he is being economically irrational by continuing to be a farmer. When expenses are calculated on a modified "businessman's" basis, without an allowance for day labor rates charged against family members, the farms generally show a net gain. In the last sample mentioned, this gain ranged from Rs. 25 to Rs. 72.40 an acre, with the single exception of one area, irrigated land in central Punjab, that showed a loss of Rs. 10.14 an acre for 1955–1956 (Punjab Pub. no. 45, 1957, p. 29). The fault in the reasoning is that it fails to take cognizance of the identity in this system between style of life and manner of work, of working conditions with living conditions. Since the village farmers do not "work" in one place and "live" in another, a villager's own and his family's maintenance are actually paid for in the course of making a return on his capital. The laborer has to be paid such a relatively high wage because all of his accouterments of life come out of it—he alone must take money out of agriculture to put it into his house.

Because his house is necessary in his work, part of the structure of the division of labor, a farmer can live in a cooler and more comfortable house. He is the first hired and the last fired. He has the least fear of unemployment and rising prices. He can supply himself with odds and ends of fresh vegetables not available to the nonfarmer. All these things surely mean he has a better life. If it is necessary for analytic purposes to mark up against the farmer a "cost" for his time at a going rate, it should be necessary for the sake of consistency to put down a "gain" for the benefits of farming as an addition to his cash income. Native estimation does this, of course, in judging the life of the farmer to be better than that of a laborer. Careful outside estimation would probably lead to the same result. As it stands, all that the "businessman" type of accounting shows is that the land could not support twice as many people as it now supports. This, of course, is no more than a quantified reflection of the importance of human labor as a determinant of production without mechanical aid and of human diet as a determinant of the cropping pattern.

The consideration of the relative "lowness" of rental prices has already indicated that the interest rates are far from exorbitantly high. On the contrary, they too are closely geared to the return from the land. This closeness itself requires explanation. In economic terms, the simplest reason that suggests itself is that the village is economically efficient—that the marginal return to each major item of capital is approximately equal to that of each other item of capital. Under these considerations, the return to land should approximate the return to other possible investments. Under these conditions and given that the cost of money should represent its best investment uses, we would naturally expect the cost of money to reflect the return to land.

If this type of explanation for the correspondence between interest and land prices seems too abstract, more concrete explanations may be found (which may in the long run be considered as mechanisms by which the more general pattern is maintained). One such reason is suggested by the analysis of the error in taking the "businessman's" point of view. As actual human work—human labor—rather than the management of funds is of great importance in the village, so too is the expenditure for food—the means of providing that work—particularly high in relation to other expenses. This is suggested not only by the inability of the land to provide the monetary equivalent of maintenance for both a "businessman" and a hired work crew, but also by direct accounting in the family budget studies, which generally put expenditures for food at about three-fifths of the total family outlays (Punjab Pub. no. 23, 1953, p. 20). In Shahidpur, the use of payments in kind for rent and wages, as well as arrangements for meals as part of "cash" payment for labor, indicate that farmers and workers place a correspondingly high importance on food as a form of income. Given this importance, and since land is the key factor in the production of food, inflationary rises in prices (inflationary with respect to the village, not necessarily with respect to the economy as a whole), which outrun increases in productivity, naturally get passed on to the price of land. So too, of course, would any "real" increase in the value of food in the total economy, whatever that might be. The farmers in the village are acutely aware of the recent trend for food prices to rise, and they consistently attempt to accumulate land and hold it, even, if necessary, by renting out what they cannot farm. They avoid unnecessary accumulation of cash, avoid saving in commerical banks, and usually try to avoid lending.

In addition to wells, labor, crops, and money, the principal items whose value is tied closely to the value placed on land are, of course, houses and other constructions. Unfortunately, price quotations on houses are impossible to obtain, and their construction costs are difficult to estimate. The government does not keep records of household property values since house values are not taxed. My village census included the question "Is the master of the house its owner?" The answer was yes in every case, and I found no instance of a person—at other times as well—claiming to rent his quarters or to rent housing to others. (I could not, in fact, find anyone to rent quarters to me, either, although I was housed without charge in the village gurdwara.) Houses seem to be infrequently rented, and to be more often lent, inherited, or built than sold outright. Labor rates have, in monetary terms, increased radically over the years, and because many of the houses antedate the current fiscal system, it is impossible to make a backward projection of investment in houses based on current building costs. I can only try to indicate their importance with a rough estimate of the replacement cost of the present structures.

With Schultz (1964, p. 96) I am inclined to think that the capital value of houses in relation to land, the amount of production diverted to buildings, is generally underrated. A sizeable portion, say about 20 percent, of the houses in current use are done in the style of the first wells. This style of building has probably been out of use for at least one hundred years, suggesting both a slow rate of replacement and a relatively high initial valuation. One new room in a farmer's house, with a cement floor, was recently completed for about Rs. 3,000. This would have amounted to about one-sixth of the total value of the establishment, to judge a comparable replacement cost of the rest of the house. The house itself was moderately commodious, a little less than average for a farmer, but slightly better than average for the farmer's side of the *abadi*, and it was about equal to a good house on the Harijan side of the village. Figuring very roughly on the basis of these appearances, the total value of the 123 houses of the village in terms of replacement cost would come to about Rs. 1,800,000, in comparison with the value of the land at the stated average price of Rs. 5,000 an acre, which would be Rs. 2,000,000. Even if we allow a half-million-rupee margin of error, this gives some idea of the role of houses as but a part of the practical basis of the farmers' emphasis on capital, and not on skill or knowledge, as the foundation of their occupation and manner of life.

The overall income level possible from the crops forces land prices up or down, while differential productivity forces farmers to invest in wells or houses to support investments in land by increasing their productive or marketing capacity. Since money is the standard by which the productivity of the different alternatives are compared, its own "value" reflects the price of land and the related objects. The conventional and socially sanctioned fact that any one of these objects can be traded for a quantity of money, and a quantity of money for any one of them, is what permits money to serve as a standard for evaluating possible adjustments among them. It is also what makes money capable of serving as a conventional device for "transmuting" land into wells or houses, according to their relative productivity, and what makes allocative choices between them as factors of production automatically adjust the value of money and keep it at a consistent standard throughout the entire market.

The village markets other than the market in land are generally linked to the market in land indirectly, through the cropping pattern, rather than directly, in the manner of the interest rate. Like the land market, the other markets take the form of a framework of standardized types of transactions within which the prices of a series of related goods are offered, understood, adjusted, and sometimes paid. It is best to begin with the cropping pattern, the farmers' response to their ecological resources and needs, in the light of the possibilities of exchange with the world beyond the village.

Crops and Cropping

The possibility that a farmer can exchange certain crops for a quantity of money, and that the quantity of money can be exchanged back for crops, brings monetary prices closely into line with the desirability of the different crops in the context of the ecology and the division of labor. This alignment, in turn, means that farmers, in constructing their households, can make or at least refine their ecological and managerial calculations in terms of the relatively simple concepts of monetary value, even though all goods are not, in fact, bought and sold.

There is an economic model for a sequence of acquisitions of capital that describes both the overall pattern of acquisition of capital and the specific biennial pattern of crop decisions that each farmer makes. Whether phrased in terms of "marginal" costs and returns, "opportunity" costs and returns, or some other methodological ideas, the basic idea in this model is that a series of decisions in relation to the acquisition and use of capital, made in accordance with the policy of obtaining the maximum benefit from each investment at each point, is also a series of decisions that will yield both the maximum overall return to capital and an equilibrium situation where the return to each item of capital in one's total "plant" is the same as that to each other item.

The pattern of an increasingly rapid development of wells at the time of the study, accompanying an apparently low level of activity in relation to the transfer of land itself, would seem to suggest, with many other observations made already, that some such general model of acquisition policies and of equilibrium conditions is in fact used by villagers in making decisions affecting major capital expenditures.

Since raising crops is the last step in the realization of a return to capital, cropping efficiency should also follow the same laws as the acquisition of the means of cropping. If land yields an equal return with each other item of capital, we should expect the pattern of crops to yield equal return for every unit of land. Even though the rising underground-water table kept the prices of land and other capital goods somewhat out of line during the period of the study, and even though at other times the equality of return to investment capital may not have been realized for other known "reasons," something like this ideal state, yielding maximum return, guided the farmers' cropping strategy.

The description of the effect of cane prices on land prices related above was based on the idea that farmers seek maximum return through realizing equal (and maximal) value per unit of land. Cane, farmers say, will be planted; land prices will rise. In consequence, since no virgin land can be brought under cultivation, grains and fodder will be in shorter supply; and then, presumably, the local price will go up. Since the differential between producing and buying is sizeable and import costs are high, as we shall see, some sort of new balance will have to be achieved. A point will be reached where it no longer pays to put new land under cane—where the benefits of planting cane are not greater than those of planting other crops, which is to say that the return from each unit of land will be the same. The average return to land, or to investment capital, will decline with further modification of the crop pattern.

The same principle apparently applied to the arrangement of crops in Shahidpur before the mill rates for cane went into effect. Late in October 1964, before the strike began, the prevailing price for gur was still rather high in relation to other crops. One average bigha's production would sell for Rs. 320 at the prevailing rate of Rs. 80 a quintal. When I asked one highly capitalized farmer why he did not plant more cane at that time, he replied that the combined value of wheat and cotton from a similar amount of land would be Rs. 251. The wheat also produced ten bundles of fodder, worth Rs. 2 to Rs. 4 each, and had a lower labor and water cost. Wheat required three waterings during a normal season, cane ten waterings, at Rs. 5 per bigha per watering. Taking all this into account, the farmer felt that there was no reason for him to plant cane in place of wheat, even in narrow marketing terms. He was making the best use of his resources at the time. Similarly, the price of maize at the same time would have yielded about Rs. 210 a bigha, for an average crop of about six maunds, slightly more than cotton paid. The income from a season of maize followed by wheat would compare favorably with that of the one crop a year of cane on an equivalent piece of land. Similar cycles, yielding similarly equal returns, can be worked out from the prices and yields of the other marketed crops listed in table 15, or the more detailed average figures of table 16, bearing in mind that the cane rate noted there is the new, legal rate. Schultz described the operation of this same rule in the crop pattern of another village: "poor but efficient" (Schultz 1964, p. 46).

Transport and Commodity Prices

Even though fodder is generally grown by the households that consume it, and is not marketed, this practice itself can be seen as an "economic" choice in response to the markets both in transportation and in cattle, in the context of the basic ecological fact that cattle are mortal.

One cannot deactivate an animal like an engine and expect to start it again days or weeks later after properly refueling it. Animals must be kept alive, even when not in use, or they will be lost completely. Cattle are moderately expensive, and it is difficult and time-consuming to acquire them. At the same time, the cost of fodder in the village is much too low to permit the price of grain or cane to offset the loss of cattle through "saving" on fodder. The five hundred rupees that an ox costs (which of course reflects its ecological importance) could rent a dozen acres of land, which would provide fodder for six to eight oxen for a year. On this basis there would be no possible gain in letting cattle starve.

But while cattle cannot economically be allowed to starve, they also cannot be fed economically on imported fodder, because of the low price per unit of weight for fodder in relation to the cost of transportation.

Under present circumstances the most practical means of hauling fodder between villages is by oxcart. The rental rate on oxcarts is keyed to their most important use, hauling the most valuable crops. This rate during the time of my study was Rs. 0.50 per maund per day. By comparison, the selling rate recorded by the state government for dry wheat straw (villagers could not give a price because of infrequency and variability of circumstances of sale) during the preceding years would indicate that its price at this time was from Rs. 2.50 to Rs. 3.00 a maund. Except in emergencies, the addition of this haulage cost to the very low fodder price makes the combined rate proportionally much too high to command buyers anywhere that unhauled fodder is available. One day's hauling adds at least 16 percent to the price of fodder, compared with a 2 percent increment to the price of wheat. The larger the increment, the smaller is the temptation to grow a "surplus" or to rely on the market. The cost

Table 15

Principal Economic Characteristics of Major Crops

Crop	Land grade	Seed rate (lb/bigha)	Fodder yield (bundles)	Grain yield (maunds)	Grain price (Rs/md)
Wheat	best	11–13	10	9–10	Rs. 23–24
Waterings: 3–6 plowings prepare soil.	average	11–13	5	6	
Chemical fertilizer common	poorest	11–13	5	3	
Official average yield: 3md/bigha					
Maize	best	3	10	6–9	Rs. 35
Waterings: average years, none; drought years, 4.	average	3	5–6	4–5	
Fertilizer: chemical to 9 bags/bigha, plus cart of manure.	poorest	3	4	1–2	
Official av. yield: 4.5 md/bigha					
Cotton	best (only)	unrecorded	none	5 maunds fiber seed	Rs. 35
Waterings: 2					
Official average yield: 1.45 md/bigha					
Cane	best	—	negligible	600 md. cane or 24 md. gur	Cane: Rs. 2/md (government
Waterings: 10					ment
Fertilizer: 5 carts manure plus					

3–6 bags chemical per bigha Official gur yield: 6 md/bigha	average	negligible	—	300 md. cane or 12 md. gur	fixed price) Gur:
Further costs for a normal "best" crop: hoeing, Rs. 30; gur equipment rent, Rs. 140; incidentals such as extra labor, Rs. 40	poorest	negligible	—	150 md. cane or 6–9 md. gur	Rs. 28/md

SOURCE: Village farmers' reports. Each figure taken from at least 3 people on 3 different occasions, public and private, in the presence of crops, with confirmation of reports in explanations of cropping patterns and practices as they were observed.
NOTE: "Grades" of land are recognized classes. "Best" is well-fertilized land with a good well, or canal, or combined water supply. "Average" is common well irrigated land without special fertilizer, away from populated area. "Poorest" is rainfall land or land with limited well irrigation and poor fertilization, farthest from populated center.

Table 16
BASIC INCOME FROM MAJOR MARKETED CROPS (in rupees)

Crop	Item	Gain	Cost[a]	Net
Wheat	Grain, 9–10 maunds	230		
	Fodder, 10 bundles	c. 25		
	Waterings, 3		15	
	Fertilizer (estimate)		13	
	Harvesting (½ bundle)		3	
	Transportation		5	
				219
Maize	Grain, 9 maunds	315		
	Fodder, 10 bundles	25		
	Waterings, 4		20	
	Fertilizer (estimate)		13	
	Weeding		9	
	Harvesting (½ bundle)		3	
	Transportation		5	
				290
Cotton	Fiber and seed, 4.8 md.	168		
	Waterings, 2		10	
	Labor (weeding and picking estimated at 3 man-days each)		15	
				143
Cane	Stalks, 600 md.	1,200		
	Waterings, 10		50	
	Fertilizer (stated)		13	
	Hoeing		30	
	Transportation (c. Rs. 9.25/md)		150	
				957
	Gur, 24 maunds	640[b]		
	Waterings, 10		50	
	Fertilizer		13	
	Hoeing		30	
	Transportation		12	
	Labor and incidentals (depreciation or rental on equipment)		40	
				495

SOURCE: Same as for table 15.
NOTE: Growing land is assumed to be of "best" grade. See table 15 (note) for explanation of grades.
[a] Labor costs for wheat, maize, and cotton are reckoned at about equal. Wheat

of transport creates a large penalty for not having enough fodder on hand, even though its local sale price is relatively low. But by the same token there is little incentive to grow more than is necessary for one's own need.

What is true for dry fodder is even more strongly true for the much heavier wet fodder and for manure, which is of course, the important end product of the fodder, and an essential part of the balance of nature in the village. The price for both of these is still lower per unit of weight than the price for straw.

The large number of cattle is an index of the importance of the allocation of manure within the village, as is the amount of fodder they consume. Other indices are the allowances of manure established for the different crops. For example, the common rate for one application for cane is 3 oxcart-loads per bigha, or 14.4 loads per acre. One maximum oxcart-load (for a normal cart) is reckoned at eight maunds (or 8 x 82 2/7 pounds). This amount is applied at the beginning of a three-year cycle of cuttings before reseeding. Grain crops often get one cart per bigha, as the water supply warrants. There is clearly a large amount of fertilizer being produced, traded, and used in the village.

Manure is purchased by two methods: "price" (*kīmat*) and "contract" (*theka*). There are three major types of contract. In the simplest, the farmer "sees" the heap which the seller has, and asks the price. The seller states his price, the farmer then gives his and finally they compromise. The farmer takes the heap away himself. In the second type of contract the farmer sees the heap and offers some amount of sorghum millet or *barsheen*. These are measured in "bags" (*pānD*) of a local cloth (made by weavers) of a certain size and kind. One such bag appears to hold about 1½ cubic yards. They agree and the farmer again takes the manure off and pays as agreed. The third kind of contract is an exchange of manure for the right to

requires more plowing but no weeding. Cotton and maize both require weeding. Cotton has no transport costs since it is sold in the village. Wheat and maize both have transport costs of Rs. 5 per maund, since they are sold in Kurali. Cane has a much higher labor utilization but uses cheaper labor. When cane is sold as gur, its transport cost is the same as the grains, since it too is sold in Kurali. For cane the transport cost is lower per maund, since the point of sale is in Khant, where there are temporary scales, which permit two trips a day.
b This price is not government controlled, in contrast to the price on cane.

harvest *barsheen* for a season from a stated amount of the farmer's land. The farmer hauls off the manure, and the seller hauls his *barsheen*.

There is one type of conventional transaction called "price." The farmer comes with a cart, and packs it himself as fully as he can. He then pays the going price, which was given at Rs. 2.50 to Rs. 3.00 rupees in 1964–1965, and at Rs. 4.60 in 1965–1966. The rupee payments apparently reflect the market value of green fodder, since one can be substituted for the other. Note that all the arrangements hold the transport cost constant by having the farmer assume it.

As was noted previously, farmers report that there is a prohibition in the village against the sale of manure outside of the village, on the grounds that the manure "comes from the land" and ought to go back to the land. In the context of the foregoing, this prohibition can be seen to be "enforced" by the same factors that limit the movement of fodder. If the value of one oxcart-load is four rupees in the village, and its weight is eight maunds, it will cost four rupees—100 percent of its value—to transport it the distance of a half-day's journey by oxcart—about five miles, allowing time for selling, loading, and the like. Since the average density of cattle in relation to the people is about the same everywhere, we should therefore expect, as with fodder, that the price for a transported oxcart of manure would result in no buyers. Thus even though the price seems low within the village, it is better than a seller would otherwise be able to obtain, so he must sell.

On the other hand, farmers prefer to buy in the village, rather than take their carts (which are often rented or borrowed) and go outside, for precisely the same kinds of reasons. These are the conditions which necessitate the prohibition and enforce it. The local market in manure is sanctioned and maintained by the market in transportation facilities in relation to the properties of the manure.

The high-priced grains, sugar products, and cane (under certain conditions) set the limits on the number of oxcarts that are essential, and in consequence set the rates for rental of vehicles. An eight-maund cartload of wheat would fetch about Rs. 208 in the Kurali market against a haulage cost of Rs. 4 a day. This increment of 2 percent is acceptable because it is less than the price differences which regularly develop between the village and points of sale within a day's travel—particularly between the village and Kurali.

The circulation of food grains that can go outside for sale is affected by other costs in addition to the cost of transportation. There is a pattern of annual regional price fluctuation that makes it unreasonable to sell food if one might then have to import it. Regional and national storage facilities and dealing in futures is apparently not well developed. Prices may rise 10 to 50 percent in a year, perhaps more if there are famine conditions or a failure of the following season's crops. The prices are usually lowest at the time of harvest, then rise until the next harvest. To sell at harvest and buy as needed would be to trade wheat for less wheat, no matter how low transport costs might become. On the other hand, to hold grain is to invest it, for debts in the village can be paid with it at the appreciating prices. Cotton is about the only crop that is regularly sold and then imported in finished form.

The seasonal pattern of price advances, the general appreciation in price of goods, and price instability (plus the factor of quality control), along with transport costs and the economies of cattle raising, reinforce the practice of growing crops in the village and conform both to local needs and to market prices. The multiplicity of local needs, together with the local level of capitalization means in turn that Shahidpur's farmers must make a large number of choices in disposing their labor and organizing their crops. Since the major needs are similar among all farm households, and since the market prices are the same for all, there tends to be a common response to them. The crop array of one farmer is similar to every other, within the limits imposed by his circumstances. The established pattern of copying the behavior of more successful farmers, already noted in relation to experimentation with new crops, is generally used in relation to all aspects of farming; time of sowing, interplanting, time of irrigation, amounts sown, and times of marketing were all mentioned in this connection. Such behavior, it seems to me, is necessitated by the complexity of the system of needs to be met, which surpasses the ken of most farmers. The situation of a village farmer is vastly more complex than that of a Southern California barley farmer, or a Midwestern wheat grower.

The Market in Labor

The cropping pattern, combined with the general necessity for economy that arises from pressure to invest in more productive goods, constrains the pattern of hiring labor throughout the year. Conversely, the pattern of labor allocation between different occupations or different social units determines the direction in which the system will develop in the future. A few examples will indicate the type of hiring arrangements that are made for direct labor, as well as their economic basis. As in other markets, rates of payment for labor are linked to production through the conventional understandings of their application to evaluated objects.

The labor market involving the most people is that for help in seasonal agricultural operations. Farmers try to organize their work to make maximum use of their own time and that of their family members who are not in school or earning money outside the village. If the work to be done exceeds what their domestic groups or other close relatives can do, they next call on one or two nonfarmers, who are usually attached to the family, to work with them, for rates lower than the daily rate but with greater security and for diffuse considerations that go along with friendship. Such arrangements may involve "partnership" for a share of the crops (usually one-seventh), or they may involve monthly wages for "servants," or they may just involve understandings of "friendship." But if the work still cannot all be done in this way, groups of day laborers are hired. The rate for this is high, and the season is short. Because of the similarity of the crops of all the farmers, the peak periods of need hit everyone at about the same time, so the village demand is great and bargaining is highly competitive. For such times there are two formal methods of payment. A flat cash rate is paid for work like weeding and hoeing, whose product cannot be carried off. A proportional rate is paid for work like harvesting, whose produce can be divided and transported. The same procedure is followed for a worker of any caste, although as noted, most of the labor of this sort is provided by Harijans.

For weeding and hoeing the farmer reportedly determines sometime in advance the number of workers he will want, the date, and the amount he wishes to pay. He then goes and meets with the people he wants to do the work. They all agree on the payment and the type and place of work, and he pays the amount in advance. Some bargaining is expected, but the wage that is current in the village at any one time is known and finally agreed upon. Argument generally involves a farmer who refuses to pay the known rate, but as it is said, the laborers can get the price in other villages. On the appointed day the laborers appear. They receive at that time certain perquisites, always understood as a standardized part of their pay. These consist in three meals and two teas for a full day's work, or two meals and one tea for half a day. It is said that there is a growing trend to give these meals to each person to eat at his house, as opposed to the practice of bringing food out to the fields in bulk and serving it as it is asked for. The reason for the change is to save against the rising price of wheat, and to avoid "abuses," such as overeating. The cash rate in 1964 was reported at about two rupees a day and rising rapidly. Apropos of the overall importance of food in household economies, the value of the food is reckoned as equal to about half the amount in wages.

For cutting crops, notably wheat and other grains, the agreement does not include a payment in advance. Instead, agreement is reached on the quality of the crop and the proportion of the cut sheaves that will eventually be taken in payment for the work done. The proportion for very good crops is lower, one "bundle" (sheaf) in twenty-five. For poor crops it is one bundle in seventeen. One meal and two teas are given. Two reasons are given for the rate difference: the better crops grow more densely and are easier to cut; and they are taller. Since "bundle" is the amount tied with a rope of standard length provided by the farmer, it is of a fixed diameter. Therefore a bundle weighs more for taller plants than for shorter plants. That is, the different "rates" actually aim at a parity of payment for work done. Because of the high value of grains included in the bundle, the smaller amount of food given with this mode of payment is also aimed at a kind of parity with labor rates at other times. (The proportion of grain to dry straw weight in bundles of wheat, for example, is nearly 1:1.) Depending on the land, a man can cut about seventeen to twenty-five bundles a day. Hence the day rate is one bundle a day, with variations according to the work done. An average bundle weighs about thirty kilos when fresh, and is valued by farmers at from five to seven rupees.

There is no point in attempting to construe such wage arrangements as part of a "traditional" caste system, as it has been described by ethnographers (Leach 1962; Kolenda 1963). On the other hand, there are many reasons for noting that these wages, like land and crop prices, are ecologically and economically "rational," in the sense that they are adjusted to the needs of the overall productive system. Wages, like the rental rates, do not consume capital. In this case, the capital is the health and resources of the laborer, and the method of safeguarding it is through the inclusion of food in the bargain. In addition, the methods of contracting, with bargaining for cash, reflect a market context, and there seems to be no reason to assume that the laborers when bargaining take more or less than they can get. A short but bitter dispute in my presence between a group of workers and the owner of a field, in which the workers insisted heatedly that the farmer had lied about the density of the crop, made it clear to me that the "bargaining" was no mere matter of form. The higher daily rate for harvesting apparently reflects the ecologically determined higher demand for labor at that time.

The same two-rupee rate for day labor that applies to weeding is also paid for other labor that the Harijans engage in, in relatively slack seasons, such as helping the masons. This rate is reportedly double what it was a year or so previously, when the sugar mill had not been in operation. The mill employs labor, on a monthly basis, about ninety days a year. Since this work is available in what was previously a slack season after the fall sowing, it doubles the amount of wage work that laborers can get annually. The canal also uses a few laborers, which has tended to further drain the village labor pool, increase bargaining power, and drive up prices.

Skilled laborers who work in agriculture do other work also. There is no clear line between people with agricultural skills and others. Since the tasks performed by individuals are always subject to change as people acquire or lose capital, the constant relationships are between capital and occupations not between people and occupations. Two examples of relatively better capitalized laborers will indicate the economic mechanisms behind the impact of a person's capital on his occupational specialization, and vice versa.

Two prominent skilled workers are the cotton-ginners and the masons. The ginner is sometimes given an agreed-upon amount annually or semiannually. For this he undertakes to do a regular type of work for the household, annually making or remaking cotton quilts and mattresses, essential on cold winter nights. Since these pack down readily and lose their insulating capability, they are normally taken apart, washed, and made fluffy again, once a year. The ginner's capital that was listed in table 13 is simple and inexpensive. A house normally has at least one quilt per member.

Apart from making quilts, the ginner's chief work is ginning cotton for home use. Cotton sold on the market, to jobbers who come to the village annually to bargain for it, is unginned. The movement of the ginners for work has been described. It should be added that their low income provided in this context is economically consistent with the fact that they have regular recourse to agricultural labor at the same usual rate as Harijans and others, and with the fact that their ginning is scheduled by farmers to fall in the slack time for labor, after the harvest.

The Masons are specialists of a different order. Corresponding to the higher value of their capital, their income is higher. Their diesel-powered threshing or winnowing devices are hired out at the rate of eleven rupees per hundred bundles processed, or about the rupee value of one bundle in fifty. Since normally about sixty bundles can be processed in a day, the daily rate is about what the mason receives in other work—five rupees. The pay when wheat or similar crops is threshed is computed at the end of the day by counting the ropes from the bundles. This rate obviously reflects the general market demand for the mason's services, and in fact appears to be the basis for his recent decision to undertake the work. The mason who owns the diesel first applied it to threshing wheat in the fields in 1963. Before that he threshed only maize, a more costly grain, in his own house compound. It is reasonable to see this move into a new area as meeting a demand that arose from increasingly intensive cropping. This provided the basis for payment at a rate that is low as a cost to the farmer in relation to the crops for a single major operation (2 percent compared with 4 percent for cutting) but high enough for a day's work to be worth a mason's while. Five to eight bighas of irrigated land, at present levels of production, yield enough bundles for a full day's pay, yet it is a small enough area to have its outrun collected in one place. On poorer land, more area would be required, and this would entail more work to move either grain or equipment. The engine is difficult to move into the fields, and the proper arrangement of the assorted machines and cooling facilities that are attached to it is time-consuming. The mason now threshes for only a few farmers who crop densely and who for one reason or another do not have cattle on hand to use for threshing (by crushing and stamping out the grain). The threshing, apparently, is productive only under marginal conditions where the needs of both the farmers and the mason have recently begun to coincide.

The mason who does masonry says that he earns about half of his income in the village, and does most of the masonry in the village. He worked on all the new buildings, three large units of construction, between October 1964 and December 1965, although some farmers said other masons had done other work for them previously. His work during this period was for a Harijan, a Brahmin, and a Farmer. He is generally assisted by the brother of the owner of the machines, who also does the blacksmith work, as was previously noted, and they both earn five rupees a day. The employer supplies food or some additional compensation. The mason also acts as contractor, arranging for the correct amounts of brick, cement, iron, and wood. Costs of these are paid directly by the employer. Since a house requires ironwork and woodwork in addition to masonry, most of the tools of all the village Masons except the miller come into play eventually, to the benefit of all parties.

Carpentry is paid for on an item-by-item basis. As in building, the rate is in addition to the actual cost of the material used, and is based on the time it takes to do the work. Again, the standard of five rupees a day holds, after the usual arguments. The mason will assist at carpentry at the common rate, just as the carpenter assists at masonry.

Various more diffuse relationships eke out the masons' income. They make small repairs for customers and friends without charge, and in return get some fodder, borrow tools, tether cattle on a farmer's land, and so on.

Like the ginners, masons are clearly in the village on business. The pattern of traveling and staying, and the range of work done by those who stay shows how the relationship between demands for the work in the village and outside affects the village labor pool, and in consequence, the village rate paid. At the same time, the specific manners of payment integrate the wages with the ecological system and with productivity. The existence of general rates that people get for the various work they do, and their willingness to work for anyone who will pay the rate argues for the businesslike, rather than "traditional," character of their activity in the village. The precise appropriateness or "rationality" of the wage rates are difficult to assess. Since it takes more capital to be a mason than a cotton-ginner or a laborer, it is reasonable that a mason's daily wage should be higher. The rate is about the same as that paid in the larger cities of Punjab, which are easily reached by the carpenters. It is also clear that the running expenses of carpenters do not exceed their income, for their houses are moderately prosperous. Beyond this, it is not possible to say if a little higher or lower rate might be more or less efficient. The same difficulty, however, would attend the evaluation of wages in Western societies of whose overall "rationality" or economic efficiency there is no great doubt. There is as much reason here as anywhere to hold that the market for skilled labor in the village is a coherent economic market in a system of such markets.

Summary

Because objects are exchanged for money, and money in turn is exchanged for other objects, the use of money as a conventional standard of evaluation creates an index of desirability among the different exchangeable goods in the village. Further, because of the portability of money, the even greater portability of expectations of exchange for money, and the great reach of "chain reactions" of exchange between areas of high and low evaluation for many goods, the index of desirability among goods in the village reflects the desirability of its goods over a wide region. This region extends far beyond the physical reach of any one person in the village and of most of the goods that are evaluated within it.

The monetary index in the village is interpreted within the context of the ecology and the division of labor. Villagers can act on the price of a good only when they know how useful it is to them, how difficult it is to produce in relation to other goods, what additional benefits can be obtained from producing it, and how useful the other goods are that can be obtained for the money. When transactions do occur, of course, they adjust the monetary index to the quantities of goods exchanged. More important, when production is planned with trade in mind, the monetary index adjusts the quantities of goods to each other. The monetary index of desirability thereby produces, in a general way, a parity of desirability and utility. At any point in time, the prices placed on goods in the village reflect past allocative choices over a wide region and permit villagers to respond to them.

The self-adjusting character that gives the economy its integrity as a message source can be attributed directly to the interaction of its two major classes of elements: the system of numerical concepts, and the conventions for applying it to objects.

The mathematical character of the economy is most directly related to its characteristic organization and function. Mathematical systems are both highly translatable and highly generative. A great many interrelated statements can come from only a few basic definitions, and the statements of the systems are highly redundant. In this sense, they are highly organized: they have low entropy and concomitantly low information, and this itself is related to the "universality" of mathematical concepts. Once the people within a division of labor arbitrarily establish the unit values of a few key items, or perhaps of just one, the values of others follow of themselves, from the numerical definition coupled with the managed ecological exchanges, without significant room for the exercise of additional choice. But at the same time, a quantitative description of an object conveys much less "information" about it than an ecological description, or a description in relation to the division of labor. It merely says it does not have either a higher or a lower monetary or exchange value in relation to other goods.

The lack of specificity and universality of the mathematical concepts built into the economy can themselves be seen to require the development of the second category of system components—the market conventions that define goods for monetary—quantitative— evaluation. The translatability of monetary values between two or more regions does not depend on their use of similar market conventions, although the efficient conduct of economic activity within the context of a single division of labor may require their consistency.

Although it would be premature here to attempt to develop a set of technical criteria to define the absolute numbers of elements of different message sources on a uniform basis, it is possible to make internal comparisons that indicate relative numbers of elements in the systems that order behavior in this community. First, it seems quite clear that the economy is more highly organized than either the ecology or the division of labor. The mathematical concepts of the economy are obviously both fewer in their irreducible logical elements and more rigidly interrelated than either the many populations, states of growth, operations, and processes of the ecology, or the social concepts, households and household strategies, and individual predilections of the division of labor. The market conventions—in that they affect fewer objects than all those in the ecology, and are not differentiated for each of the different elements of the division of labor that they refer to—are also general and vacuous, even though they are not rigidly or logically related to each other and there is considerable freedom for innovations permitted in their use.

The relatively low information of the economy does not mean that it is less important for the village than the ecology or division of labor in some general sense, or less worthwhile as an object of scientific attention. It means, rather, that the economy differs in function from the other two systems. Precisely because of its relatively low information, its inability to uniquely specify each object in the other two systems, economic information can frame comparisons and permit actors to judge between otherwise different and incomparable objects and their associated courses of action. Conversely, it is precisely the relatively low organization, high entropy, and high information of the ecology and division of labor that provides the practical need for such a comparative frame of reference through which people can communicate and coordinate their many highly specific and technical activities. The great freedom to combine options and modify definitions and actions that is inherent in the ecological system and in the division of labor (though to a somewhat lesser extent) is channeled and organized by the more restricted, broad, and widely accepted informational code of the economy.

The ecology, division of labor, and economy of Shahidpur appear to be systems of increasingly high organization, fewer functionally differentiated elements, and therefore of increasingly lower information. The economy obviously has markedly lower information than either of the other two.

These formal relationships, with their functional implications, provide a way of seeing common ground beneath opposed positions in an important general question that has been of persistent interest to economists and anthropologists alike. Does the economy encompass all social aspects of transactions (as Alfred Marshall and other "political economists" suggest, and as is implied in the modern practice of speaking of good will, "social costs," and the like as part of the "opportunity cost" of obtaining a good)? Or is the economy, as Karl Polanyi has said, "imbedded in society"? As we should expect, there is a major element of fact in both views. There is a sense in which the economy encompasses society, and a sense in which the economy is surrounded by noneconomic factors affecting its use. The real problem has always been to find a way to specify each sense in a way that does not preclude recognition of the alternative as well, and this is what an informational orientation seems to permit. Basically, the systems are separate. The economy is not essentially a part of the other systems, nor are they a part of it. Since price is not inherently linked to other considerations, such as a place in a life cycle as Duesenberry suggests, price cannot be considered to the exclusion of those other factors in making a major decision. In this sense, then, economic decisions can be seen as occurring in the context of noneconomic factors—because the systems are separate, not because they are one. At the same time, however, the vacuity of economic categories explains how they can be effectively thought of, and used, as general relations that encompass and compare options that have many different specific characteristics defined in the other systems. In this sense, the economy can be thought of as including other types of information, as it is in the assumptions that Duesenberry sought to modify. But again, this is because the systems are separate, not because they are integrated. Because of the differences that can arise only as part of their separateness, and because the economy has fundamentally low information value, the effective content of any economic decision involves the physical exchange of goods in a concrete setting, governed by culturally defined market conventions, as "substantivists" in economics and anthropology have persistently suggested.

Breaking ground for winter wheat.

Mustard-and-barsheen crops.
Right-hand field shows effect of manuring.

Harvesting wheat on land irrigated by well.

The *durwaza*, main village gate at north entrance to the *abadi*.

Threshing wheat with bullocks and a drag.

Village street, with entrances to doctor's office, shopkeeper's residence and shop, patwari office, house of a Farmer.

Roti being prepared for free kitchen of 1965 *diwan*.

Wedding party of Harijan caste.

Chapter VI

The Sikh Religion as a
Conscious Sociological Model

Just as many specific formulations of comparative prices are generated from the mathematical conventions and marketing practices of the economy, so too a large number of seemingly specific social descriptions are generated from the simple and highly ordered systems of premises described in this and the succeeding two chapters. Each chapter describes a "conscious sociological model" and its main implications. A conscious sociological model is a system of information that is generically like the systems already noted but specifically different in several respects. Like the other systems of information, these are broadly recognized systems of conventionalized elements that are chosen and acted upon in the creation of recognized differentiated actions. And as with other systems, the actions thus formed feed back into the system and maintain it for future utilization.

Conscious sociological models differ from the systems already described in several ways. First, their elements are primarily conceptual. Even though there are "rituals" that demonstrate their use, somewhat as markets apply the mathematical concepts of the economy, the rituals apply the concepts primarily to each other. That is, they demonstrate conceptual integration more than conceptual application. Second, and most important, the putative referents of the concepts of these systems, the things they purport to describe, are groups of persons and the roles and obligations of their members. Third, their formal organization and content together are such that they provide for reflexive characterization of the user as well as of the described object. That is, when one makes and enacts a choice of available characteristics of the social reality described in one of the systems, by that same fact one enacts a characterization of himself. If one speaks to another as God, one is put in the position of worshipper. If one uses a kinship term, one elects at the same time to be the reciprocal relation of the person or object named, and so forth. Such reflexity of characterization does not occur in the nonsocial systems of information. When one considers an object wheat or barley, one's own definition of oneself does not change. Nor does one's self-definition change when one sees objects in terms of price rather than in terms of their ecological characteristics, or in one price range rather than another. Finally, the conscious sociological models are highly organized systems of very low information. These general, formal properties and their functions can be examined in greater detail after each of the specific models used in the village and its special features are described.

The reflexivity and low information of social conceptions are directly related to their use in the division of labor. These systems provide the conceptual resources that people use to define themselves as interrelated members of housholds, castes, religious groups, factions, and of numerous other related and derivative groupings. Although these groupings, or rather these conceptions of groupings, do not dictate relationships, they are treated as if they do by those who manipulate them in the constant adjustment of the balances of cooperation and competition. They are the language of control and cooperation, of morality and power, just as the numerical system of the economy is the language of allocative choice.

Of the three principal models, the religion illustrates most clearly the point that such models are orderly in and of themselves, and are important in and of themselves—and not because they are conceptions "of" something substantive that is itself important. One cannot by any arguments confirm that the conception of God and the related entities of the Sikh religion as it is known in the village are abstracted from the villagers' observations of God himself, and no such claim is made in the religion itself. Learning the religious conceptions is clearly a matter of learning a standard picture of God and then being able to apply it in "reality," learning to speak of concrete objects as symbolizing all or part of it. It is learning to do what Wittgenstein would call playing a certain "language game" (1965, part I). Like all of the conscious sociological models to be described, the religious conception is a model "of" reality *only* putatively. Objectively, it is a restricted set of terms and images that are publicly promulgated and utilized "for" the determination of accepted definitions of situations. Its elements are said to have socially relevant referents, but the referents may often be, by their own definitions, not objectively observable. In all cases, because of the vacuousness of the terms, the stated referent will be only one among many possible accepted symbols or representations of the concept. The religious conception is only "of" God, but religious books, icons, people, and rituals are all taken as symbols of this concept. Beyond these conventionally recognized objects of religious significance, less standardized symbols—concrete objects and actions of many kinds—may be seen in terms of the religious system from time to time, as it may suit the circumstances.

The Basic Model

The ruling conception, the basic premise of the conscious sociological model of the Sikh religion, is a particular conception of God in relation to his disciple. This conception is embodied in current ritual and lore, which includes what we can consider an "ethnohistorical" account of the development of the religion itself. The simplest and most accurate way to convey the central concept and its implications is to summarize this history.

The conception was formulated in the second major doctrinal statement of Guru Nanak, almost five hundred years ago. Nanak was the first of ten personal Gurus who guided the development of the Sikh community in its first major historical period. His doctrine, which laid the basis for the theology of the movement, was: "Only God is the true Guru" (Narain Singh, ch. II). This phrase has many precise and powerful implications that derive from the meaning of its terms in the body of general Hindu religious philosophy and from the specifically Sikh exegetical works of Guru Nanak and subsequent Sikh religious philosophers.

Outside the Sikh traditions a guru is considered to be a religious or moral preceptor, an actual human teacher, not God, and not a god. The term is applicable to any teacher, of any religion, but it would not apply to a nonreligious teacher. In this context, Nanak's doctrine suggested a new point of view. To identify God as the only *true* Guru implies that other gurus are somehow "untrue," at least insofar as they might claim special or exclusive authority. This naturally also means that no particular set of religious practices, which a guru would explain and stand for, has any special authority either. This reformulation of the relationship between the concepts of "guru" and "God" encapsulates an entire school of thought, called *bhakti*, which is itself built upon one of the principal ancient schools of Indian theology: Vedanta. The term *bhakti* literally means "devotion." The tradition of concerns it designates takes off from Arjuna's discussion with Krishna in the Bhagavad Gita (Narain Singh, p. 21; Radhakrishnan 1967, p. 99).

Arjuna, in the Gita, asks why he should worship Krishna in particular, and why he should take part (at the bidding of Krishna) in the battle in which all are involved. Why should he contend against others, fear some things, seek some things, and fulfill his obligations, if indeed all objects and acts are aspects of one underlying God? The answer was first given by Krishna verbally, and was then demonstrated. Krishna assumed the staggering variety of only his own shapes and revealed, thereby, the profundity of the one formless God himself, and how difficult he was to reach. In effect, the answer was that a person should struggle, should fulfill his particular obligations, and should worship the particular personal God appropriate to him, because in that way the nature of the formless God is revealed to him by a personally suitable means. There are so many things God underlies that most men cannot hope, and need not try, to see him directly, or through all his manifestations at once. This theme was developed into the idea that different religions are thus necessary as different forms of devotion (bhakti) to the one formless God that underlies and surrounds each person—which leads to Nanak's theme in turn. The bhakti movement proper was a major ecumenical and reform movement affecting all religions, in and around the fifteenth century, and was particularly concerned with providing, on the basis of the old concepts, a common ground between Islam and Brahmanic Hinduism. Nanak was closely allied with Kabir, a major Muslim thinker in this movement, and many of Kabir's writings appear in the

Guru Granth Sahib, the Sikh sacred scripture. It is not at all unfair
or improper to say that early Sikhism itself was part of this movement. Indeed, Nanak's first pronouncement, which the second was
meant to explain, was "There is no Hindu; there is no Moslem."

In Sikh writings, Nanak's theme was systematically elaborated.
Nanak's poems, and most of the poems of his successors that have
been collected in the Guru Granth Sahib, each take as their subject
matter one or a few religious practices, household practices, occupational practices, or common occurrences, and then show how each
can be used to convey a sense of God. In this way, they repeatedly
make the point that each form can be used to worship, which is to
learn, and each can be used hypocritically or uninstructively.

The particular concept of a formless all-embracing God that
defines the problem of Arjuna and the solution of Krishna and bhakti,
is the God described in the literature of the Vedantic philosophy,
older than the Gita, which in turn develops logically out of certain
of the later Upanishads. God, in this tradition, is seen in a framework
that Westerners could regard as more epistemological than religious,
and more pragmatic than ethical. The Vedantic theology is pointedly
described by Radhakrishnan as "monistic," in contrast to "mono-
theistic" (pp. 16–17). Its fundamental concern is not with God as
a distinct object, nor with morality, and certainly not with "faith" in
the Western sense, but rather with all perceptions of reality. In this
sense "God" is much what it is in Whitehead's *Process and Reality*:
the fixed reference point against which, or in which, the constantly
changeable, individual, perceived forms or objects are ordered. It
is the background against which any particular "form" is to be perceived—and must in that exact and strictly logical sense be itself
"formless." It has been presumed since the beginning of this line of
analysis that an understanding of the nature of this formless background of perception will yield an understanding of the nature of
perceptions themselves, and thereby of all the particulars that are
perceived. This, in turn, has been understood as related to the problem of delineating right or adequate courses of practical action, like
the problem of "form" in the Western tradition that has closely associated epistemology with the philosophy of science since Plato's
time. What has not been seen to lead from an understanding of the
formless God itself has been what we call "moral" action as a special

class of action. The concerns of Arjuna reflect this "gap," recognize it and formulate it as an addition or adjunct to the Vedantic philosophy rather than as an integral part of it.

Nanak's conception that only God was the true Guru was elaborated during the leadership of the nine succeeding personal Sikh Gurus, over a period of about 250 years, through the writing of new theological poetry, the development of rituals, and the development of the Sikh tradition of history that is the principal vehicle of exposition and exegesis of theological doctrines—just as the above sketch of bhakti and Vedanta is exegesis of their doctrines that follow the broader historiographic model. After the fifth Guru, however, the doctrines of Nanak had gained enough adherents to become an independent and potent political force in Punjab in their own right, and had become the object of Mohammedan concern and then suppression. In consequence, the fifth and later Gurus developed the key elements that mark the Sikh community today as a self-perpetuating and militant body, capable of providing its own leadership without centralized personal "guruship."

Changes included the development of a distinctive script, compilation of a single authoritative sacred text, development of a system of temples and their management, and development of military tactics and of a military establishment, regular and irregular. All the different reforms were brought under their present well-ordered conceptual rationale in a series of ritual innovations by the tenth and last Guru, Guru Gobind Singh, in the early part of the eighteenth century. The keystone of his accomplishment was the Granth, which he took to completion and which he then declared to be the successor to his own spiritual authority—not merely a historical record of the words of the Gurus, but their physical embodiment—a teacher in its own right. This is the sense in calling it the Guru Granth Sahib, an honorific name such as one might give to a person called Granth, whom one held as a revered teacher (Guru) and lord (Sahib).

The Guru's transfer of his spiritual authority to the Guru Granth Sahib was accompanied by the transfer of his administrative authority to a self-perpetuating body of followers. These changes provided for an end to the system of personal gurus, and provided at the same time for a rapid expansion of the Sikh community through initiation and instruction of new members. Appropriately, they are most clearly embodied in the ritual of initiation that Guru Gobind Singh created and first used on Baisakhi day, the first day of the Vikram calendar's new year, in 1701 (Macauliffe 1963, V). This ritual conceptualized the changes in terms of the model of the Guru that goes back to Nanak.

The Guru selected the five first initiates by asking if any in the congregation he had assembled would offer their heads to the Guru. These became the nucleus of the new community initiating others in turn. The Guru himself was their first new convert. He asked them to initiate him, as their first act—signifying their complete authority thenceforth.

Five previously initiated Sikhs conduct the ritual in the presence of the Granth. When they act thus, they are said to represent, or act for, the Guru. They first prepare a sweet liquid, called *amrit*, which is stirred with a *kirpan*, a particular type of weapon that has traditional military significance and ranges in size from a small dagger to a sabre. Then, always in the presence of the Granth, each initiator takes some of this liquid, by hand, and places it in the mouth of each initiate in turn for him to swallow. Next, each initiator in turn sprinkles a bit of the same liquid from his fingers onto the face and eyes of each initiate in turn, in a similar manner. The initiators explain these actions and also the particular obligations that a Sikh assumes. They ask the initiates if they understand them and are willing to accept them. Eating amrit is said by them to signify equality among Sikhs. Eating in this way—a common theme at all Sikh services—requires the initiate to contravene, and thereby abandon, the rules against caste interdining associated with conventional Hinduism. In place of caste, he accepts the idea that the entire community is a body of "sons of one father," the Guru. They are "common sharers of the Guru's patrimony." All Sikhs are enjoined in the ceremony to call each other *bhai*, "brother." The ramifications of this highly charged phrase are combined with the significance of the second principal act—sprinkling. Sprinkling amrit signifies the spirit of martyrdom of Sikhs, the second major theme in the rituals. The act specifically recalls that each of the first five initiates offered to "give his head as an offering and proof of his faith" (Macauliffe 1963, V, 91). The idea is that since they have done so in a spiritual sense, thereby publicly renouncing ties that all living people have, such as ties to caste and, by implication, to family, they might at any time be called upon to "give up their heads" physically, in defense of the Guru, under martial circumstances symbolized by the dagger. In the initiation, they renounce the only reasons one could properly have, in terms of the ethics derived from the Gita, for resisting such a call.

The two themes of equality and martyrdom interlock, partly because they both spring from and give substance to the underlying conception that the community represents the Guru and God in the traditional sense. The community, Granth and Sikhs, are intertwined as the locus of truth and as a sustaining medium, the basis of individual existence. Eating the amrit signifies this, saying in effect that Truth (the Guru) sustains an individual just as a patrimony—the property a man inherits, manipulates, and depends on to earn a living—sustains him.

The ritual act of eating the amrit from the Guru recalls a very ancient and widely used analogy for the relation of the disciple to God in Vedanta. The disciple is represented as like a fish in relation to water. He depends on the water, and is part of it. Yet he is also different from water, and the difference itself is essential to his individual existence. If he were to approach the water either in magnitude or quality, he would be destroyed as a fish. Gobind Singh's treatment shifts emphasis only slightly from Nanak's earlier and more intellectualistic conception, which emphasized the liberating rather than the sustaining aspect of the truth. But both aspects of God, or Truth, have always been interrelated in the Vedantic tradition.

The Sikh concept of militancy follows directly from the identification to the Guru as a sustaining precondition of individual existence, and of the Guru with the community of Sikhs. Militancy—risking one's life—is logically necessary in defense of that which one's life, or individual existence, depends on. Since Truth, in all its special philosophical senses, is a precondition of individual existence, it is therefore both appropriate and necessary to risk individual existence to maintain or defend it. If one aspect of this Truth is embodied in the community, the community must be defended at the risk of life.

These concepts are the premises of the religion, the major elements structuring the conscious sociological model of the religion as a highly organized message source.

Major Implications and Their Symbolic Expression

The simple and highly ordered concepts of the religious theology are preserved and promulgated for use in a highly redundant system of conventional symbolic representations. These follow a continuum of varying degrees of formality, from the highly stereotyped iconography of the religion's buildings and their use, through small verbal and behavioral usages that are incorporated into everyday behavior.

The design and usage of the Sikh temples, called gurdwaras (*gurduārā*, house of the guru) express particularly the conception of God's place in the world. These are large structures, generally products of massive community involvement. Their floor plan exhibits certain regularities, apparently symbolically appropriate to their significance, although there is no explicit architectural convention comparable to the cruciform ground plan for Western Christian churches. The buildings generally involve concentric walkways, either in the form of rooms within rooms or rooms within corridors or courts. The central room in each system is the one devoted to the Guru Granth Sahib itself. The setting is generally so arranged that each Granth appears to be a center of attention and activity from a large surrounding region, extending far beyond the outermost walls of the gurdwara. Central rooms do not, for example, look out upon another such room, or upon a blank wall. Generally, instead, if one looks outward from the dais of a Guru Granth Sahib, one sees a series of doorways and arcades, progressively less closely tied to the Granth; and finally, beyond the last, one obtains a suggestion of the world outside the gurdwara. From a main room at the Golden Temple at Amritsar, for example, the view contains the Granth, several small arcades around the Granth's main room, a walkway around the room containing main room and arcades, a tank surrounding both temple and walkway, a second walkway beyond the tank, then the residential buildings for visitors to the shrine, which line the walkway around the tank, and finally the outer wall of the gurdwara, which is surrounded by the city of Amritsar, whose presence is suggested by treetops and a few rooftops. In Shahidpur, the gurdwara has barred but open windows looking out on all four sides, and all major services are held out of doors. There is no sense of enclosure or isolation in a purely religious environment, such as that conveyed by the dark interiors, stained windows, and closed doors of Western churches or synagogues.

The furnishings of gurdwaras and the practices of worship within them also express the concepts of the theology represented by the architecture. For example, it is now a common practice to brightly illuminate the immediate area of the Granth itself with a sodium vapor or flood lamp, (usually just in front of the Granth, over the congregation), leaving the surrounding arcades, or even the corners of the same room, in increasing shadow. In Shahidpur, the same effect was obtained with my own kerosene pressure lamp. It was often requested for religious services at night, where it was placed on the dais with the Granth (even though many of the readers know their parts from memory), thus casting the rest of the building, and the outside, into darkness.

The themes recur again, naturally, in the symbolism of the Granth itself, the central object that the gurdwara houses. The Granth is always kept upon a dais higher than the level of the congregation, and is treated with reverence, fanned in summer and covered with a heavy cloth in winter when not in use—just as one would take care of a revered teacher. Tobacco, whose use a Sikh foreswears in the initiation ceremony, is never brought into its presence. On the other hand, weapons "from the time of the Gurus" such as kirpans are generally displayed in its vicinity, often on the same dais. All these usages recall the symbolism of the initiation ritual, with its definition of the Granth as the successor to the last Guru, its injunctions to the initiates, and its definitions of martyrdom and the nature of God and the defense of God. The related ideas of equality and the sustaining character of the Guru are symbolized by a distribution of ceremonial sweets near the Granth and at the end of each regular service, and by a free kitchen that is always maintained on the gurdwara grounds. The sweets given out near the Granth are called *preshād* and are the same as those used to make amrit. During regular worship, they can be obtained outside the gurdwara. Those who come to worship bring them in, and give them, any amount, to one of the *bhais* upon approaching the Granth for the first time. He takes them, puts them in a common collection, and then gives back some out of the collection—an action that has the same symbolic effect as the mixing of servers and initiates in the rite of initiation. The sweets handed out at the end of a service are called *kRāpreshād*, and are made of wheat flour, ghee, water, and brown sugar. The mixture is cooked before the service and is allowed to sit under the dais or otherwise near the Granth while the service is being concluded. It is then stirred with a kirpan and served out to the congregation—again symbolizing sustenance drawn from the Guru in the precise sense noted. The free kitchen serves meals outside the area where the Granth is kept, to all who come. Its maintenance follows an injunction of several Gurus. It has the same significances as the amrit, since the caste of those who prepare, serve, and eat the food is unknown, and since the food comes to one through the Guru —the community. Eating it, too, signifies the recognition of the Guru.

The conception of the two aspects of the Guru, warlike and spiritual, is manifested especially by the personnel associated with gurdwaras—two kinds of Sikhs described as "typical" in Punjab. Those who devote themselves wholly to the Sikh religion, apart from individual "saints," fall into two types called *bhāī* ("brother"), and *nihāng* ("reckless"). Each is the antithesis of the other, and each symbolizes a segment or aspect of the complete idea of the Guru. The *bhais* symbolize the conception of the Guru in relation to Sikhs, the *nihangs* enact the conception of the Guru, or the community as the Guru, in relation to non-Sikhs. Their significance corresponds to the significance of the Granth and the weapons, respectively, in the gurdwara.

Bhais are attendants in the gurdwara. They generally wear white, with perhaps some blue trim. They exhibit a gentle and scholarly demeanor. They escort people about, conduct services, serve food, and so forth. They display no weapons. The kirpan, or dagger, which Sikhs must wear, is generally concealed under their shirt.

By contrast, *nihangs* generally guard the gates of the gurdwara, and seldom go inside to sit. They wear saffron and blue garments— traditional martial colors. They carry all manner of ancient-style weapons. They exhibit an aggressive and hostile demeanor. They do not generally read the Granth, and seldom attend services. Their principal "Sikh" activity is to attend various outdoor fairs, where they stage mock battles, have contests of horsemanship, and engage in other shows of martial skill. It is not insignificant that *nihangs* tend to be young boys or old men, outsiders to the main force of active working men that make up the community as a whole. They are not noted for religious learning; nor do they teach.

At the highest level of organization *nihangs* have the aspect of a sect apart from the general community. They have a head gurdwara of their own in Amritsar, of a unique design, which represents their order. But they have no hierarchy of lesser gurdwaras, and no real organization as such. Significantly, this one major building is incomplete and has every prospect of remaining so. They are, thus, outside the regular gurdwara system, but not complete by themselves, just as weapons signify the external aspect of the community when defending the Guru but have no primary and unique meaning in isolation.

Nihangs are associated with the *bhais*, but are of secondary religious and political importance—their importance comes from their association and not from their own qualities. The *bhais* are the center of the community organization just as the book is the center of religious worship. They are central to the community just as the book is to the gurdwara. The *nihangs* are associated, but not identified or united, with the gurdwara and the community just as weapons are associated with the Granth.

Given the complex redundancy of the graphic expressions of the religion, it should not be surprising that the behavior of those who come as occasional worshippers themselves sound the general theme of the centrality of the Guru and the community in the secular world. In all gurdwaras, at all services, those entering come through a door that is always open. They approach directly to the front of the dais upon which the Granth is kept, where they bow in show of respect, and only then take their place among the rest of the worshippers for as long as they care to remain. From there, of course, they go back, away from the Granth, to their normal occupations. All this emphasizes the general idea that the Granth, and the Truth of all religions, is present in and is part of and oriented toward the everyday world of those who come to it. It is a source of general wisdom and sustenance, of enlightenment and strength. Religion is not an isolated area of concern, or an isolated and esoteric set of truths. There is no "kingdom of God" cut off from or different in kind from the "kingdom of man."

In view of the content of the themes emphasized in these widely known and used symbolic manifestations, it is not surprising that they are currently viable in daily affairs throughout Punjab, including, of course, Shahidpur. The five marks of a Sikh that initiates agree to wear in token of their acceptance of their obligations are worn as a matter of course by most villagers who consider themselves Sikhs, whether or not they have undergone the formal ritual itself. The name "Singh," also enjoined in the ritual, is similarly used to show loyalty to its theology and ethic by both initiated and uninitiated alike. The conception of the Guru in relation to the community, and the ideas of equality and of martyrdom, are formally represented and expressly discussed on religious occasions. These range from family-sponsored *akhandpats* (*akhānDpāt*) within the village, through annual village fairs, to large ceremonies and fairs at the major temples nearby that attract thousands. The fairs generally mark the anniversaries of principal events in Sikh history. For example, the creation of the community by Guru Gobind Singh itself is celebrated each year on Baisakhi day at Anandpur Sahib, about fifty miles north of Shahidpur.

The national and local religious rites represent and promulgate the concepts of the religion in a concise, and highly redundant, symbolic form. In addition, they provide occasions wherein the concepts of the religion can be applied to matters of daily concern, giving them implications for daily situations. Every regular religious service has a period set aside for what is called *sikhia* (*sikhīā*), literally "study." At this time, speakers address those assembled in what is understood as a discussion of religious principles and their importance to members of the community. Very frequently, for example, the theme is the importance of preserving the community itself. There is an established oratorical style for these talks of "illustrating" the principles with discussions of current persons or issues known locally or publicized in the press. Some of these illustrations strike a popular chord. They are widely discussed and sometimes become the center of major controversies. Any such widely established "illustration" must be considered by us as a manipulated symbol of the concept it illustrates, a new "synonym" for the standard name of the concept that is defined in terms of the theological system in the religious literature. The significance of the object at the time it is discussed becomes, for the moment, and for those who accept it, part of the nuances of meaning of the theological concept itself, so that from the point of view of most of those who identify themselves with the religious community, there is no clear distinction between the general concepts of low information and their elaborations thus stabilized in publicly expressed religious consensus. By this process, the religious ideas are constantly given new and viable policy implications, and are in turn maintained as a viable framework for discussing policy matters of broad personal concern wherever the rituals are made to occur in this form.

As one important practical application of religious ideas, the relation of *nihang* to *bhai* and of the weapons to the book in the gurdwara has a symbolic parallel in the current practice of seeing the Sikh community as a single, "national," political entity. The major leaders of the *panth*, the Sikh community as a political entity, such men as Master Tara Singh or Sant Fateh Singh, adopt the manner and dress of *bhais*, and work within the gurdwaras in both a symbolic and a practical sense. Their political views are promulgated in terms of the ethic of the religion, and the gurdwaras themselves, particularly on the occasions of major religious fairs, provide the platforms from which these men make their views known and from which they assess their support. Each group contends for leadership by arguing that its specific policies are those "truly" consistent with the principles of the religious teachings and the spirit of sacrifice. The capitol of the Sikhs, the religious and political seat of government, is the Golden Temple. (The proper Punjabi name is Durbar Sahib, "Sir Court.") It is the meeting place of leading religious and political bodies, as well as a monument to the strength and devotion of Sikhs.

The recent, successful campaign of Sant Fateh Singh (elected chairman of the Sikh religious organization in 1964) for partition of the former Punjab state along linguistic lines was argued squarely in terms of the religious ideology. It provides a good example of the general ways in which the concepts of the ideology are utilized to organize important daily concerns at many different levels.

In his spoken and written argument, the Sant relied closely on Nanak's ideas of tolerance and equality of religions, and of course implicitly on the theology behind it. He contended, repeatedly, that

Master Tara Singh had been wrong to emphasize Sikh rule, and that a Punjabi subah consistent with Sikh ideals both could and should be based on absolute religious tolerance, making no invidious or preferential religious distinctions. He also argued, again in terms of the religious ideas, that the demand for a subah was based not on political ambitions but entirely on the need to avoid discrimination against Sikhs, to protect the Truth and the religion. He argued against Master Tara Singh by pointing to past actions of his that indicated political motives in conflict with these religious ideals. Similar arguments, similarly relying on the wide acceptance of the basic religious concepts, covered many more particular issues of policy, but the most spectacular uses of religious ideas were less verbal and more dramatic.

Sant Fateh Singh's campaign, like many of Master Tara Singh's before him, centered on a hunger strike and threat of self-immolation in the late fall of 1965. In the religious context, this form of action was an expression of his willingness to sacrifice himself. It suggested that the Sant was defending the Guru and the continuation of the Sikh community, and implied that the community he represented was being threatened. Had he been allowed to die, this implication would have been confirmed, and a time for physical sacrifice would seem to have developed. The government would, in effect, have shown hostility or indifference to the welfare of the Sikhs. Widely announced support for the Sant's view of the significance of the issue made it clear that this would have triggered wide and forceful demonstrations, which the government of India could not then afford.

The connection between the specific issue of a Punjabi-speaking region and the concept of defending God lies in the association, in the debates, between the Punjabi language and the Gurmukhi script in which the Guru Granth Sahib is written. The religious writings are considered by most Punjabi Sikhs to be embodiments of the Punjabi language par excellence just as sacred writings in the Devanagari script are considered to epitomize Hindi. Teaching "Punjabi" in the Gurmukhi script thus provides access to the religious texts, whereas teaching some other language cuts off the religious writing from the mainstream of social life, particularly from government and the schools. The issue of an "official language," which is by definition a written language to be taught in publicly supported schools and used in tests for government offices, is thus intimately bound up with the general influence of religious teaching and respect for religious writings. The issue is especially clear for Sikhs since theirs is the only religious literature in Punjabi (that is, in Gurmukhi script), while numerous sects have literatures in Hindi (that is, Devanagari). In effect, the preservation of Punjabi is specifically associated with the preservation of the Guru Granth Sahib as a viable force in civil affairs, which amounts to preservation of the Guru in terms of the equation of the Guru and the community as represented in the ritual of initiation.

In addition to the specific issue of a Punjabi subah, religious ideas have also been utilized by Sikh leaders to articulate and organize support for various matters of policy respecting, particularly, economic development and land reform. These issues reflect utilization of the religious concepts in organizing agricultural activities and interests within villages, including Shahidpur, throughout Punjab, and they feed back into the village practices in turn. But since these usages are connected in practice with uses of the factional ideas in ways that complement the religious ideas, their discussion will be deferred until chapter 8.

There are, however, some stereotyped indications of the relevance of religious ideas to agricultural and economic practices in the village that should be mentioned directly. First, I should point out that the caste name that I have consistently translated here as "Farmer" is called Jat in Punjab in general, and in Shahidpur and similar villages it is explicitly and consistently described further as "Sikh Jat." Village Farmers insisted, when asked directly, that it was a different caste from "Muslim Jat" or "Hindu Jat," indicating that they recognize something about being Sikh as being pertinent to their particular type of farming. The amount of consensus on these views, and its importance, is suggested by the unanimous use of Sikh surnames and other personal symbols within this group as noted in describing the division of labor. By contrast, no other caste of the village appends the term Sikh to their caste name in the same way. Nor does any other large group adhere so strictly to the religiously defined symbols of membership in the community. The Mason does not say his caste is "Sikh Mason," nor does the Barber say he is "Sikh Barber." Village farmers have definite ideas on the decisive features of their occupation—they consider themselves superior to Muslim and Hindu farmers specifically in matters pertaining to independent, small-scale, irrigation agriculture, including the management of wells and the raising of wheat. In fact, there is a strong statistical association in Punjab between the proportions of Sikhs in the rural areas of the eighteen districts of Punjab (as they were constituted at the time of the study) and the proportion of land watered from irrigation by mixed sources (Spearman's Rho coefficient of .66), a correlation nearly as strong between rural Sikhs and the proportion of cropped land devoted to wheat (.50), and successively less strong correlations with wheat yield per acre (.34), and the number of cattle per hundred acres (.28). Within the state, Sikhs are concentrated in a continuous section of the central plains, bracketed by Hindu-dominated areas in the mountains to the north and east, and in the very arid regions to the south and west where the water table was too low for wells to be practicable, and more drought-resistant crops replaced wheat. This pattern is commonly known, though the statistics were derived only from my own preliminary analysis of census data from the 1961 returns—on the basis of which, in part, the original selection of Shahidpur as a typical Sikh village was made.

In addition to the names of castes, and general opinion on the relationships between religious beliefs and farming proficiency, there are a few explicit ritualized usages that point to specific religious ideas in association with equally specific objects of agricultural significance. There are, for example, monuments to village "martyrs," called *shahids* (the same term as that used in the religious context to signify what I have translated as "self-sacrifice"), which are built at well sites and which are described by farmers as appropriate places to leave first-fruits offerings at each harvest. It is also said that each group of men who leave the village to go to another for a wedding should stop by the main *shahids*, or some *shahids*, and ask for blessings from God. Other rituals, for village cattle and for sons, are described as being to thank God for their health and to pray —for the welfare of the village—that such blessings will continue in the future. Finally, wheat porridge is served after all Sikh rituals, and wheat breads are the standard fare at the free kitchens every gurdwara maintains. By these symbols and others which are used in casual speech and interaction, the ideas of martyrdom and of a patrimony upon which individuals depend are linked with irrigation management including wheat as an irrigation crop, and with the maintenance of human and animal populations in this type of village system.

Summary

There is a sharp and perhaps paradoxical difference between the relationship of the religious model to behavior and the relationship of the ecology or economy to behavior, a difference easily overlooked if they are not treated together in a comparative framework. The ecological system and the division of labor have irreducible terms or elements that are highly specific in "information," in the sense that in order to properly demonstrate "understanding" of them, to properly symbolize them, a person must go through a detailed and time-consuming set of activities. "Wheat," for example, is an irreducible element. Its properties cannot be derived from any other element or set of elements alone. To demonstrate knowledge of wheat one must grow it by a system of operations specifically connected to this crop and none other, and these operations, in turn, maintain wheat as part of the ecological message source. The paradox is that such elements are not the sort of thing usually considered to be directive of human behavior. They are not "normative." The ecology does not consist in a system of statements about what its elements "should" be, or about what people should be or do. Rather, they are descriptions of the way things are, descriptions closely tied to operations and tools.

By contrast, the religious information lacks specific directive force in relation to behavior, but it is specifically "normative" and applies directly and explicitly to people. The religious information does not say what those who appear to be Sikhs have been observed to do, but rather what a "true Sikh" does—that is, what a person should do in order to be a true Sikh. Similarly, the conceptions of a Guru do not dispassionately record observation of apparent Gurus, but reflect what a Guru *should* be, and what a person who acts for the Guru *should* do. Despite this, the idea of a Guru is symbolized by objects as diverse as the Granth itself, older men, teachers in relation to students, fathers, political leaders, soldiers, and, of course, other conventional nonhuman icons—to name but a few more common examples. Similarly, the conception of the Sikh community is represented by groups as diverse as the totality of those who support the Sikh leaders in either their religious or political aspects, or both; by groups of men who share wells in the village; by labor unions; and, as was indicated in describing the division of labor, both by "members" of each faction and by those who argue that factions do not exist or are unimportant in village life. Finally, the conception of "devotion" or worship, the relationship of a disciple to a Guru, provides a general model for the expression of respect that can be and is employed in relationships between nearly every type of person and collectivity in the community, as well as by the community as a whole in relation to others, and by people as Sikhs in relation to non-Sikhs. The concepts can not in any way be construed as deduced from, or as "describing," their diverse usages, as if the usages had causal or logical priority.

The low entropy of the religious model in relation to choice permits this wide range of application of its component ideas. Logically, since the elements in the system are few, and their interconnections are rigid, the use of each element can be given only limited "information"—only limited utility for designating unique courses of action to maintain the system. The ecology, although highly organized as a biological system, is too vast and complicated to be adequately known by any one person, so that its effect as a message source is less determinate—it has more entropy. Choosing one element to symbolize, such as growing wheat, does not determine the choices available to most other elements in and of itself. This lack of integration from the point of view of the user permits the different elements of ecology to be given their detailed individual programmatic significance. But, again, it only *permits* it. To explain why the "permitted" potential is utilized it is necessary to look beyond the formal properties themselves. In the ecology and in the division of labor this poses no problem. The designated objects themselves provide the incentives for utilizing the informational capacities of the formal system and provide sanctions against those who fail to do so. Wheat is food. But what provides the incentive for utilizing systems of low information?

There is no apparent intrinsic benefit in properly utilizing the symbols associated with the religious model, but there are numerous extrinsic benefits that may be obtained. For example, the hospitality of the gurdwaras, their free meals and lodging, is more than a symbolic expression of the idea of the community as a patrimony shared equally by Sikhs. It also makes the gurdwaras the principal system of public accommodations for the rural people of Punjab. There are no hotels or motels in the rural areas, and even tea shops are scarce except along the main roads. Market towns generally have active gurdwaras instead, where visiting farmers stop to eat and talk. The larger gurdwaras generally attract commercial fairs to their religious gatherings, even if no market town is in the area. Finally, the smaller gurdwaras not in market towns, like the village gurdwara of Shahidpur, are also important for local gatherings and for personal travel, on business or pleasure, to visit relations, seek work, or visit courts and offices. Taken together, gurdwaras are a primary foundation of the pattern of high population mobility that characterizes the Sikh tracts. Their important function as a political forum, already noted, is tied to this, and each reinforces the other. The donations given to the gurdwaras, logically symbolizing the concept of self-sacrifice for the community, also must reflect satisfaction with the efficiency of the system in relation to the important material services it provides.

Similarly, there are perfectly good material reasons extrinsic to the religion for referring to the group that one shares a well with as if it should respect the idea of "martyrdom"; and there are extrinsic benefits to be gained by utilizing the model of respect relations provided by the concept of "devotion," the relation between disciple and Guru. Superficial reasons are to please others, or to obtain some end through cooperation. Underlying these are the more basic kinds of reasons Hobbes saw. There is, for example, a need for requiring people to be able to identify each other as continuing social beings, morally responsive to each other and to commonly held ideals or principles. Such extrinsic reasons at all levels refer back to the previously described ecology, division of labor, and economy. The enduring interpersonal relations built up with the low-information systems are necessary to organize the transmissions and application of the more "precise" information of the three high-information systems.

The religious model is too highly organized for the descriptions of people, its putative referents, to have significant directive effect on behavior; but this itself means that they are general enough to enable the putative referents to be referred to repeatedly in a wide array of circumstances in order to convey a sense of enduring human or social relationships that "transcend" or "underlie" large numbers of objectively different kinds of objects and actions.

Chapter VII

Kinship as a Conscious Sociological Model

T he system of concepts that defines relationships subsisting
among people on the basis of their place in a system of
putative kinship groups and kinship relations makes up the second
conscious sociological current in the broadest consensus in Shahidpur. The broad functions of this model are identical to those in the
model of religion. This model permits people, acting as individuals,
to agree on a set of enduring relationships that appear to underlie
their actions and that give their actions a dependable moral basis.
The conscious model of kinship differs from that of the religion only
in its form and its specific putative content. The kinship model has
more elements, and the putative referents of these elements are biological rather than theological.

The relationships between the present approach to kinship and
the approach of established theories in social anthropology bring up
some new aspects of the nature of information systems in the present
sense, and they have some long-range implications for the relationship between kinship theory and theory pertaining to religion, as well
as to the third type of system, to be described in chapter 8.

The present approach, considered only as a theory of kinship,
falls partway between two principal divergent views descended from
a position first formulated by A. L. Kroeber in 1909. Arguing against
Lewis H. Morgan's practice of deducing residential patterns from
terminological definitions, Kroeber held that terminologies were

purely "psychological" phenomena, and not in any way "sociological." "Psychological" in this sense referred, I believe, to the sense that the German term *psychologie* had in the school of *Völkerpsychologie* of Virchoff, Bastian, and Wundt. It was linguistic in the sense meant by European philologists of the nineteenth century, who were partly involved with the sounds of speech and grammar, but equally concerned with what we now distinguish as "semantics," as well as with myth and cultural cognition in a very broad sense. In the context of this tradition, it was perfectly appropriate for Kroeber to say that kinterms were "psychological" entities "determined primarily by language" (reprinted in Kroeber 1957, p. 181). Kroeber kept the same idea, but chose a more understandable way of conveying it in an American context when he later reformulated his position. In a 1952 summary and review of several of his earlier papers, he changed "psychological" to "semantic." He held that "kinship terminologies are patterns of semantic logic" (p. 172).

Kroeber's 1952 position would have been identical to major aspects of my position in this analysis were it not for his added caveat that "kinship is a quite limited little universe held within a rigorous biological system" (p. 171). This preserved, by hypothesis rather than by observation or logic, his initial "conclusion" that terminologies and institutions were somehow unrelated, for it had to be presumed that neither marriage rules, nor residential patterns, nor religious or political groups could similarly be held within the same "biologically" bounded compartment.

Although the idea of "biology" is logically extraneous to any concept of semantics, it was integral to Kroeber's methodological approach to kinship terminologies. Kroeber proposed to compare terminologies by examining the different ways they organized eight "categories" of relations that he presumed to be more or less universal. These categories, such as "difference between persons of the same and of separate generations" and "sex of relative," made up the biological system that "held" terminologies, in the specific sense that it limited the meanings terms would have.

Kroeber's analysis into "principles or categories" was developed by G. P. Murdock into the technique of transcribing native kin terms as sets of "kin-types" (1949). The basic type-symbols include Mo, Fa, Br, Si, Da, So, and a few modifiers for age and other similar relations that might be needed on occasion. These are combined into strings such as Mo-Fa to designate specific positions, and these strings may be further combined into sets to designate the gloss of a specific native term. This technique, with the closely related use of a genealogical tree, has been a mainstay of the methodology of field elicitation of kinship terms, and the principal means for indicating the sense of terms to scholarly audiences.

Kin types in turn were developed into the basis of the technique of "componential analysis" by Goodenough (1956) Wallace and Atkins (1960), and others. This technique applies comparative frames like those in linguistic componential analysis to configurations of kin types. The technique is to substitute kin-type sets for the terms to be analyzed, then to arrange them into an economical pattern.

"Components" are then derived by inspection of the kin-type patterns, and represent the minimal number of principles by which the semantic patterns or domains represented by the kin-type configurations can be generated. Goodenough began with a simple, two-dimensional diagramming format for arranging terms. More recent modifications of this basic method have included the use of notational conventions from transformational linguistics (Buchler and Selby 1968, chap. 9).

Kroeber's view that terminologies were "psychological," not "sociological," was duplicated at every stage in the development of this particular line of analysis. Goodenough considered this analysis to be part of the general study of linguistic form that he called "descriptive semantics" (p. 216). Wallace and Atkins, reviewing their own position and that of their colleagues, took the position that "the semantic structure to which we refer is a structure of the logical relationships of definitional meanings among terms and does not pretend to describe such phenomena as marital exchange or authority relationships" (p. 60). "Psychologically real" analysis of kinship terms based on componential analysis may or may not be "structurally real," depending on the ingenuity of the analyst in arranging kin-type glosses and picking the parameters implicit in their arrangements. There is, however, no essential connection between the two types of "reality" (p. 78). The implication is that "marital exchange or authority relations" are not represented in semantic systems, that somehow "structure" in kinship terms is different from "meaning" in systems of definition.

Several important treatments of kinship terms based on different theoretical premises show quite different results. E. R. Leach, for example, compared several subsets from different terminologies, treating them as comparable "mathematical" patterns of "organizational ideas that are present in any society" (1961, p. 2). These patterns, in addition to terms for kinship positions, include concepts of "marriage," "descent," "influence," and family organization: matters that are closely and directly linked to what Kroeber and the componential analysts would call "institutional" rules. Leach was obviously dealing with organized systems of definitions, of concepts —semantic patterns. Unlike Kroeber or componential analysts, however, Leach made no important use of kin types or of similar devices to limit these patterns. David Schneider has articulated the implications of this line of analysis in a general attack on the necessity of assuming a biological basis to the analysis of kinship systems as "cultural systems" (1965b; 1968).

The principal difficulty of Leach's and Schneider's analyses stems precisely from the way it shows terms and structure to be interrelated. Because of this the practical analytical difficulties in their type of study are not limited to a narrow area. What Schneider and Leach, and those with whom they have been concerned, say about terminology is bound up with complex larger arguments on social systems and social structure in general, including the debate between "alliance theory" and "descent theory." In this context, the complexity of concerns surrounding the analysis of such small sets of terms as Leach describes, or such subsets as are involved in defining a lineal group, virtually precludes exhaustive and systematic treatments of whole terminologies.

The mode of analysis used to describe the Sikh religion as a system of definitions that is also a system of information provides the basis for a simple and operational middle ground between these two approaches. It yields an analysis more limited than that of the structuralists, and more operational. But the religious model seen this way is not artificially disconnected from institutional rules and concepts.

Precisely the same technique can be used in the elicitation of kinship systems. In order to connect the concept of an information source, or a conscious sociological model, to kinship systems as semantic systems, one must bear in mind a point that componential analysts sometimes lost sight of—that a "word" in semantic analysis should not be confused with a word in the context of phonological analysis. In semantics, the basis of assorting data is synonymy. All forms with the same definition are treated as equally representative of the same semantic unit, regardless of their sound characteristics. In phonological analysis, the basic unit of concern is a range of similar sounds that are phonologically, not semantically, conditioned. It is something of a truism in logic and philosophy that the sound characteristics of a particular "word" have no intrinsic or inherent relation to its semantic aspects. Semantic words may have many sound representations, and a given set of sounds can have many different meanings. Semantic words, in effect, are concepts. The technique of direct elicitation by continuously asking for explanations until replies become circular is perfectly appropriate to the semantic sense of word, and its lack of bearing upon kin "terms" in a phonological sense in no way impairs this appropriateness.

The procedure used to analyze the religious system was to solicit basic religious ideas and ask for their explanations. This yielded other closely related ideas that could in turn be inquired into. Before long, once most ideas had been identified, a point was reached where the ideas elicited to explain some ideas were the same as those elicited at the beginning of the inquiry. The most basic definitions formed a logically closed system.

The Kinship Terminology

Figure 3a presents the basic pattern of definitions of the Punjabi terminology, the complete set of categories for any person's kinship relations. This pattern functions as a basic premise of the system, analogous to the basic image of God surrounding the disciple in the religious model. Figures 3b and 3c give special synonyms that are used for the affinals of male and of female egos for some purposes. The maps were constructed according to two operational rules that derived from the basic concept of a semantic word. The first rule was to use no symbols that could not be given clear Punjabi names and

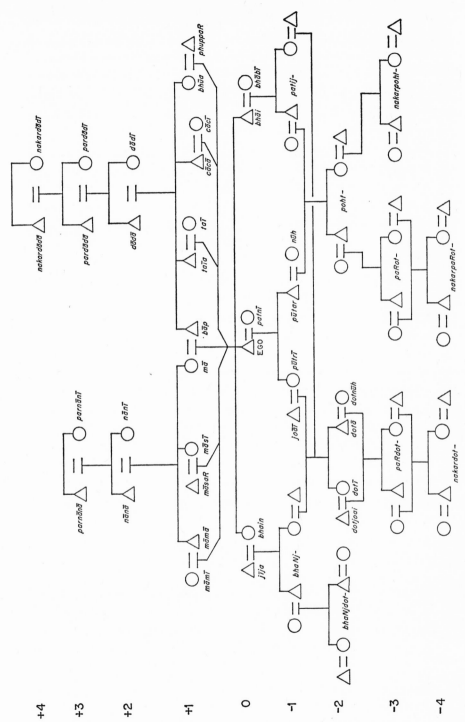

Figure 3a. Semantic map of Punjabi kinship terminology—main terms.

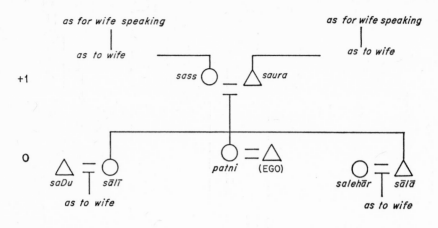

Figure 3b. Semantic map of Punjabi terms for affinal kin of male.

definitions by informants. The second was to use the minimum number of such symbols that could convey the full range of implications agreed on by the users of the system. (These are the same procedures that were used in eliciting the religious and factional systems.) Following these rules, the map was elicited and constructed in the presence of a large group of villagers, after some preliminary work to identify clear examples of commonly used terms to serve as the bases of questioning. Elicitation proceeded outward from ego, beginning with the six relations directly linked to ego: *ma* (*mā*), *bap* (*bāp*), *bhai* (*bhāi*), *bhain*, *putar* (*pūtar*), and *putri* (*pūtri*). Each of these in turn was taken as ego, and the gathering was asked, "What are his ——— to ego?" where the frame was supplied with each of six central terms in turn. The answers showed most consensus on what turned out to be the formal or standard phonological symbols, with scatterings of divergent colloquial or informal usages. The most standardized forms were taken down in the Gurmukhi script so that most people could read it, and these are the terms transliterated here. As this procedure revealed new positions, each of them was inquired into in turn, using the same procedure. The map was thereby traced outward in every direction until positions were reached that were described as endpoints, or that were wholly defined in terms of positions already elicited. The first end-points thus reached were on the +1 generation, and showed up as a number of redundant loops of

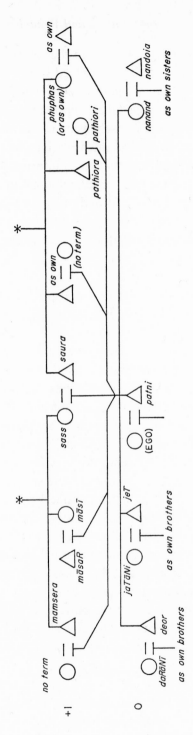

Figure 3c. Semantic map of Punjabi terms for affinal kin of female.

terms. These loops were simplified into the forms presented during the first elicitation itself, and the simplified form (used here only in +2 and above for reasons of pictorial convenience) was discussed with the informants and received their approval. Later other villagers were asked to exhibit some comprehension of the map and to supply any missing elements. In further intensive interviews with villagers who had previously supplied genealogical information, the map was used to predict terms that designated relations at different points would employ for each other. This and other procedures sought any types of relations that might be excluded from the map. With the exception of some affinal usages that are properly regarded not as new positions but as synonyms for positions the map includes, the map as initially constructed on the basis of the first group interview withstood all these tests for completeness and predictive power. Direct elicitation of semantic systems is not only easy but remarkably accurate.

In addition to the terms themselves, all the graphic symbols used in figure 3 were agreed on in the initial interview. These are triangles, circles, single lines, equal-signs, and two-dimensional space, and they represent the Punjabi concepts *ādmī, ūrat, sākhī, shādī,* and *nazdiki,* respectively. They can be rendered into English as "male," "female," "blood relationship," "marriage," and "nearness" in the order given. No additional symbols were considered necessary for each position in the map. These concepts that structure the map form the common parameters underlying the differentiated positions. They may be regarded as native "components" of the terminology, elicited directly without benefit of kin types and without recourse to the theory of meaning that has underlain many difficulties in componential analysis. But these components are not to be regarded as exhibiting universal "biological" features in any sense stronger than that in which the basic ideas of the religion can be said to represent a universal "theology"—which is to say that these ideas simply resemble our own ideas of biological descent more than they resemble other ideas we may have.

The conventional symbols F, B, S, H, will represent father, brother, son, husband, and the symbols w, d, m, s, will represent wife, daughter, mother, sister, respectively, in the following description of the way the kinship map predicts and describes the choices of significant symbolic behaviors in the creation and maintenance of social relations of kinship. In this context these are not to be understood as kin types—they are not in any way the equivalent or "meaning" of kinship terms from the terminology. They pertain to another phenomenon entirely: they describe links between people, such as exist in actual genealogies, as villagers conceive of and report them.

A genealogy is not a set of terms; it is rather a set of people, known and named individuals, who are reported as being related to each other through marriage and descent, or in this case, by *shādī* and *sākhī*. Genealogies record a unique sequence of events. Inder Singh was born of Anok Singh after Santokh Singh was born; he was born once; his time and position of birth cannot change, and it will never recur. He married one particular woman and had two sons. She died, he married again and had one more son. Such is the stuff genealogies—but not terminologies—are made of. Terminologies contain no such personal information. Terminologies are conscious sociological models, but genealogies are not, both because they are not present in wide consensus and because they really do not purport to describe recognized social groups. People who are "in" one genealogy may use any of several terminologies in designating their relationship to each other when they might meet, just as they may for any of several reasons elect to use no kinship terminology at all, preferring to establish a relationship on some other basis. For example, people in Shahidpur choose between English, Punjabi, and Hindustani kin terms, with their different semantic imports. People who are relations but who meet on occasion in occupational or political capacities also use such terms of address as "headmaster" or "Sardarji" (an honorific or polite general name by which Sikhs are addressed). Even within a terminology, different terms may be chosen. A person was addressed as "headmaster" by a villager on one occasion. This villager, it later developed, was the headmaster's terminological "grandfather" *dada* (*dādā*) by strict genealogical reckoning, even though he was younger. On some occasions, the genealogical relationship was appropriate and was referred to by appropriate usages that put the elder man in the inferior position. But on other occasions it was more proper for the young man to call the older by the term *cācā*. The original, non-kinship, usage I had heard was considered proper and appropriate on still other occasions.

Several visible features of the map provide assurance that it has "psychological reality" in a number of senses. The definitions parallel an elaborate phonological ordering of the standard word-forms presented. (This is a second reason for considering these as core forms to which phonologically disparate synonyms are equated.) The phonological pattern duplicates the spatial ordering seen in the map and represented by the general symbols. From ego's generation upward, for example, terms occur in pairs. Suffixes in this group distinguish only male and female terms (as represented in the diagram by both equal-signs and consanguineous lines between "sibling" pairs). Coincident with this phonological pattern, each term applies to a class defined as including both affines and consanguines. Contrasting with this system, the −1 generation and those below use a four-way system of suffixes, two for males and two for females. These permit and carry the definitional distinction of four types of positions: affinal male, affinal female, consanguine male, and consanguine female. In both groups a system of prefixes, (none), *par-*, and *nakar-*, mark the generational distance from ego. Finally, each columnar group thus framed by prefixes and suffixes is duplicated or marked phonologically by rhyming stems, and similarity of sound thus approximates similarity of descent. For example, the matrilateral superior kin +1 are designated with the stem *-nān-*, the patrilateral equivalent with the rhyming *-dād-*. The matrilateral kin of +1, mother's kin, are all designated with stems rhyming with *mā*: *māmā*, *māsaR*, *māmi*, and *māsī*. Their suffix pattern, too, both links them to and separates them from their superiors. Similar points can be made for the patrilateral group, and for the inferior kin, *-dot-*, *-paRot-*, *-paRdot-*, where the rhyming and grouping are obvious in the map. These linguistic patterns, in supporting the "spatial" arrangements, support the semantics, because the spatial relations have pervasive cultural meanings that appear in the use of the system.

Use of the Terminological Map

My informants stressed that the terms at the top and bottom of the map are the ends of their lines. The father of *nakardada* in +4 is described as "nothing" to ego—not a relative. The same is true for —4 *nakar-paRota's* son or daughter. There is, thus, no presumption in the system that a person can always be classified by tracing up to a common relative and then back down, as in our Western terminologies. Rather the relationships to remote kin have to be traced laterally out through nearer links. The map thus presumes a "social" rather than purely "biological" network in the world to which kin terms are applied.

The main generative mechanism that permits distant kin to be reckoned laterally is the configuration of terms, at each level superior to ego, that distinguish sex but not specifically affinal as against consanguineous status. Consider, for example, the configuration in the patrilateral side of generation +2. The term *dadi* (*dādī*) designates all those who are "sister" and all those who are "wife" to *dada*. And *dada*, in turn, names all those who are "brother" or "husband" to *dadi*. This is understood as a logical circularity that generates an unending chain of potential patrilateral relations. If *dada* has a wife and sisters, each of these is *dadi*. (The merging descent lines from 0 to +1 show that all daughters of +1 relations are "sister," so that this alone is a large domain.) All who are brother to them, not only the first *dada*, are in turn *dada* to ego. All who are sister or wife to each of these, in turn, will be further *dadis*, and so on ad infinitum. This type of extension occurs, of course, not only on the +3 level but at all superior levels, for two reasons. First, all of the male-female pairs on these levels are understood to be constructed with the same formal properties as the *dada-dadi* pair. Second, all generations ancestral to an unlimited class must themselves be unlimited by definition, as must any classes descendant from such an unlimited class.

The matrilateral terms are arranged in precisely the same way as the patrilateral terms. The +1 terms also embody the same logic, although the pictorial conventions used here do not reflect it, for convenience of representation. This means that ultimately, in terms of the logic of genealogical reckoning alone, the matrilateral and the patrilateral terms will have overlapping domains. Every male on ego's +2 generation can be classed either as *nana* (*nānā*) or *dada*, and so on throughout the map—or they could be so classified if the meaning of the map and its terms stopped with genealogical relationships alone.

The semantic, or logical, chaos that would arise from over-lapping domains does not arise in practice, because the terms are seen not only in relation to kin types but also in relation to the "institutional" rules for descent, inheritance, marriage, and residence. These rules further refine the concepts of the separate positions, and amount to a series of unambiguous guides for choosing between potentially conflicting categories, including matrilateral and patrilateral categories. First, the general marriage (or "incest") rule stipulates that a man may not marry a woman if they have any of what are called the *pūra cār* in common: father's parents' parents and mother's parents' parents' kin groups. This rule is understood to mean that either a matrilateral term or a patrilateral term, but not both, will apply to any superior relation. It says that if ego is legitimately conceived, then *by definition* his or her matrilateral kin and patrilateral kin are unconnected. Given this, the next relevant rule is that if a known genealogical link exists, address will be on the basis of the relative through whom it is traced most closley. If no such link exists, the next relevant rule is that people from mother's village are addressed matrilaterally. (This rule assumes the rule of patrilocal residence upon marriage, and also assumes the application of "sibling" terms to covillagers along with the prohibition of intravillage marriage.) Finally, if residence is not known, it is the general rule that patrilateral terms and not matrilateral terms are to be used for polite address. Within the context of these rules, it is still possible for certain cases of what is called "double-relation" (*do sākhī*) to arise, as in the example noted above. They are managed contextually, through the choice whose general sense is most desirable in the behavioral setting of the relatives at any point in time. With these ancillary rules, and only with them, any alter can be classified for ego. They operate like the rules for operation with zero, or the rules for manipulation of signs, in mathematics.

The map, when understood in the light of these social rules, can predict any pair of categories that two people will use toward each other. If their linking genealogical relationships are known, one simply starts at ego and traces the most direct set of genealogical links onto the map. For example, mF is *nana*. This can be seen by starting at ego, tracing the first link to his m (*mama*), and the next link to her F (*nana*). Similarly, mFFsdH is also *nana*. This is derived by beginning at ego, following the consanguineous line to m, then up to her F, thence again to his F. From him, the consanguineous link to his s is traced, thence down to her d and finally across the affinal link to her H—*nana*. The reciprocal of each of the terms can be obtained by reading backward along the genealogical chain, which should be constructed with pencil and paper apart from the terminology. The reversed mF chain, starting with mF as the new ego, is dS or dd. Turning to the map, and starting again at ego, ds can be seen to be *dota* (*dotā*), dd is *doti* (*dotī*), both the reported reciprocals of *nana*. Similarly, reversing mFFsdH (for a male ego) yields wmBSdS. Beginning with ego on the map and tracing first the affinal link to w thence the consanguineous links to her m (same as ego's), her brother, his son, his daughter, and her son, we again arrive at *dota*.

By extending this process of reasoning, the map can be used to generate a list of kin types that constitute the genealogical domain of a term. Thus *nana* obviously contains mF and mFFsdH. In addition, by its definition, it must also contain mFB, mFwB, mFsB, mFBwF, mFsBwB, and indeed an infinite series consisting of all possible pathways to the *nana* position—all ways to be a +2 generation matrilateral male.

Classification of persons or generation of domains do not, however, always depend on genealogical linkages. People without such links to ego can also be traced, and domains apart from genealogical domains can also be generated. For example, a male of one's own village who is older than ego's father but younger than ego's father's father would be *tāiā*, and his wife would be *tāi*; a man of his age in his mother's village would be *mama*, his wife *mami*, and his father *nana*.

To generate a nongenealogical domain, we can select any position and ask what general extragenealogical characteristics will be exhibited by those we map exclusively into it. Because of the many implications that can be drawn from the relevant institutional rules, the answer to this question can be quite elaborate. For example, *nana* is any man of ego's mF generation associated with her village of birth. By simple logic, such a male can be described as being old and respected and as having a fairly clear relation to ego, through his mother. One's *ma* has a residual right, legally and traditionally, to maintenance in her village of birth, and hence an interest and a position in its organization. Because of this, the men from this village have an interest in her welfare. The senior men, *nana* to ego but *bap, taia,* or *caca* to *ma,* would be the ones upon whom the obligation to protect the woman's interest would fall, and who must be depended on since they hold the property rights in her village. Ego's relation to *nana* can be described exactly as flowing from this dependence on his mother and her dependence in turn on her father and village as "insurance" and support in her husband's home.

Similar implications can be drawn out of the basic definitions and institutional concepts for any other term. The concept of *ma* is obviously tied in closely with that of *nana,* while the terms *dada* and *dadi* designate the residual class of those who are not *nana* or *nani* on the +2 generation. Their properties are more complex and various. When selected terms are used, they suggest these other implications. Used in conjunction with related terms that are defined in the institutional rules, the exact sense intended can be differentiated from the general implications in each case. "Real" *dadas,* who share "property" with ego, can be differentiated from "nominal" *dadas,* who do not, and so forth.

Although it is significant, with respect to Kroeber's position, that terms can be used in an institutional sense even for those with whom no genealogical relationship exists or is implied, there is a more fundamental and critical point. The organization of the terminology as a whole shows that not even the simplest genealogical connections, such as mF, can be mapped into terminological positions without the assumption of the institutional rules that keep the semantic domains discrete and clear. In this important sense, the terms are inseparable from the "institutional" concepts or patterns of the society: from the rules of marriage that separate matrilateral from patrilateral kin, from the distinction between genealogically remote ancestors and "relations" who are either affines or consanguines, and from the rules for address and associated rules of respect based on generational "age." Because of this, I would rearrange Kroeber's formula.

Kroeber saw terminologies as systems of concepts that were linguistic and yet existed "in a rigid biological framework" divorced from the institutions of the society. I would have to say that what the concepts are embedded in is a mnemonic framework. In this case, as in many others, the mnemonics is phonological, but it is conceivable that other mechanisms, such as rituals, might also be used, as they are for the religious concepts. The general concepts of the terminology themselves are identical to those of institutions—they are embodied in institutional rules and rituals just as they are in the phonology. Biology, as represented by Kroeber's eight categories or by the analogous insistence on "kin types" as a basis of componential analysis, is essentially extrinsic to the terminology in a very specific sense. Although the formal structure of the terminology permits it to encompass genealogical relations between people of a society who are reckoned as direct kin, its constituent positions are broader, more general semantic conceptions. A kinship term, as Schneider said, "is not *only* a term for a kinsman" (Rivers 1968). While it cannot be said that biology frames or limits the meaning of terms or terminologies, it can be said that terminologies put genealogical interrelationships of individuals into a larger institutional framework of concepts.

Kinship Groups: Implications of the Terminology

By a process that will be examined in the following chapter, the indefinite number of possible groupings of domains that can logically be generated from each system of low information are reduced to a few well-established and widely promulgated derivative models, most of which were mentioned in the description of the division of labor. The more prominent of such derivative models in the kinship system are models of the household group, the *parivar* ("family"), of the individual life cycles for men and women, of the *patti* (*pattī*), of the *got* ("clan"), and of the *jat* (*jāt*) or *brādarī* ("caste").

Each derivative model is built up from a segment of the terminology and a particular interpretation of its domain. Each such domain is connected logically with a particular concept of "property" —*jāidād* in Punjabi.

The importance of the concept of property in defining a kinship group is based on the semantics of the terminology itself. *Bap* and *ma* on the +1 generation, ego on the 0 generation, and ego's children are the only positions whose domains are relatively limited, capable in themselves of serving to delineate an effective corporate group. All other domains are unlimited, so that insofar as limited groups are to be organized consisting of kinsmen their membership must be delineated by criteria external to the terminology itself. A group of *dadas*, for example, that contains fewer than all possible *dadas* must be defined with a characteristic that *dadas* can have in common but which is not the concept of *dada* itself.

The sense that *jaidad* has in Punjabi is only imperfectly rendered by the English term "property." In the Indian laws written in English the somewhat fuller phrase "ancestral property" is used, and provides more of the sense. But the clearest way to describe it is to review in more detail the principal institutional rule in which it occurs. This is the rule of inheritance.

The rule of inheritance is actually a comprehensive rule of ownership. It pertains to much more than the disposition of property of people who die. The rule is that all sons inherit equal shares with the father in the property of the father, that they acquire these rights from birth, and that the rights of sons preempt the rights of brothers. For example, if a man had six acres, and one son were born, both he and the son would own three acres each from the moment of the son's birth. If a second son were born, father and sons would own two acres each—one-third of the original holding. None of them could sell his share without permission of the others, and in the event of a sale by one party the others could exercise their right of preemption and force the buyer to sell back to them at the price he had paid. Sons could even preempt a sale by the father to his own brother. If one of the sons or the father were to die, the process would be reversed. His share would be divided equally among the two remaining co-owners, and if one of the last two were to die, the survivor would become the owner of the whole original unit. If one of the sons should have a son of his own, his share would in effect be "anchored" into his own line. He and his own son would each own one-half of the one-third of the original holding, but if he should die, his personal share would go only to his son, not to his brother. If he had had several sons, all of them would have to die before the brother of the original father would reclaim control over the land. But if one of the original brothers had no sons and the other had, his share would devolve, upon his own death, on the brother with sons, and the sons of this brother would thereby automatically inherit equivalent portions with their father.

Technically, this rule of inheritance does not apply to "self-acquired" property—defined in the law as any property acquired by a person with his own resources in his own lifetime. All property a person inherits is automatically ancestral property. In practice, in Shahidpur, property that a person acquires is very difficult to distinguish from that which he inherits, since most of his capital and resources are inherited and others have shares in them. Within a few years, property is considered to have the characteristics given to ancestral property in the law. Significantly, the village terms that correspond to the legal terms "ancestral" and "self-acquired" translate literally simply as "old" and "new."

Given the inheritance rule as a part of the conceptual system of kinship, it follows logically that groups with property in common have ancestry in common. Groups with different property logically must have different ancestry. In accordance with this cultural theory, different kinds of conceptions of property can be used to define different kinds of groups with correspondingly different kinds of common ancestry.

The Parivar

The definition of the *parivar* rests on an interpretation of "property" in the sense of the effective managerial units of capital (described in the division of labor) combined with a kinship group defined as the *putars* of a *bap*, the only position in the map whose domain can include no more than one person. The common definition of the *parivar* is "a group of kin who cooperate in some common property," where property is in turn defined as a farming establishment, a shop, or some similar unit. This definition seems to place almost the whole weight of effectively defining the boundary on the concept of property, rather than on kinship criteria as such. Anyone, no matter how far removed, can be in the *parivar* if he contributes property and helps with the property, and anyone, no matter how closely related, can be out of the *parivar* if he does not help with the property.

Actual household groups called *parivars* exhibit a great deal more structural regularity than the common definition suggests. As was noted in the division of labor, they show a well-established pattern, in that no group censused in the village had two sons who in

185

turn had sons of any substantial age. No household group had more than one line of sons of a son of a father, with whatever brothers, wives, and daughters may have been attached to the men. A household unit may therefore be structurally described as a single patriline with occasional unmarried or childless consanguineous males and with consanguineous and affinal females. It is never more than a single patriline.

The uniformity of the structure in households can be attributed to the clarity of the basic inheritance rule and to its enforcement in courts of law. Clarity of the law and uniformity in its enforcement means that the particular type of conflict of interest in local groups that is implicit in the rule of inheritance is sanctioned and uniformly becomes explicit in sanctioned practice. True common interest in property exists only when the possibility of devolution exists—when any member may be the ultimate holder of the entire reconstituted unit of property upon the deaths of those he shares it with. Once it becomes clear that two or more sets of people exist and that a person in one group has no practical chance of reacquiring the share of the other group, conflicts of interest arise. A person naturally wishes to devote time only to that portion of the total property that he will receive benefit from—or rather, he will (in the long run) be forced by competitive pressures to channel his efforts only to these goods.

After my census of the village was completed, I asked villagers if they recognized the pattern of residence and had any name or explanation for it. Naturally, they did know of it, despite the vagueness of the definition of the *parivar* commonly given. Their explanation was that although the men did not want to divide the household when two brothers each had sons with an assured prospect of reaching maturity, their wives fought each other and thereby forced them to take up separate residences. The explanation of this in turn is that women rely for their support on the obligations of their sons to them, even more than on their husbands. Women thus naturally may be expected to feel, more clearly than men, the conflict of interests that two sets of sons create and would naturally be expected to express it. Whether women in fact instigate quarrels is less important than the universal recognition, among women and men who report their behavior, of the pattern of segmentation. This reflects the detailed relevance of the concepts of the terminology and of property beyond that included in the conventional and rather vague definition of the *parivar*.

Male and Female Life Cycles

Expected male and female life cycles are suggested in the rationale of household fission. They follow from the map and the conception of property when the question is asked: How are the positions around ego filled as ego ages?

The prominent people in a person's life are in the higher positions on the map when he is young, and in the lower positions when he is old. Or, a person moves "upward" through the map in time, when seen from the perspective of the general community (always of average age), as well as from the perspective of the other living members of his or her family. Like the general community, the *parivar* also persists through time and normally maintains an average age. Ego appears to move up through it in time, in relation to its other members.

As a man goes through life under these circumstances, he is faced with a continual readjustment of his relationships with the group with whom he shares rights in property. Readjustment is forced by the process of aging itself, and by the waxing and waning of strength and ability that it brings. When young, the man is dependent on his grandfathers (perhaps) and his father and father's brothers. He must respect them, and the expression of respect in this phase of his life takes the form of submitting to their guidance and instruction. As ego grows and his strength grows, he contributes more and more of the physical labor of the household, and respect takes the form of following orders, of deferring to the superior judgment of his many elders. Gradually, however, he assumes the responsibility for policy as well as labor, particularly if he comes to have sons of his own on whom he will have to depend in his own later years. His respectful relationship to his remaining elders comes in time to be transmuted into a form of extreme mutual deference, almost avoidance. Often, if possible, the older man moves out of the house, to avoid interfering in his son's life (the deference owed him would of itself constitute an interference and make his presence disruptive). He "governs" by governing least, by assenting to his son's wishes, though he always retains formal control and is to be consulted on all policy matters. By the time this stage is reached, the son himself will generally have reached middle age, and his own son will in turn have reached, say, his early teens. A man tries to work until the last day of his life, to avoid being a burden on his sons. And sons, by the time a father is this old, try to defer as much as possible to him and treat him with great care and solicitude— mindful perhaps of their own future and of their watching sons.

Women have a quite different life, though it follows from the same conceptual premises of the kinship map and the conception of property as a working unit. The rule of marriage, which assures the continuity of membership and residence of the male group and thereby makes the process of aging the chief force men must adjust to, necessitates a radical readjustment in the woman's life at the time of marriage. The prohibition against marriage within the village, male ownership of property, and continuity of residence for males form a pattern within which a shift of residence for women at the time of marriage is logically structured.

A woman is born in the house of her father. She shows respect, not by learning to work the land, but by practicing the talk and manners that will lead to her finding a secure marriage. The parents raise their girl that she may leave them, which gives the relationship between parent and daughter a color quite different from that between parent and son. There is, from the Western point of view, a strange and touching, partly romantic and partly tragic character about it, bitter always mixed with sweet, the show of love always mixed with knowledge of future parting. A girl works in her house while her brother works in the fields. As she approaches marriageable age, about twenty, the sense of future parting becomes more prominent, and the girl is treated with greater and greater solicitude. She is given lighter work and better clothes, not only to make her happy herself, but also to make her more desirable as a wife through showing her person and her family in a good light. A well-dressed girl is both pretty and the mark of a successful family, who would be valued as kin. Attractive girls may become involved in local romances, as well as marriage, and their parents are put to great pains to prevent this. The longer they wait for a good match, the greater the risk of a premature liaison in the village with the possibility of pregnancy of the girl and frustrations of the parents' efforts. On the other hand, early marriages provide more time for the fortunes of the groom's family to fail. These years in a girl's life are tense and romantic, and a girl in the family is both a good thing and a great deal of trouble.

With marriage, the girl begins the process of shifting her concerns and allegiance to a new household in a new village. Because she owns no property and is dependent on men who do own it, she has to assume a cooperative interest in her husband and her brothers, even as her father must be giving ground to his sons at the same time. Later, if she has sons, she will become most concerned with them because of the peculiar logic of the inheritance rule.

As a man has sons, his own share in his property diminishes proportionately. The first son leaves him with a half of the holding, the second with a third, and so on. A woman, on the other hand, gains in power and security with the birth of each son. She is wholly dependent on sons in later life, as her husband is, but with the difference that the relation between son and mother is supposed to take precedence over all other concerns. She gave the son his early health and security, and is wholly reliant on him, having no property of her own and less claim on her husband's property than her sons have. Need imposes obligations, and this particular need, because of its connection with sacrifice for the sons, is doubly binding. The reported zealousness of mothers in pursuit of their sons' welfare reflects this exact point. In later life, while the husband—as *bap* and then *dada* —may spend more and more time in the fields, the wife moves more and more solidly into a position of power and authority within the house and assumes a position of more and more importance in the internal economy of the village. From daughter-in-law in the household, she becomes *ma* and then *nana*. The mother of several sturdy and wealthy sons in a household is an employer of household help, and several families of inferior means may depend on her wishes.

The life cycles of both men and women, with the details of the structure of the *parivar* they are connected to, are represented in several rituals, besides stereotyped common knowledge, songs, and oral and written literature. The male life cycle is summed up in the ritual of *lori* (described in detail in the next chapter). A group of men of the village build a fire at the village gate, using dried cow dung (which comes from the soil). Then they go to each house where a male child was born and collect a certain amount of brown gur. They pray for the life of the boy and go on to the next house. After visiting all the houses in this manner, they return to the fire, say a general prayer for the birth of more boys in the coming year and the health of those now born, and distribute the gur to the children of the village. Giving sweets in this way is a stereotyped way to symbolize the spreading of good news. The ritual states the dominant fact of the man's life: each man depends on the continuity of births in the context of a local group of aging men that persists through time.

The woman's life cycle is represented in the marriage rituals, as is the man's, and in three women's rituals that occur annually. The contrast between men's and women's funeral rites, too, repeat the contrast between their life cycles in the context of the conception of the *parivar*.

The marriage rituals are a complex sequence of rituals, too long to be recounted and analyzed here. But the general theme of the most relevant subset of rites, different from the religious gathering that solemnizes the relationship between the bride and groom, is sounded in a small ritual at the end of the sequence. After the major ceremonies are over, the goods that the bride will take to her new house are packed in the vehicles of the groom's party, and the groom's people themselves prepare to leave. Finally, from her house in the village, the bride comes to go with them. She comes wailing loudly, in the midst of a group of female relatives, friends, and servants. Her mother, beside her, consoles her and tells her of her future and why she must go for her own good. Her elder sister (anyone in the category *bhain* if actual elder sister is not available) supports her and guides her physically, for her face is covered. Her friends and her mother's friends crowd around. Among them come the Sweeper's wife carrying a broom, the Potter's wife carrying a pot, and the wife of the Barber carrying some sugar and a special coconut wrapped around with red yarn, to be taken to the bride's new house. The bride enters the vehicle with the wife of the Barber. Then all her remaining relations and supporters push the vehicle to start it on its way. The wife of the Barber will accompany the bride to the new village and come back with her the next day. After that, she will be fetched to her new home by her husband.

No methodological hocus-pocus is required to see that this ritual juxtaposes two parts of the normal life cycle of a woman: the time when she is a bride and the time when she is the mother of a bride. The tyrannical mother-in-law, who some analysts have said inspires the girl's weeping, is after all but a woman like her own mother, and what she must aspire to be as she herself becomes the mother of sons in the course of time. Indeed, the mother's consoling is exactly to this effect, as it is described. In leaving the servants behind, the girl demonstrates their connection to her mother as head of the house, not to herself personally. She thereby acknowledges her present state and future expectations. As we should expect, there is no equivalent ritual of parting for men. Rituals enact in a compressed form the conceptions that apply in general life.

Three rituals held annually in the village spell out three slightly different parts of a woman's life cycle. The ritual of *tij* (*tīān* or *tīj*), held in June–July (the third month of the main Indian solar calendar), the ritual of *karue* (*karūe*), held around the end of October, and the ritual of *behairi* (*behāirī*), held about the beginning of March, enact the structural position and concerns of a girl before marriage, a newly married girl, and a mother of small children, respectively.

Tij occurs during the day and calls for the young girls of the village, their newly married friends who may have returned to the village for a visit, and their brothers. Their brothers put up swings in certain trees, and the girls swing and sing songs. The ritual occurs as the monsoon rains have begun, when the crops and trees are moving into mature growth, and the ritual, in this vein, is clearly in exaltation of the freedom and pleasure of being a young woman likewise just entering maturity. It is a joyful and also a romantic and a sad occasion. The songs the girls sing are, paradigmatically, in praise of the season and of their brothers.

Karue is celebrated at about the time of winter sowing, in homes. Married women eat no "food" (staples) from sunup to moonrise. This is said to be because they "think" it is good "for the welfare of their husbands." If she is living at her husband's house at the time, the woman is visited by her brother, and if she is at her own house, her husband visits. Either brings sweets when he comes. If the husband visits, his wife's kin joke with him, trying to embarrass him. In the evening, just before moonrise, the women gather together on roofs or in courtyards. Men are excluded, and are not supposed to be around. The women take a *karua* (*karūā*), a large vase-shaped clay jug with a tall neck about seven inches wide. They put some earth in the bottom, then put in their hands and trace circles in the earth in the bottom with their fingers while singing the special songs of the occasion. These are described as "generally in praise of their families." From the manner in which they were referred to, they would seem to be of a lusty or forthright character. I was told I would blush if I heard them. The women next fill the *karua* with cotton or "anything white," and add some *shakkar* (brown sugar) and ghee in a small bowl. This is taken to the home of a Brahmin and given to him. On this occasion, girls put on gold bangles.

The cast of characters of this ritual are the principal people in the life of a woman just after marriage, whose chief support in life is divided between two households, each of which supports her position in the other. She has, as yet, no children, only brothers and a husband. Gold bangles are associated with weddings, and this and other points in the ritual signify her closeness to the time of marriage. The Brahmin signifies her low position in the village, but even at this it is better than having no position at all—as the wedding rites depict the bride. The songs and the jug, to judge from other usages where white objects appear, suggest her newly proper concern with sex and romance. White cottonseed is sometimes used to wish for fertility at weddings, for example, as rice is used in America and England. Romance and fertility will naturally lead to having children just as the beginning involvement in the caste exchanges will lead to a fuller position in later life.

Behairi occurs toward the winter harvest and toward the end of the year in the *vikram* calendar normally used. Whereas the ritual of *karue* is "for" husbands and families, this ritual is "for" the children. The roles in the ritual call for it to be celebrated by mothers of young children. As with the previous ritual, the description to follow comes almost verbatim from field notes taken from a male informant, supported by others and verified by observance of the physical remains of the behavior described.

The principal focus of this ritual is the village *mata rani* (*mātā rānī*), a large, brick, house-like building, near which are small "houses" called *than* (*thān*), made of three bricks each. In a low spot beside this shrine, near the *than*, is a clear area. Alone, or accompanied by her children, the woman of the house rises at dawn and brings two cakes of a special bread and a cup or tumbler of water mixed with *chole* (chick-peas) to her *than*; she cleans it off with a cloth, and then faces it and prays for the welfare of all children. She places one of the cakes upon it, along with some *chole* and water from the cup. She next goes to the low area, the "pond," where she pours out some of the remaining water onto the ground and makes a bit of mud. She puts some of this mud on her own forehead as a *tilak*, and takes some with her. On the way back, she gives the remaining bread to her Sweeper, who has stationed himself in the way with a white hen in a basket (recalling the imagery of the white cotton in the *karua* jug). The Sweeper may bless the children in return. She goes farther and meets her Potter and his donkey, also stationed in the path. There, whatever *chole* and water remains is given to the donkey. When she reenters her own house, she uses the mud she has brought to place a mark, *tilak*, on the head of each of her children in the house. To complete this evident process of drawing out the isomorphism between the *mata rani* as conscious symbol and the village as its conscious referent, she gives more cakes, identical to those already left at the shrine, to the Sweeper and Potter later in the day when they come to her house, and to the Cottonginner as well. She also feeds the same type of breads, *chole*, and other special foods to her family that day for lunch. Most important and significant, the *mata rani* worshipped can only be the one of the village where she and her children and husband live.

Briefly stated, the action at the shrine portrays the woman as attached to and representative of, a house among a group of houses; as a feeder or preparer of food for that house; as a person responsible and concerned for the welfare of children; as a person with children; and as a person in a system of related household groups. It is significant that the *mata rani* is said to "be" the goddess who brings smallpox, a disease described as "coming from the mother." The house-like large structure represents the goddess; and the Potter's donkey is her traditional "vehicle." The actions subsequent to the visit to the shrine make it plain that there is an isomorphism between (1) the *mata rani* and pond, the shrine's "houses," and the actions there, and (2) the actual village, the house of the woman, and her concerns there. The mud and the second visits of the Sweeper and Potter are the lines connecting the elements of the shrine to those of the actual village. And the implication is unmistakable: the woman at the shrine stands for the same woman in the village—a woman at this special time of life. This would be a woman who has long since stopped attending the festivities of *tij* in the village associated with her childhood, her *peokā*—"father's." It would be a woman who probably would no longer feel comfortable with the songs and concerns of *karue*, who would not be homesick in the village of her new husband but secure in the village of her children. It would, finally, be a woman who would, perhaps while praying, be looking forward to the growth and marriage of her own children and to her participation in marriage rites in the place of her own mother some few years before.

Rituals through the year call for women at different stages of the life cycle and represent their concerns at each stage by the required actions. The annual cycle of rites portrays the life cycle of cares, hopes, and responsibilities.

The rituals provide economic characterizations of the implications drawn out of the basic concepts of the kinship terminology and of property, and stabilized in consensus. Ideas thus presented in rituals are known to be publicly acknowledged, and can thereby form a first line of understanding in interpersonal communications. At the same time, the rituals provide a vocabulary of standardized symbolic manifestations that can be used to invoke their conceptions. From the elaborate preparation of the ceremonial food of *behairi* and a *than*—which is an expression of concern sometimes when a woman's child is sick—to the wearing of bangles, the singing of songs, or the simple use of terms to designate roles in the rituals, the elements of the rituals provide material for structuring major and minor daily events in ways that a villager can confidently expect to be familiar to others. The number of rituals that reflect the ideas of life cycles and of the *parivar* may be taken as an index of the use made of the particular aspects of the basic terminology and concept of property they embody.

Not all derivative models are as viable as the *parivar* and the life cycles, and not all are as well represented in established rituals. In such cases, the direct derivation of the model from the terminology and the general concept of property is particularly clear.

The Patti

The model of the *patti* seems to have about as little viability as possible for an idea so widely current. The term literally means "division" and refers to a segment of the total number of village households, a "division" of the properties of the village that are organized into households. It is represented in no rituals, in the sense that *patti* membership is not a requirement for participation in any ritual, nor does any ritual make mention of *pattis* either as units or as a general concept. The concept is standardized only in the revenue record and in the origin story of the village that is told by Farmers, which is the story of how Shahidpur received its name. I shall substitute the name "Shahid" for the name of the person in the story, so that the story will correspond properly to the name I have invented for the village.

The Farmers of the village group themselves into six *pattis*, each consisting of several families and at least two distinct lineal groups. Each *patti* is described as being descended from one of six sons of the village founder, Ram Datta Singh Shahid, whose name indicates that he was a Sikh Jat like those now farming in the village. It is significant that no one "knows" the names of the sons and that no one can trace their links to any one son in particular. The nearest anyone came was when, with considerable excitement, a villager informed me one day that he had inquired of his elder kin and traced his line back to the village founding. After he had named the first known ancestor of his line, he concluded by saying, "And his father was the son of one of the sons of Ram Datta Singh Shahid." He still had not found which son or the name of the missing link. In short, the story cannot be construed as one derived from documentation of historical fact.

The revenue record of the village divides the villagers into three *pattis*, not six. Villagers say that each of these *pattis* is an arbitrary grouping, by the government, of two genealogical *pattis*, purely for purposes of administrative convenience. Be this as it may, the practice is traced in the record itself back to the founding of the village— though it is described quite differently than in the current origin story. The revenue record was first established in 1887, in accordance with a standardized process called a "settlement." In it, government officials came to the village and recorded its landholding pattern, its rules and customs, its family organization, and the story of its origin as it was told at the time. At that time, according to the record, there were three *pattis*, not six. These were composed of the families of Brahmin landholders, not Jat Sikh. And the founder of the village, some two hundred years before, was Shahid Das (a Hindu name), not Ram Datta Singh Shahid. No sons of Shahid Das were mentioned.

The model of the *patti* cannot be derived from history, and it cannot be derived from objective "structure," since *pattis* never act as collectivities. But it can be easily derived from the definition of the *parivar* within the terminology. Note that it logically follows from the concept of the *parivar* that there will, in time, be groups of families with similar properties as an initial family divides and its property is split among different descendants who add to it and pass it on to the other descendants. Logically, the existence of one family will give rise to the existence of several families more closely related to each other in similarity of property and nearness of descent than to other families. The name *patti* is neither more nor less than a name given to this implied group of families. It is a verbal hook on which to hang a reification of a logical possibility implicit in the basic concepts of kinship as they are applied to the definition of a *parivar*. The names of specific figures in geometry, such as "isosceles triangle," serve a similar function.

The Caste

The conception of caste is more often used in describing people and objects, and more often represented in ritual, than the idea of the *patti*, though it is much less important and prominent than the concepts of the *parivar* and of the life cycles.

A caste is described and represented in rituals as a group of kin with a common social rank and occupation in a region. Castes are considered to be endogenous. No two castes have precisely the same rank, or precisely the same occupation. There is some feeling that castes in a village or region ought to form a harmonious system of complementary occupational groups, and that if they did they would constitute a kind of utopian system, self-sustaining and self-perpetuating. Unlike *pattis*, described as descended from single individuals who form heads of families, like each son of Ram Datta Singh Shahid, castes are described as being descended from groups of men. One of the points in the origin story of the village as it is told in the village is that it links the name of the village, the name of the founder, and the name of one of the principal ruling clans of the Sikhs to each other. This places the village Farmers within the caste descended from the group of Sikhs that came as a military confederacy, settled the area, and established the ruling house.

The description of the division of labor indicates that the concept of caste cannot be construed as derived from the characteristics of "actual" castes or actual history. The term caste (*jāt* or *brādarī*) names a model derived directly from the inheritance rule and the forms in the terminological map that generate classes of kinsmen with unlimited membership. The definition of a caste names the implied properties of the maximal group of kin—the maximum domain of marriageables or affinal kin designated by the unlimited terms—given the ideas of property, the rules of marriage, and the inheritance rule.

Since the rules of marriage and inheritance make common property the mark of common descent and vice versa, it follows that if there is a maximal group of "true" *dada* and *nanas* and their ancestors and descendants, all ought to have the same kind of property. The same kind of property in turn implies the same occupation and, on the basis of it, the same social rank. And since no two occupations can yield exactly the same return, no two social ranks are identical. That is, given the kinship terminology, the marriage rule, and the rule of inheritance, a maximal group of kin should logically have the properties normally attributed to a caste.

Implications beside these can also be deduced from the general ideas that serve as the premises that underlie or support the idea of caste. These too find assent, to a greater or lesser degree. For example, the strong generational clarity of the map, together with the idea that respect inheres in generational positions, leads some to see each caste organized internally as if it were a layer-cake arrangement of discrete ranks. Each person belongs to one generation or the other in each caste. This implies that there is a kind of equality among all groups within a caste, in that any member in one clan, *patti*, or family has an equivalent number in all others. Such equality within a caste was in fact reported spontaneously by a fair number of villagers (and nonvillagers). Marriages, for example, are described as not being between people of different rank. Differences in rank were consistently denied in Shahidpur, even by people who admitted that the groom's family was wealthier than the bride's (the desirable relationship). What is being denied, apparently, is only inequality of such generational rank with the caste.

For another example, links by affinity and consanguinity between people of one type of property can be taken to imply that each caste is an isolated breeding population, a kind of small race. In fact, racial differences were adduced by some villagers in connection with occupational differences, and vice versa. Harijans, for example, were sometimes said to be unable to make a clear sibilant sound in the manner of the Farmers. The unusually dark complexion of some Sweepers in the area of Shahidpur was said to be a racial characteristic of Sweepers in general.

The current, though not highly standardized, conception of the village as one containing a system of interrelated castes carries the implications from the basic kinship and property conceptions one step beyond the derivation of the conception of a maximal group of kin itself. Since any functioning community must have different occupations, and since different occupations imply different castes, the castes of a community should logically be both different and complementary in some way. The content and character of a whole system of possible caste relationships similar to those that have been extensively described in the anthropological literature can be inferred from, or adduced in terms of, the more basic concepts. Needless to say, these and other derivations from the fundamental kinship terms, relations, and rules can have no more foundation in observed or historical "fact" than those basic conceptions themselves.

Beside the rituals mentioned and a few others, the caste conceptions are stabilized and promulgated in a large body of folklore. There are, for example, innumerable descriptions of the significance of different castes for augury. If one is starting on a trip, it is good to meet a Sweeper, and one should continue. But it is bad to meet a Brahmin, and one should start over, because the first is dominated by, but the latter is dominant over, oneself. Fading off into daily life, the usages and conceptions appear as baseline assumptions behind descriptions of people and groups such as make up the division of labor and many interpersonal dealings intended to be of a business-like character.

Other Current Implications

The order of the "descriptions" of kinship units is an order of premises, postulates, and deductions like that of geometry, not a descriptive order like that of geology. The stability and apparent clarity of the description of each kinship "group" is derived not from the objective clarity of each group as a real entity, but rather from the simplicity and formal orderliness of the concepts from which it is deduced. The name of each "group" is, in reality, the name of a particular configuration of logical manipulations of the basic concepts of the system. It is a name given to a special reification of the system, just as "isosceles triangle" is the name not of an observed object but of a special set of formal deductions from the premises of the Euclidian system. The definition of a caste is a reification of the implicit description of the maximum domain of true kin at the edges of the kinship terminology. Similarly, the definition of a clan can be considered to reify an implication of the sharp division between matrilateral and patrilateral sides at the center of the terminology. Since the marriage rule requires village exogamy, matrilateral and patrilateral kin terms designate at least two different kin groups in at least two different villages. The members of each such localized group of people are within one caste by definition. Further, they are more closely related to one another than to others in the caste. One's matrilateral consanguines must by definition be more closely related to each other than to one's patrilateral consanguines. The definition of the clan affirms no more than this. It summarizes these implications of the general terminology, just as $a^2 + b^2 = h^2$ summarizes a derivation from the basic concepts of squares and right triangles.

It may be added that a person's clanship is often vague and is presumed to suit marriage arrangements rather than be looked to as a basis of such arrangements. In the three weddings for girls held in the village during my stay, no informant knew the clan of the groom, even though the informants included fathers and brothers of the brides. Similarly, during the census operations I asked each of about twenty men for his wife's *got* name. None knew, though all assured me it was "different." This all accords logically with the difficulties in reckoning patrilineal connections that are inherent in the structure of the map. The map provides no terminological method for determing actual patrilineal relationships, and known linkages of actual descent are never sufficiently deep to explain the common clanship of many people.

Summary

As the form of the religious message source can be seen to be the basic image of the disciple and the Guru, together with the subconceptions that are produced by the addition to it of special interpretative ideas, so the form of the kinship system can be considered to be the form of the terminological map, together with the special structures produced from it by the addition of concepts that, in effect, block off some of its elements and emphasize others. This is a system of many more elements than the religious system, but one of equally rigid order. In comparison with the ecology, division of labor, and economy, it is a system of relatively low information, so similar to the religious message source in this respect that their general functions in behavior are practically identical.

Each principal and derived kinship conception is used by each villager to organize his social setting, to group many specific ecological, managerial, and economic acts into a few long-term social patterns. By mapping others and himself into the terminological positions, and construing those positions as part of the different kinship models, a villager can map himself and others into what he sees as a powerfully complex and orderly system of "real" and enduring kinship groups. For example, by construing *bhai* as "sons of one father," he can map others of his generation with respect to a category "true *bhai*." They either are in it or are some other such group connection to another father. Given certain assumptions, this is equivalent with mapping them into his *parivar* or into other *parivars*. Construing *bhai* in other ways, he can map males of his age level into his village, or some other village; into his caste or some other caste, and so forth.

Each specific model of a kinship group, when actual people map each other into it and express agreement to each other on its relevance, can become the definition of a communicative situation of long-term interactive significance. In providing the basis for the definitions of the different units in the kinship structures, the kinship terminology and the conception of property also provide the means by which these units are integrated into a single kinship system.

In the complex logical structure of the kinship terminology, every person who can take the perspective of ego and see himself, at once, as part of a *patti*, a family, a clan, and a caste and a group of kinsmen, can also see, and trace, a continuity of personnel among these different groups. This continuity holds even if the definitions of units may be doubted, disputed, or changed in some degree, so that the system allows for its own dynamic readjustment to changing uses and needs—such as may be presumed to be constantly occurring in the background of the division of labor. The process, on the whole, is well documented. Indian village ethnography to date has largely been concerned with recording or developing the many different aspects and implications of these operations, and the ways in which visible objects or actions or verbal behavior are taken to symbolize and sanction different pictures of all or part of kinship "society."

Since kinship is the most complex of the conscious sociological models, it most clearly indicates the scope for analysis that such systems provide and the promise they hold out of showing not only new types of ordered phenomena but even new modes of order itself. There is—in the dynamic interplay of the kinship terminology, the institutional concepts and units, and the symbolic conventions—a new world, a new area for scientific mapping. It is a world as vast and as "real" in its own way as the world of physicists and chemists, but it is a world whose reality, like theirs, exists in its own terms—a reality of semantically stabilized information and of the exigencies of symbolic conventions. We should never believe either that it derives from some more "objective" reality or that a more objective reality is patterned by it and contains it. The convenient path of following the usages of natives, speaking about caste as if it were something other than a conception, or about family structure, should not obscure the point that one is actually deriving one's data from observing the people that claim these notions, rather from observing groups in some noninformational, "absolute" sense. No one has ever objectively or disinterestedly seen a caste and observed its structure. No one has known by historical analysis that he is in a certain caste. No one has ever seen a system of interacting castes with unique properties and occupations, or a system of families. People "know about" any given unit not because they have seen it, as they see cows or crops, but rather because they see that others claim to know it and because it is in their interest to act as if they do too.

This is not to say that the conceptions come first, and that families, *pattis*, castes, and so forth are patterned after the conceptions. The difference between this view and the equally untenable view that conceptions are derived from quasi-physical, objective entities is merely verbal. Both assume that there is an independent concrete reality that corresponds with the conceptions but is detached from them. In fact, there are no objectively observable concrete groups that can be considered to be castes in any important sense, and there is no need to postulate them either to explain the existence of a stable and widely known concept of caste groups or to explain the confidence that villagers have in their perceptions that behavior is ordered, in some situations, by caste. Similarly, there are no "concrete" families that are different from, though parallel to, the conceptual families. There are times, however, when people speak and act as if there were castes. People speak as if families existed and had concrete structures of rights and duties, and they make their actions accord with what they say. Conscious sociological models by themselves neither require nor create a corresponding concrete reality, nor does reality require or create ideas. The models, semantic systems of definitions, are present because they have unique properties of their own that are useful. They in fact provide an essential ingredient for the organization of action—a basis for stable classification of people in sanctionable contexts. The system of low-information class labels that can be generated is so encompassing that villagers cannot evade it, yet so flexible and dynamic that they cannot but find it both unbreakable and useful, whatever their needs.

Chapter VIII

Parties as a
Conscious Sociological Model

The putative referent of the third and last major conscious sociological model current in Shahidpur is a system of two opposed and more or less clandestine social groups. In Shahidpur, these groups are named parties, a term evidently borrowed from English. In the literature that has been concerned with them as they appear throughout South Asia, they have been more generally called factions.

Just as the religious model shows most clearly the way models can be considered without regard to their "real" referents, and the kinship model shows most clearly the way models can generate complex systems of social relations, so the party model provides an opportunity for an unusually clear look at another feature common to all the models. Although all models are capable of being manifested in the context of other systems of information—including other models—the party model, because its putative referent is a "secret" group, and to some extent because of its especially low information value, is particularly well adapted for such manifestation. Within the village, in fact, it is hardly ever manifested publicly except in combination with other models.

The unusually close relationship between the manifestation of the party model and the manifestation of other systems of information has been reflected in the unusual tradition of analysis that has grown up around the preferred term, factions. In this tradition—which is without parallel in the analysis of kinship or religion—factions within a village have been seen "in terms of cleavages in its [the village's] structure" (Beteille 1965). Yadava, for example, reflects this orientation when he observes: "The pretentious posture of unity presented by the village Kultana to an outsider soon starts crumbling on establishment of some rapport with the people. Cleavages cut across the community at various levels. Some of these divisions are temporary and short lived while others are lasting, tending to become a feature of the village social organization. The villagers are painfully aware of this" (Yadava 1968, p. 899).

The "pain" of awareness of parties is directly related to the manifestation of parties as something underlying the "unity" presented by other models. One cannot openly and directly manifest an idea of something hidden, secret, and "painful." Or, since parties are defined in the conscious model as inherently hidden and painful, they must logically be manifested covertly, at the same time that the models they appear to "undermine" are manifested overtly. This is done through the formation of collectivities (to be described).

The Basic Model

Since the model of parties is extremely simple, it is best introduced by some of the stereotypic "observations" about parties that it generates in Shahidpur. "Always in Sikhs there are two parties." "We must join together to protect small and weak people against opportunists." "People in one party are enemies of the other." "A person's friends are in his party, his enemies are in the other." "If two people fight, it is not necessarily a party matter. But if one person is helped by his party, the other person's party must come and help him." "Panchayat members support people of their party in cases." "In a case, you testify for people of your own party." "They are not in the same party—they are not on speaking terms." "Friends help one another." "Everyone is in one party or the other" (no one is in both parties). "There are no village parties." "It is not right to ask people who their friends are or to talk about parties in public." "The parties go from high to low."

Court cases, fights and disputes of any kind, and support at family affairs are all commonly said to be party matters. Parties crosscut kin divisions. People in different castes may be in the same party; brothers or father and son may be (and sometimes are) in different parties. Candidates for public office, including the elected positions that control the Sikh gurdwaras, are supported by one party or another in the village.

The first villager who attempted to explain how the different points made about parties fitted together drew the following diagram, and subsequent discussions and my own ability to seem knowledgeable about parties to villagers make me certain it is the conscious model:

Party:	A	B
Issue:	yes	no

It can be noticed first that there is no hierarchical dimension in this diagram, nor are there "boundaries" representing exclusive or complete enclosures of membership. The groups are sharply demarcated only in their opposition to one another. And in that, the demarcation, as it is drawn and described in the village, is fundamental and complete. One says yes, the other no. They say yes or no on some issue that is generally described as a matter of principle.

The precise sense of "issue" is the key to the whole picture, and to the pattern of manifestation of the model. An issue is not some proposition to be approved among a body of possible propositions. Definition of opposition by stands on issues in that sense would logically lead to a shading of hostilities, not a polarization. Instead, an issue is one of the Sikh leaders, one of the two people contending for control of the chief governing body of the Sikh community. At the time of this study, the two men were Master Tara Singh and Sant Fateh Singh. Such men are issues in the sense that they take public stands on a number of proposals—"issues" in our own sense. They thus come to represent complex issues. Still, one can vote for only one man. One man must dominate, the other must lose. Hence, through symbolic summarization in the persons of the leaders, stands on issues become polarized.

Everyone who supports one man repeats his stands. To differ on any point would be to set up another party, since the leader is the symbol of the party and the focus of the alliances that make up the party. The issue is the man, the man is the issue, and of course both represent basic principles.

This sense of leader and of issue fits logically with there being two leaders and no more, with the leaders' being not village but national or communal leaders, and with their supporters' being polarized into two opposing camps, each trying to dominate the other.

The sense of an issue explains how the diagram represents the village parties, and how these parties have the specific properties they are generally stated to have. There are two parties in the village because there are two "among Sikhs." There are Sikhs in the village, some of whom favor the one leader while others favor the other. No one can support both or neither and still be in parties. Each group is the enemy of the other because each is trying to dominate the other. Yet there are no formal village divisions of the national parties and, naturally, no public village leaders to symbolize their existence. In order to be overtly recognized, the village leaders (instead of more or less prominent "followers" of the two men who are the issues in the contest) would have to differentiate their own positions, on behalf of their village, from the position of the national leader of their party. Logically, however, such a differentiation would have the character of a disagreement: the local leader would be taking issue with the national leader. But such a disagreement with a national leader, because it *is* with a national leader, is a disagreement on an issue. Hence the would-be village leader would actually appear to be in conflict with the national leader, thus splitting the national party. There would still be no village party, but only an attempt to raise a new national party (that would be quickly wiped out). Thus, given the conventional definition of an issue as the struggle between leaders, there is no logical way to publicly define local parties. A public statement using the idea of a local party in an American sense would be as confusing as the idea of a triangle whose angles did not add up to 180 degrees.

Major Implications of the Model

The logic of the concept of an issue might not have the force it has in interpersonal relations if it were not that the idea of conflict closely associated with it has no parallel in either of the other current conscious sociological models. As it is, the other two models not only do not provide for the formal and overt expression of conflict, they proscribe it. Each model, and the rituals that express its elements, stresses cooperation and harmony—defined differently, of course, in each case. Each, in effect, rules out the possibility of conflict in the world it describes. Caste and kin are in harmonious cooperation based on their distinct properties; members of the religious community are equally sons of the Guru, equally subordinate to a single ethical ideal and sharers of that ideal and of the other aspects of the community as their common "patrimony." Accordingly, when conflict occurs and must be organized, there are no ideas to use except those of the party model.

But since the formal and explicit creation of rituals or other public party expressions is ruled out by the sense of an "issue" within the party model, as well as by the moral injunctions of the two other models, there is only one logically appropriate way to express such conflict—by the use of the symbols already defined in the other models, in new ways that are neither proscribed nor prescribed in those models. This is easily done, and villagers explain that villagers in the same party maintain their nonparty relations, while villagers who are in opposition "break" them—the idea reflected in the anthropological concept that parties involve "cleavages" in other organizations. When two people are in one party, or when one or both are in no party, they express whatever relationships they desire in the manner already described. They call each other by kin terms, caste terms, or terms with religious associations. But when they are in opposite parties, the expectation is that they will literally not be on speaking terms. They will not use the established modes of address at times when these might otherwise be appropriate. Since people who are in opposed parties do not speak and do not cooperate, a hidden pattern of what is called "help," or friendship, naturally emerges. People support the rituals of those in their party and attend the weddings of those in their party. Rituals thus overtly of a religious or kinship nature covertly assume a party significance, reflected in the configuration of those who attend. These carry over from purely personal rituals into a few major village rituals which become, in effect, arenas for testing the relative strength of the two groups of men who have aligned themselves against each other under the rubrics of the party leaders.

The same groups of men who express party commitments by

attending each other's rituals and putting on major public shows of party power have other more direct interests as well. Those who claim adherence to the party model tend to be involved in agriculture, either as landholders or as laborers as noted in the division of labor. Their party interests stem, in most cases, from their desire for land or help, or for security of employment. I will discuss these interests shortly, but they are at present of less theoretical importance than a more detailed understanding of the precise role of the concept of parties in the organization of rituals. Just as rituals provide the primary assurance of consensus in the use of the other two models, so too they provide the principal standardized expression of, and instruction in the use of, the party model. Still more important for us, they provide the most widely agreed upon form of public instruction in the accepted and understood ways in which several systems of information can be combined.

Collectivities

For the present, a collectivity can be described as a recognized group of individuals (not roles) with common interests who assume some sort of social identity and putative common purpose. Since the low-information systems that provide the means of creating widely articulated social goals are different from the high-entropy systems that set individual interests, collectivities in this sense necessarily involve the concurrent use of multiple systems of information.

In Shahidpur, collectivities that form through the use of the factional model as one of their information sources regularly use religious rituals as a principal means of expressing their power, interests, membership, and social purpose. Accordingly, these rituals are considered to represent a situation that underlies all the party activity of the village—indeed of the region. Two such rituals, one of which has regional significance, provide a convenient starting point in describing the general processes by which collectivities are formed, and by which collective behavior is organized. Then the method of organizing smaller and less formal sets of actions, involving fewer people or engaging in more restricted behaviors, can be readily indicated, and some intimation of the total complexity built up with the relatively simple conscious sociological models can be provided.

The ritual of *lori* is described by villagers as unique to the village and of strictly local interest. The contrasting ritual called *diwan* (*diwān*) commemorates a major historical episode in the life of Guru Gobind Singh. The incident is of general significance to all Sikhs, and the ritual widely known, drawing speakers from all over the Sikh tract and visitors from several miles around Shahidpur. *Diwan* is explicitly described as part of a linked series of rituals that ultimately involve several of Punjab's most important gurdwaras and people of great importance.

Lori is held in mid-January. Around dusk, a "volunteer" committee of interested people from the village, generally understood as being Jat Sikhs, collect cow-dung cakes and build a fire in the entrance to the village gate. Then they go to each house on the Jat side of the village where a boy has been born. At each, they ask the master of the house for "sweets," lumps of brown sugar. When they receive it, they say a prayer for the house and for the long life of the son. After every house has been visited, the men bring the sugar back to the fire. There, once again, they say a prayer to God for the long life of all the sons and for even more sons to be born in the village in the coming year. They then distribute the sweets to any children from the village who ask for them.

The mode of prayer and the Sikh affiliation of the group membership constitute the specifically religious elements in the action. They invoke the religious image of God and the religious community on which individuals depend. Sons are interpreted as an aspect of the sustaining community, a part of the patrimony that comes from the Guru and for which thanks are given.

The factional model is manifested covertly by the party composition of the group of Jats who perform the ritual actions, and other actions they perform that are neither prescribed nor proscribed in the stereotyped ritual format. The *lori* of 1965 fell just a few days before the Shromani Gurdwara Prabandak Committee (SGPC) elections, which were hotly contested by the two parties. The group of "volunteers" who participated were all adherents of the dominant faction in the village, the group supporting Sant Fateh Singh. The leader of the ritual was a brother of one of the most important men in the party. The ritual group stopped at his house, and was given a special cake of sugar, called *bheli*, much larger than usual. This in turn occasioned mention of the giver and his cause in the final prayer, wherein the future prosperity of the village was linked with the election activities. To the best of my knowledge, the other party did not regard this use of the ritual as strange or untoward, although naturally they did not like the specific content it was given. Everyone was aware of what had happened and of the double significance of the total event even though few people attended. In fact, prior knowledge of the event played a role in preserving the outwardly religious appearance by obviating the possibility of overt conflict during the ritual events, since the opposing faction systematically avoided the activity. The mechanism for obtaining this general consensus is the same as in the *diwan*.

The *diwan* is held in December, in the village gurdwara compound. A fair associated with it is set up on the surrounding common land, in front of the village gate. This *diwan* is part of a series of similar events commemorating the flight of Guru Gobind Singh from a Moghul siege of Anandpur and the loss of his four sons in the flight; the history of these losses is the theme of the *diwan*, its rationale, and the overt subject of its orators and singers. The story, briefly, is as follows.

Some years after the invention of the ritual of initiation, Guru Gobind Singh had become a political threat to several hill kings who looked for protection to the imperial court in Delhi, and therefore a threat to imperial sovereignty in the area. Accordingly, various military contingents were drawn together in 1705 under imperial authority, and a series of battles were fought around Anandpur, culminating in the siege. Failing to break the siege, the Guru fled with a small band of Sikhs and the two eldest of his four sons. His mother had previously left with the two youngest sons to seek safety in the south. The Guru reached Chamkaur, about seven miles north of Shahidpur, where he was forced to make a stand. Here, his two sons were killed in battle, to protect him and the religion he represented. The Guru himself fled, with two Sikhs, after the loss of his sons, but only after declaring that any five Sikhs constituted a priesthood, a Guru, in the future, and after circumambulating the five Sikhs he left as a rear guard to show that they, like fire and the Granth, were sacred—circumambulation being a traditional means of receiving blessings from the central object of worship, as in the

Hindu and the Sikh wedding rituals, both of which had been previously established. The two youngest sons and the Guru's mother had meanwhile been betrayed to the Moghuls by a Brahmin they had stayed with, and were subsequently brought before the governor of Morinda, the town about seven miles southeast of Shahidpur, and thence to the higher-ranking viceroy of Sirhind. There, on being invited to convert to Islam, the boys defiantly proclaimed their loyalty to their own faith and their father, declaring it to be more valuable than "worldly ambition" (see Macauliffe, 1963, Book V, chapter 22). Thereupon, they were executed. When the news reached their grandmother, who was at Fategarh, a few miles farther south, she also died.

Commemorating these events, the first large fair and *diwan* is held in and around the gurdwara of Chamkaur, where the Guru defended himself. Then, in sequence, smaller *diwans* are held along the routes of the Guru and his two youngest sons, on subsequent days. Shahidpur's *diwan* is three days after the Chamkaur *diwan*. The last of the series is another very large gathering in the gurdwara at Fategarh, seven days after that in Chamkaur. Each *diwan* is a formal religious convocation. Its speakers and singers are expected to commemorate the events that took place nearest the village or city and explain and extoll the general religious principle of martyrdom, or self-sacrifice, that the events exemplify. Technically, the exhortations take place in an extended *sikhā*, the period set aside for religious instruction just before the conclusion of a regular morning service. The morning service is held, and then a full day of speaking is interposed, until late in the evening or early the next morning when the final closing prayers are said. During the whole time, therefore, the place of convocation constitutes a gurdwara, and the general religious model of the disciple in relation to God and the community is manifested through the conventional material symbolism of the Guru Granth Sahib in a high place, by the speakers, and by demeanor appropriate to this setting, as well as through the theme of the oratory itself.

As in the rite of *lori*, the model of parties is presented in this ritual covertly, in matters not of direct religious significance. As in the *lori* rite, these include the composition of personnel and aspects of verbal behavior that are neither prescribed nor proscribed in

religious terms. Like *lori*, *diwan* is organized by a "volunteer" committee. The committee arranges for the speakers, sets their schedule,
and sometimes collects fees to be given to more prominent and desired orators. It sets up the *langar*, the free kitchen that every gurdwara must maintain for all who come, representing the same ideas
as the feeding of amrit in the initiation ritual. It hires sound equipment, sets out straw to sit on in the gurdwara yard for those who will
hear the service, and in general does what the occasion requires. The
committee, its principal supporters, and the speakers it brings in
consistently represent the dominant party. The committee members
are known in the village and its environs, even though most of them
do not participate overtly in the public activities. The party affiliations
of invited speakers are known by their prior activities, or by their
having received endorsement from, or given endorsement to, some
more famous religious leader at some time in the past. (Newspapers
and other media consistently report such endorsements.) Although
explicit comparison of political issues between the parties is avoided,
each speaker expresses his convictions, while adhering to the overt
theme of martyrdom, by comparing past acts with present policies
or people, or by interpreting the principles of past acts in such a
way that they clearly concord with his party's policies and not with
the policies of the other party. In the 1964 *diwan*, before the election
and before *lori*, one of the speakers was himself a local candidate for
the committee that would in turn elect the SGPC. With directness
that some remarked on as inappropriate or arrogant, he spoke explicitly of his own candidacy and of the man he was supporting, Sant
Fateh Singh. But even without this, the drift of the occasion was
clear to any who wished to see it. Members of the opposition party
in the village were conspicuously absent from the event, as they are
from similar rituals whenever they occur, so that the speaker's words
only accentuated a significance built into the occasion while it was
being organized.

The Sant Fateh Singh party in the village, as its speakers in the
diwan indicated, interpreted the ideas of martyrdom and equality
as broadly applying to economic and social matters, and as implying
support for consolidation of holdings, for giving lands to Harijans,
and for a number of similarly populistic, or perhaps socialistic, governmental policies. The party was generally acknowledged to be

closely tied to the Communists (particularly the "right," pro-Soviet Communists) in "secular" state politics. Many of the supporters of Sant Fateh Singh also supported Communist candidates, as the local candidate did, or they themselves ran as Communists in the state elections at about this time.

The opposing faction supported Master Tara Singh, and was generally considered to be aligned with the Congress party and to be opposed to consolidation and other similar programs for land reform and land redistribution. Although its position was less clear than that of the dominant faction, since it lacked access to public platforms in Shahidpur, its members seemed to hold that religious equality and self-sacrifice did not apply directly to landownership. They spoke privately, and occasionally in public, as if they preferred a more laissez-faire economic philosophy, but one with security of legal rights in ownership. It was thus the more "capitalistic" or "conservative" party, in an English or American sense.

Volunteering, the process by which the sponsoring group forms, is an important process, reflecting as it does the considerations people generally exchange in forming groups to manifest party relationships. Volunteering begins when a few people decide that they would like to sponsor an event. They are, generally, people already active in factional conflicts on other matters. The first volunteers seek advice and commitments from others, who may either refuse help, give help freely and be satisfied with their leadership, or give help on the basis of some explicit *quid pro quo*. If more than one group has initiated activities in Shahidpur, they eventually either join forces or continue to build up their individual support until one group outweighs the other and the weaker party peacefully defers to the stronger. Physical confrontations have occurred in nearby villages, villages with new immigrants—people who do not know each other well. Multiple speakers' platforms have been set up in some of the larger gurdwaras, some in more preferred spots, some in lesser locations, such as outside the walls of the compound.

With each step in soliciting support, with each new person coopted or dissuaded, the covert political platform of the ritual becomes elaborated and fixed in a double process of building and sanctioning a constituted group. New speakers are suggested by their particular friends. Some such speakers are invited, and some accept, some refuse. Some villagers favor fees for some, while others doubtless do not, and so forth. Everything leads to the final well-ordered show of control in conflict that "underlies" the ritual itself. By the time of the performance there is a clear line between the supporters of the event and their major opponents. Their respective reasons for support or opposition are generally both known and implicit in the overt event, so that final policy meanings read into both models in the ritual are bound up with the "meanings," the known interests, of the collectivity that supports it.

The activity of *diwan* involves the volunteers in a system of considerations and rewards that extends well beyond the village. They may expect some consideration from the public figures for whom they provide a platform. In 1964 these included politicians, young orators and singers, a magistrate, teachers, writers, and civil servants. Consideration may be expected from the SGPC committee if the village's faction is successful, perhaps in such matters as support for local schools. (The local candidate was headmaster in the local higher secondary school, privately financed primarily by villagers in the area. He ran against the headmaster of the school in Chamkaur, allied with the opposite party.) And through increases in regional visibility, village men become more likely to affect regional and even state policies of interest to themselves, and to manipulate the governmental machinery in their favor. Such exchanges of consideration mean, in effect, that the village ritual is a single instance of the promulgation of the models over this whole wide region where they operate, a range of promulgation logically consistent with the content of the model itself.

Sanctions

The outcome of the actions that lead to a final ritual performance, with its cast of cooperating participants and nonsupporters, is significant precisely because the actions themselves occur, each one, in a *personal* context. Each villager tenders or withholds support, and decides on its exact type and quantity, by referring to his personal needs, circumstances, or desires that such action might serve— needs that arise in his fields, in his family, and in his efforts to hold or modify his circumstances. Activities of litigation, often referred to in explaining ritual groupings, figure prominently as a more direct means by which such needs are fulfilled.

At the time of the 1965 *diwan* there were three major court cases being fought by villagers, and several score minor cases, most of which went back to 1964. One of the major cases involved charges against the village *sarpanch*, brought by a local Block Development Officer who is associated with the opposing party (the Congress-aligned party). The second case was a countersuit brought by the *sarpanch* himself and the brother of the leader of the *lori* ritual (discussed on p. 209) against the same official. The charge was false arrest. Each of these cases involved about a dozen villagers as witnesses on both sides, in addition to the plaintiffs and defendants. The third case was a writ petition submitted by twenty-one villagers to the High Court of the State of Punjab to quash the consolidation proceedings then in process. The consolidation proceedings were being conducted at the time by a civil service officer under the guidance of a local advisory board, a majority of whose members represented the dominant party. Seventeen of the twenty-one petitioners were identifiable with the weaker party, while two were identified with the dominant party (though not in prominent roles). The latter maintained that the petition "was not a party matter." All of these cases involved rights in land.

Since these conflicts are organized through manipulation of the conscious political and religious models that *diwan* represents, they are relevant to action in respect to that event. For example, the five hostile witnesses in the case against the *sarpanch* were in that context defining themselves as the "enemies" of the *sarpanch* in the opposing faction. They were therefore logically also the enemies of the *sarpanch* when the latter was involved in organizing the 1965 *diwan*, since parties are defined as enduring groups with exclusive membership. Naturally, they did not directly support the *sarpanch's diwan* committee or the *diwan*. Of course, this could have put them in the awkward position of appearing to oppose or reject the religion itself —which is doubtless one of the points the dominant group would have liked to make. To preclude this interpretation, and to show that he rejected only the dominant group and not the religious principles, one leader of the opposition party, a major witness against the *sarpanch*, sent his daughter with a village assessment for the free kitchen, although he carefully avoided appearing at the ritual himself.

Collectivities cannot impose sanctions on behalf of one model or interpretation of a model, unless its members make allocative choices in additional systems of information.

The nature and extent of the choices in other systems that are made in imposing the factional model and factional interpretations of the religious model can be obtained from the following two tables. The first provides a correlational analysis showing elements of choice that are associated in Punjab as a whole with choice of the Sikh concept of community rather than choice of the Hindu concept—the principal point of differentiation between the two traditions. The second compares the situations of villagers who have publicly undertaken to support each of the two village parties.

Table 17 suggests the context of the choice of claiming adherence to the Sikh religious model, by a process of reasoning similar to that used to describe household strategies in the division of labor. In this case, however, the data is drawn from Punjab as a whole, as described in the censuses of 1951 and 1961. The correlations presented in the table implicitly compare Sikhs with the total rural population of the state and suggest the broad sets of common interests among all Sikhs within which the smaller party conflicts take form. In the census-taking procedure, Hindu, Sikh, Christian and

Table 17

AGRICULTURAL CONCOMITANTS OF PROPORTIONS OF SIKHS
IN RURAL DISTRICTS OF PUNJAB, 1961

Item	Coefficient
Proportion of Sikhs in rural population in 1951	.96
Proportion of total crop area irrigated	.66
Proportion of wheat to total cropped area	.504
Wheat yield per acre	.344
Number of refugees in 1951 (Sikhs 1951)	.306
Number of cattle per 100 acres	.282
Proportion of cropped area under bajra	−.157
Proportion of females enumerated in village of birth	−.285
Proportion of cropped area under gram	−.438
Proportion of males enumerated in village of birth	−.498

NOTE: Coefficients are Spearman's Rho coefficients of rank, correlation calculated on the basis of 18 districts, following the 1961 census.

Parties as a Model

"other" are the designations for religious affiliation. Of these, the first two categories are by far the most viable in terms of both popular opinion and numbers. Hindus make up 63.6 percent of the total state population, Sikhs 33.3 percent, according to the 1961 census. Effectively, then, when one has chosen to return oneself as "Sikh" one has rejected the label "Hindu." The census procedure allows us to ask, "What characterizes the situations of those who declare themselves to be Sikhs rather than Hindus when they must choose one or the other?"

The correlations presented in Table 17 derive from a larger set of trials designed initially to find all major factors correlated with the proportion of Sikhs in the rural areas of the eighteen districts of Punjab as it was constituted at the time of the census (and the field study). Each district was ranked in relation to proportions of Sikhs and the other variables, and the latter ranks were compared with the former using Spearman's Rho coefficient of rank correlation. The correlations presented are those whose implications are clear in indicating the nonreligious situations of those who adhere to the Sikh model. To translate the coefficients into words, the correlation between Sikhs in the rural population of the eighteen districts in the 1961 census and Sikhs in the rural population of the same districts in 1951 can serve as a benchmark. Since the population is considered on other grounds to be very stable, we can by comparison call the correlation coefficient of .96 that describes it a "very strong" association. Compared with it, there is at least a "strong" correlation between Sikhism and an ecological configuration like that in Shahidpur, based on irrigation using mixed water sources. This is reflected in the strong positive correlation with high wheat acreage, wheat yield, and the density of cattle, as well as in the negative correlation with rainfall, and, more strongly, the proportion of cropped areas under bajra (pearl millet) and gram. Wheat is the principal staple crop grown with irrigation, while gram and bajra are the summer and winter staples grown with rainfall alone. The cattle density reflects the higher overall level of capitalization with irrigation farming, which requires more draft animals for cropping and for turning wells, as well as more milk animals for the higher population density.

The remaining data pertain to population mobility. Sikh villages tend to have more immigrants who were refugees from the parts

217

of Punjab now in Pakistan, and Sikh villages tend to have fewer residents born in the village residing there permanently, and therefore more people from other villages. These two figures are doubtless related to some extent, since refugees did not generally return to villages of their birth. It may also be supposed that the higher capitalization and intensiveness of irrigation farming is associated with a more widely integrated market in labor and skills, and more movement to adjust to fluctuations in the labor market.

While it is obvious that Shahidpur exhibits a pattern of high Sikh religious activity that we would expect to occur with intensive use of its type of irrigation and crop cycle on the basis of the correlations, and that Shahidpur's factional activity as well as the religious activity both help to create these general trends and are shaped by them, the theoretically most important point lies at a somewhat deeper level. It is not entirely true to say that Shahidpur is a Sikh village rather than a Hindu village, that its people are Sikh rather than Hindu. That distinction is made only in certain contexts, and it is those contexts, rather than an absolute either-or identity, that are indicated by the general correlations. The contexts are those that the villagers themselves identify—those of certain cooperative aspects of irrigation agriculture revolving around the management of land and wells, the same contexts within which factions operate, the same as those relevant to the rituals. But there are other contexts, defined in other rituals within the village, where the Sikh ideas do not hold and where the specific problems of irrigation management do not enter. In these areas, the type of ideas used are the same as those used in agriculture in the "Hindu" areas, and one can speculate that the general cooperative patterns of relations also resembled those called for by rainfall farming as contrasted with irrigation farming. The ideas are primarily kinship ideas; the arrangements are primarily arrangements between strongly autonomous village households.

Other rituals follow the pattern of *diwan* and *lori*. They are managed by men, have overtly religious actions, and are concerned with agriculture and factions. They include a small ritual "for cattle," similar to *lori*; the ritual of *akhandpat*, which is usually sponsored to commemorate happy family and economic events such as completion of a new well, or the undertaking of a new job; and some of the rituals associated with marriage (which is itself the only life-cycle event with specific Sikh religious recognition). But in contrast to these there are other life-cycle rituals, such as funerals, where men and women have active roles, and numerous local rituals, like *tij, karue,* and *behairi,* that are generally concerned with families and human fertility, but not specifically with characteristics of agriculture. In these, women are dominant. They assemble the materials, enact the rite, and are often the only adults in the immediate audience. These rites lack standard Sikh religious elements and are not considered Sikh rites. Neither are they the object of factional activities. In fact, they generally refer to such caste occupations as Brahmin, Barber, Potter, and Sweeper, which are not operative in actual irrigation work and which are barred from mention in religious contexts. In effect, it is not that Shahidpur represents the Sikh portion of the statewide trends, but rather that the village represents in microcosm aspects of the entire pattern of trends—not as patterns of segregated people but as patterns of situations organized into exclusive collectivities. Village factional activities have an obvious bearing on statewide uses of factional models and the segregation of broad patterns of interests, and the religious manipulations in the village likewise contribute directly to the general pattern. But however important these actions are in practical terms, their theoretical importance is immeasurably increased when we see that in effect they are merely special cases of a process that all village collectivities seem to engage in—the process of evolving information systems by the continuous adaptation of their elements to the segregation of and competition among collective bodies.

The ritual segregation of religion and agriculture into one sphere of interconnected concerns has many parallels in daily behavior and nonritual usages. The appellation Jat Sikh itself, which the farmers invariably used to name their caste, rather than simply Jat, indicates that they see themselves as occupying a distinct occupational niche as Sikhs, as noted above. In the same contexts, they distinguish the Sikh area from other areas. The implication of a connection between the religion and farming practices is unmistakable. Sikhs who farm see and feel that their religion is directly relevant to their farming. They see their role as farmers to be specifically related to their religious identification, unlike at least some of their other roles, such as householders or fathers. The one Brahmin in the village who owned irrigated land and a share of a well insisted that I record that he was a "Brahmin by caste but not by religion," and further insisted that I accept a book, in English, explaining the tenets and nature of the Radhoswami sect, to which he adhered. The beliefs of this group center on the activities of a communal settlement in Dyalbagh, Punjab. The settlement's practices and ethics stress equality, the dignity of labor, self-sacrifice (in the Sikh sense), and community-mindedness. They embody a close parallel to the Sikhism of Nanak and the early Gurus, while the Brahmin's distinction between "caste" and "religion" itself stems from the thinking of Gobind Singh that made kinship and Sikhism alternative models, each appropriately embodied in a distinct set of village rituals.

The conscious model of caste that has religious status in Hinduism—with its emphasis on family and lineal purity and obligations, with complementary relationships of dominance and asymmetry between ritually differentiated groups—is apparently inappropriate to the fluid, general, but equal reciprocities that irrigation demands —as the Brahmin mentioned above seems to have felt. Sikhism, with its conceptions of martyrdom and obligation to the entire community, provides an organizational charter by which the necessary cooperation can be agreed upon. One who claims to be a Sikh claims a framework within which he can be expected to honor general practical obligations and defer individual and family requirements. It is in peoples' interest to claim this, and it is in their interest to prevail upon others to do so. This interest is expressed when villagers intercede to dampen factional quarrels, or when minority groups claim that party politics should not be brought up in areas that are matters of general fairness and equity and not party matters. Although 63 of the 126 groups involved in management of working farms have two or more members in one of the two village factions, 20 other such groups have at least two members in opposed factions. These people are often not near kin to each other. In such cases, the religious model is the most appropriate available organizational charter (assuming that direct conflict does not bar its use).

Within Shahidpur the sanctions associated exclusively with adherence to the Sikh religious model are mild. The Brahmin's qualified ideological conformity, insofar as it is not part of his factional activity, appears to have been induced, rather than coerced, by the prospect of better relations with the Jats he shared a well with and, during the time of the study, by the prospect of obtaining the chairmanship of the village government-sponsored cooperative loan society. Cooperative effort is required to impose forceful sanctions, and these, in Shahidpur, become matters of opposition between factions.

The distinction between the two village parties, like that between Hindu and Sikh at the statewide level and between Sikh and kinship/caste in the village, is only made in certain contexts. People enter the collectivities from time to time by assuming factional identities. The interests of the opposed "groups" describe the contexts in which such factional identities are enacted.

The interests of the factional groups within the village can be seen in a comparison of aspects of their household populations and landholding resources. These variables, which were indicated by the analysis of the division of labor, are major determinants of household managerial strategies.

Table 18 compares the land security, income, and population of the two groups of men who have publicly and actively aligned themselves with the two parties in Shahidpur. Land units are bighas (one bigha is equal to 5/24 acre). Population is expressed as a direct count of all the members of the households of those villagers who are actively and unambiguously identified with one party or the other. The Sant Fateh Singh faction has thirty-six active supporters, twenty-three of whom are landowners. The opposition party, aligned with the Congress party, has twenty-nine supporters, seventeen of whom own land. In terms of division of labor, the compared variables show an opposition between a large group of small landholders in a relatively tenuous position and a smaller group composed of more secure, larger landholders and their nonlanded supporters. In terms of the ecology, we see two groups balancing out land in relation to labor to obtain overall efficiency.

The first row of statistics of the table compares the land controlled through ownership with the land controlled through mortgage arrangements in the two factions. The comparisons indicate a striking difference in the ability of the two groups of men to rely on their own capital resources. The men of the opposition faction hold on

Table 18
LANDHOLDING AND POPULATION OF SHAHIDPUR FACTION GROUPS

Item	Statistic	A Master Tara Singh faction		Total village	B Sant Fateh Singh faction		Percentage comparison
		Absolute ratio	Decimal ratio	Decimal ratio	Absolute ratio	Decimal ratio	Statistic A / Statistic B
1.	Mortgaged land / Owned land	37.80 / 420.80	.09	.24	144.40 / 299.55	.48	19
2.	Crop share / Total land	421.30 / 458.60	.92	1.00	499.20 / 443.95	1.13	81
3.	Total land / Owners and households	458.60 / 96.00	4.75	3.27	443.95 / 160.00	2.76	172
4.	Crop share equivalent / Owners and households	421.30 / 96.00	4.39	3.27	499.20 / 160.00	3.12	141
5.	Crop share equivalent / Total faction population	421.30 / 152.00	2.77	2.52	499.20 / 299.00	1.67	166

mortgage an area of land equal to 9 percent of the area they own. In contrast, the Sant Fateh Singh supporters hold on mortgage an area equal to over 48 percent of the area they control by ownership—a far greater relative amount on a smaller and less secure capital base. As the comparison column on the right shows, the proportion of land held on mortgage in relation to land held in the opposition faction is only about 20 percent as great as the proportion of mortgaged land in the Sant Fateh Singh faction. Since land can be occupied on a mortgage arrangement by lending its owner just one-half its selling price, twice as much land can be occupied on mortgage as can be bought with a given sum of money. But, only half as much money is necessary to displace the holder of such a mortgage as would be necessary to displace an owner. Further, the lender must return the land on demand. A person is never forced to sell in the same way. This means that these statistical differences between the two groups represent very different division-of-labor situations.

The second statistic, crop share equivalent in relation to the total land, indicates the relationship between ecologically useful "income" and controlled resources. A crop share equivalent is a share of the crop of a unit of land expressed as a portion of the area of that land. Thus, for example, if a person owns four bighas of land and has a partner who receives one-fourth of the crop in exchange for his work, the owner would be recorded as having three crop-share equivalent bighas, and the partner would be listed as having one. This closely follows the sense of the various local tenancy arrangements, all based on sharecropping in different proportions. The implication of the close approximation to unity of the income to land ratio of the two factions is that both ownership and mortgaging are converted into ecological materials. People acquire land for the crops it yields. Since the statistic for the opposition faction is smaller than unity, all of its income potential is not utilized within the group. This suggests that a margin of security has been obtained by them. Conversely, the ratio for the Sant Fateh Singh faction, which is slightly greater than one, indicates that some income is obtained from land that is neither mortgaged nor owned within the group—that is, by tenancy or partnership. The Sant Fateh Singh faction, on the whole, does not possess a comparable margin of safety based on ownership of capital resources. A comparison of the two ratios indicates that the utilization of resources to produce direct income in ecological terms in the opposition group is about eighty-one percent of that in the Sant party.

The labor supply represented by household members, like other major ecological resources, must be efficiently utilized. The third, fourth, and fifth comparisons indicate the scope of the influence of this characteristic. The comparison between owned land and the population of the households of landowners in each faction brings out clearly the land shortage implied in the first two statistics. The landowners of the opposition faction own 172 percent as much land per capita as the landowners of the Sant faction. The higher risk arrangements noted are a reasonable, indeed necessary, means of manipulating the division of labor to find employment for the labor surplus.

The comparison of crop share equivalents per capita in the two factions shows that even though the Sant Fateh Singh faction derives somewhat more total income from its resources, this income per capita is still markedly less than the income for the opposition. The opposition has 141 percent of the per capita income of the Sant group—the gap is narrower than the gap in per capita ownership but still great. It is most interesting and significant that the gap between the two factions in respect to the final figure, the ratio of income per capita for all households in the faction, becomes wider again than the gap in income per capita for the landowning households. The total opposition income per capita is 166 percent that of the total income per capita—landowners and workers and their households—in the Sant group. This indicates that the larger numbers who have taken land on tenancy in the Sant faction have been offset by the much greater numbers of nonowners—129 against 56 in the dominant group. This increase offsets the continuing trade-off of family income for nonfamily support, either political or economic, in the opposition faction. Even with this last apparent sacrifice of income, the per capita income level of the opposition group remains above the overall village average of 2.52 bighas per person—taking all agricultural land and all permanent village residents as an approximation of the population from which factions are drawn—while the per capita income of the total Sant group is substantially below the average of the village.

In ecological terms, the two faction groups appear to be at opposite ends of a continuum from high land per capita to low land per capita, and to be responding to pressures that force them toward a balance. The land-rich group has to trade off income for support or labor, in order to avoid underutilization and possible loss of its land and capital. The labor-rich group has to acquire land to achieve adequate utilization of the labor resource it has in plentiful supply. Division-of-labor adjustments within each group, such as taking land on rent or hiring regular landless helpers, apparently cannot completely erase the different ecological imbalances, so the groups carry their differences into public action. Each promulgates a version of the general model of self-sacrifice, one calculated to create consensus that will yield the kind of cooperation its own members need. The general situation of related interests creates the coherence of factional concern: rituals define the general framework within which cooperation and conflict take place; political policies are efforts to gain support for one group or the other among the noncommitted; and court cases are specific attempts to acquire or hold specific pieces of land or to incapacitate or discredit particular political opponents.

The sanctioning processes that form rituals and other large events guarantee a high degree of consensus on the application of the religious and political models to agriculture—or to whatever else they might from time to time be applied to. At the same time, the sanctioning processes provide a standardized form and interpretation of the models and of the collectivities adhering to the different models as formulae of their common purpose and interests. Finally, the process of building a sanctioned form of the models is a process of sorting out interests. It involves "picking" those specific concerns that will move people to declare public hostility out of all the graduations of difference between them, and it is carried out through sorting, reconciling, and assimilating individual promises and offers of help, support, or opposition. The sanctioning aspect of the symbolic activity is of extreme importance, for it is the means whereby the ideas are finally *applied* to situations. Whether or not individuals privately believe that the conscious sociological models describe their own activity, the rituals and their meanings give villagers practical assurance that people in public will act as though the models did indeed naturally and logically fit their mutual interrelationships and policies regarding the management of agriculture.

Summary

The relation between conscious social models and collectivities cannot be fairly or adequately described in terms of the distinction between "ideal" and "real," or any of its analogues that hark back to Durkheim's distinction between social groups and "representations," or between "norms" and regulated behavior. Once free of this restricting conception of the nature and function of conscious sociological models, we can see their proper importance and can return, their full range of properties in mind, to some particularly relevant current issues in the analysis of social structure and behavior.

Conscious sociological models can only be construed as "ideals" in the limited sense that some natives *say* that some of them embody some principles that action should follow, in the manner described by Barbara Ward (1965). But when such commendations of a model are made, they are themselves objectively only a piece in a larger complex and important social process, the process of grouping individual interests around a few general intellectual charters, and of establishing the charters as foci of coordinated behavior. Making such a statement is part of the process of saying what the order in behavior shall consist in, of gaining agreement on the point, and thereby of ordering behavior into patterns with interpersonal significance at many different levels. But not making it, as when villagers condemn themselves for factional activities, is equally part of the same broad process. In both cases, behavior is said by members of communities, almost in so many words, to consist in a set of symbols of "underlying" principles—the principles represented in the models. And since this position is sanctioned, actors are, in the process, literally forced to see behavior in just this way—as exhibiting a recurrent underlying meaning describable in terms of conscious sociological models.

In the process of gaining consensus on key principles, villagers engage not only in manipulation of conscious models, but also in manipulation of their perceptions, and through them of their actions concerning information systems other than the social models themselves. Groups, to enforce consensus, must form by the process of sorting out basic choices from peripheral ones, of identifying certain aspects of the total world of each actor as areas for common endeavor and neglecting other areas. Elaborating, or "filling in," the models by defining individual needs means that those who form collectivities shall articulate or describe perceived and practical needs, defined in terms of the systems—the conscious models—even while relating the models to practical needs. There is, thus, constant mutual interpretation and adjustment between all the systems of information that contribute to each collectivity.

Since a collectivity is an agency whereby a social model is interpreted and imposed, and since the collectivity thereby necessarily uses the concepts and logic of the model, its exact form (insofar as a form can be specified) varies according to the nature of the model, the other information systems it is tied to, and the types of sanctioning activity required to impose it. Sometimes a definite "corporate" structure might be required; at other times hardly more than a conjunction of people vaguely defining themselves as "the same" would suffice. The collectivity might be named in the sociological model, or it might not—but in no case will the relevance of the model end with the description of the collectivity. The models help organize individual action, individual expectations, and interpersonal communication of the significance of individual actions. Through the application of sanctioned backing to the use of conscious sociological models, individuals create a means for morally and conceptually organizing their behavior. By adapting single models to their various and scattered concerns, they produce the collectivities whose principal characteristics have been recognized in practice by anthropologists since field study was first undertaken. It would be difficult to find any point better documented than the flexibility of forms of collectivities and their resistance to study by methods which isolated them from conscious models, from their own material concerns, and from general interpersonal interaction. In every area and every period, anthropologists have been driven to find clear groups as counterparts of their structural models, and have failed to find them. But we have been unable to dismiss their importance. The Australian section arguments were one form the problem took; others were the search for a corporate lineage in Africa, the debate over Polynesian residence, the argument that resulted in Leach's distinction between "localized" clans and "pure" structural clans in Kachin, and the involved search for concrete counterparts of the occupational castes of the Indian jajmani system—by no means exhaustive of the literature. The recurrence and inconclusiveness of these debates can be seen as evidence for the view that the processes of gaining social consensus that exist in Punjab are universal, since they show both the importance and the fluidity of collectivities in relation to the social models promulgated in communities.

As the complex relationship between collectivities and models became apparent in literature, a line of analysis developed that bears closely on this one. Leaving aside direct concern with collectivities, investigation focused instead on the analysis of particular significant actions and objects, in the context of rituals, public debate, and ordinary behavior. But as this was pursued by Bateson, Turner, Schneider, and others, two seemingly contradictory points were made. The first is that behavior embodies and represents social ideas, social meanings. Behavior is a symbolic process. But on the other hand, Schneider (1968) has made an express point of arguing that the contrary of this does not hold. Social structure, in his view, is a symbolic system that must be analyzed apart from patterns of behavior (pp. 4, 5, 6). Social structure, he insists, is a "cultural system," a "system of symbols and meanings" whose relationship to patterned behavior or "real" groupings of people, if any, is problematic (pp. 5, 7ff.).

The apparent contradition between the view that behavior is inherently symbolic and the view that symbols are inherently separate from general behavior disappears when each of the positions is seen in terms of the relationship between conscious sociological models as systems of low information used in conjunction with systems of high information. As low-information systems, the conscious sociological models are systematic by themselves, without reference to behavior. But since they are low-information systems, they never really occur in any widely accepted form except through manipulation, and in a process of imposition, which involves the use of behavioral elements that reflect high-information systems. Schneider can be seen as having focused on the American kinship model and its implications as implications alone, in the manner of chapter 6. He can be seen as presenting a summary of commonly expected applications of some basic conscious model of American kinship. By contrast, Turner and the others can be seen as presenting a summary of the high-information activities that might be drawn together by natives as symbolic expressions of some set of ideas: all the activities recalling the actions of the Naven ritual or those that resemble or recall the apparatus of the Ndembu drums. But in these cases, the analysts make no attempt to describe the basic models directly. I suspect that the internal difficulties of each analysis may be resolved by a recognition of their actual complementarity. They are not really conflicting "total" theories, although they may appear to be so in an organic, single-system framework of theory. They are, rather, accounts of two aspects of the same process of ordering behavior that is found in Shahidpur.

Analysis of collectivities as coordinated manipulations of several information systems permits the internal order of systems of structural meanings to be related to the symbolic character of daily activities precisely because it avoids postulating a deterministic relationship between social structural models and patterned behavior. It permits the experience, if not the theories, of analysts of social structure to be integrated with the newer analysis of behavioral symbolism in a single frame of reference. Collective behavior expresses not mysteriously self-perpetuating universals but the sanctioning power rooted in the concrete needs and resources of interdependent people: users of the ecology, the division of labor, and the economy of the community. In this respect, primitive societies share their fundamental similarities with our own, where any act responds not to one cause or determinant but to multiple pressures, of many kinds at many levels, even though the basic ingredients of the picture are simple and clear. The concept of a conscious sociological model, like the older conception of a "social contract" that it resembles, requires us to accord a degree of theoretical importance to sanctioning behavior that corresponds to its practical importance, at least in the case at hand. The broader concept of an information system permits us to coordinate our analyses of conscious sociological models and their ritual and nonritual expression with analyses of the ecological and economic contexts within which people work, cooperate, and quarrel, in a way that generates a complex and apparently useful overall picture of the nature and basis of ordered social behavior.

Chapter IX

The Analysis of Behavior

While social scientists can afford to ignore some of the aspects of communication theory that were most important to its authors—namely, the mathematical definitions of noise, feedback, code systems, and channel capacity—we require more sophistication in other areas than the original theory provided. We cannot accept the assumption that "the brain" is a message source, and that messages consist merely in "written or spoken words, or of pictures, music, etc." selected from it (Shannon and Weaver 1964, p. 7). Weaver recognized that not all words and the like are messages, and that the selection of those which are messages depends not only on the presence of a brain but on uniformity of what brains do. But it was not his province to explain this uniformity. To social scientists, on the other hand, it is of the utmost importance to find how operative consensus becomes established concerning the use of words and other symbols, and to find how these social forms become part of the biological functions of individual human beings—how "understanding" is created both collectively and individually.

The six message sources in Shahidpur seem to tell us a great deal about how people of the community come to know things, what it is they know, how they come to feel they know it, how they can act as though they know it, and how they can expect others to know it. The concept of a message source, used descriptively, permits many parts of the larger puzzle to fall into place. But it does not resolve all the problems. The present model of a community as one using several message sources external to individuals requires us to provide not only for the selection of symbolic elements but for the selection of message sources themselves and for their combination. We need some explanation of the mechanism by which each system maintains its integrity despite its being combined with others in behavioral sequences. Our modification of Weaver's concept of a message source to fit social needs requires, and permits in turn, new levels of complexity in the analysis of communicative activity.

While the analysis of the combined operation of information sources in behavior is more complicated than the description of single message sources, the additional challenges yield greater rewards in terms of a sense of scientific discovery. It is here that the microscopic applicability of the broad concept of a message source to social behavior begins to show itself most clearly, and it is here, too, that the benefits of this approach to well-recognized and important problems in social theory are most apparent. There is, of course, no major tradition of social analysis concerned with message sources as such. But the analysis of the social aspects of individual behavior is the focus of many of the best-developed bodies of literature in social philosophy and social science.

As the conception of behavior required by our understanding of the several message sources in Shahidpur unfolds, we can begin to see more and more points of basic agreement between it and analyses of other communities and sets of behaviors in what have been the two dominant and largely conflicting theoretical approaches to social anthropology and to social science since at least the beginning of this century.

On the one hand, we see the process of self-definition from individual adaptive and creative behaviors that was so important to Franz Boas and G. H. Mead; on the other hand, we can see some grounds for Durkheim's views of the identity between extra-individualistic entities and pattern in individual behavior. In the present case, however, there is no conflict. We are not constrained by our theory to see individual differences and individual freedom as suggesting a lack of order at the societal level. Nor are we required to see the existence of well-ordered societal entities, some of which are very similar to Durkheim's "collective consciousness," as suggesting that individual actors are uniform and passive. Instead, we see a complementarity: order at the societal level gives structure to individual freedom; and free, exploitive, and nonuniform individual action in turn preserves that order.

It seems to me that there are three main questions pertaining to analysis of behavior, and that they all are more clearly discussed in the context of an overview and comparison of all the six information sources of the village than they are in relation to one system or the other. The first question is, How do actors who learn the systems learn to combine them in ways that do not lead to the eventual amalgamation of one system with another? This involves the question of the relationship of individual abilities to the use of the systems, since the answer to the question requires us to show that the systems are so constructed that their use by everyone from the village idiot to the village genius is shaped by the models (sources) themselves in such a way that the integrity of the sources is maintained.

The second question, or problem, is to show how a situation—a "unit" of behavior—is organized. What are its limits, how are the areas of freedom and constraint structured by the several sources reflected in it?

And finally, in view of the first two questions, it is necessary to deal with the problem raised specifically by the previous chapter. How do the many situations entered into by individuals from time to time come to be recognized by those in the community as aspects of the action of a collectivity? How are actions and behaviors aggregated into perceived patterns, and—a closely related question—how are we as outside analysts to deal with behaviors that seem "real" to us but which are not recognized by members of the community as forming patterns in their own right? All of these are important questions, with major bodies of literature pertaining to each. Although no pretense can be made toward dealing with them fully, it is important to show that some resolution, or at least some clear position, with respect to each is implicit in the present study.

Individual Uses of Message Sources

How can people of greatly varying individual sophistication be recognized as full-fledged members of the community and the established systems of information, and contribute to their maintenance so consistently that no one system becomes confused with the other?

There are two related answers to this question, both of which lie in the formal properties of the systems themselves and have already been suggested. First, there are the properties of the systems that enable them to articulate sanctioning behaviors, which in turn permit a few to impose the several systems on the generality of those who use them and thereby standardize consensus on them at any time. These are aspects of the systems whereby the interpretations of the more far-sighted people can supplant confusions that might arise in the actions of the less astute. Second, there are generalized system properties quite apart from the capacity of the systems to be used in sanctioning behaviors. These system properties affect all users directly on a day-to-day, minute-to-minute basis. The best way to describe them is as set, separate, operational "rules," one of which is uniquely associated with each system. Each describes the general orientation a user should have toward the selection of any element within the system to which it pertains. The rule of each system is slightly or greatly different from the rules of the other systems. And each rule, each general orientation, is itself a direct reflection of the information value of the system it refers to—of its structure and complexity. It is in fact an artifact of the organization of its system. For convenience and consistency, each of these rules is best described in terms of the way it directs users of the system to relate the concepts and words of the system to other systematic objects. That is, we are describing them as the ways in which "words are *made* to refer and signify in virtue of some underlying consensus and given rules of operation" (Nadel 1951, p. 43).

Each of these rules is simple and capable of being "followed" and exploited at many different levels of sophistication. Yet as long as each one is followed, at whatever level, the system that generates it will be maintained, adapted, and preserved.

Rule of Objective Primacy

In the system of highest information, the ecology, the basic rule for responding to its elements can be described as a "rule of objective primacy." It is taught, as part of this system, that words and other more conventional "code" items take their meaning from the natural objects to which they purport to refer. For example, the meaning of the word "wheat" and all of its logic and implications are to be considered identical to the real properties and the biological and ecological effects of actual wheat plants. When the concept of "wheat," or any other object in the system, does not carry entailments parallel to the biological effects of actual wheat plants—when the concept does not match the behavior of its referent—then the rule requires the concept and its implications to be altered.

The rule of objective primacy permits the specific sanctions inherent in the ecological system to operate. It says, in effect, that users of ecological information are to imbed themselves in the system of homeostatic relationships and to adapt their communication, co-operation, and action to its requirements. What is thus information-ally "true"—what should be acted on—is equated with what is ecologically productive. Finding that a technique is more or less productive than was supposed is taken as sufficient cause for modi-fying the verbal instructions in the system, for altering the pattern of what is taken to be true and what is taken to be untrue.

Although the rule of objective primacy is not enunciated ex-plicitly, like the description of wheat or of plows, it is enunciated implicitly in almost all discussion of the ecology, in instruction, and in practice. It is reflected in the stress laid on careful observation of the effects of variations in culture. This was clearly brought home to me when a young farmer explained slight variations in color of three fields of wheat by indicating the different fertilizing practices that had been followed. It is reflected in a strong bias toward experiment among all those who can afford it. The father of the farmer just mentioned, for example, learned that I had some American garden seeds for maize and asked me for them. I gave him a handful and thought little more about it. After a brief absence I returned to the village late in September, when the fall harvest was well under way. The father then reminded me of the seeds. He told me I had given him ninety-five seeds. He gave twenty to his brother-in-law, a good irrigation farmer who lived in another village. These served as what we would call an experimental control. The remaining seeds were planted in a good plot of irrigated land. He showed me the plot, where only seven seeds had produced plants, the largest a dried dwarf of about seven inches, with the barest beginnings of a single ear. None of the brother's seeds produced any result at all. The obvious conclusion was that the local varieties were greatly superior. The experiment reveals a clear and well-established sense of scientific procedure, and it shows how that practice is frequent enough to have been encompassed in kinship interactions. Those who cannot themselves afford to experiment, or who cannot obtain new seeds or other resources, carefully watch and closely copy those who can.

Over and above the highly empirical character of ecological information—the desire to base what one says and conveys upon accurate observation of the objects of the ecology—there is another pervasive sense in which the rule of objective primacy is part of the ecology. It is imbedded in what I have called the "specialist" character of the ecological system, which is tied to its formal complexity and size. The system is too large to be encompassed in the direct knowledge or in the time and resources of any single individual. Since knowledge is held and conveyed in memory and practice, rather than in writings and written protocols, the system is too large to be systematized and codified in a single intellectual scheme. In the absence of codification and the development of consensus on systematic underlying principles, complex knowledge assumes a more pragmatic character. The principle that replaces codification is observation, the rule of objective primacy.

A person can utilize information in the ecology, in accordance with the rule of objective primacy, at many levels of complexity and competence. A child who plays by copying his father in clearing an irrigation channel is responding in accord with it, as is a laborer who digs out a set of pits for the making of gur. Both are simple tasks that can be done in accordance with spontaneous procedures given the tools available plus very simple instructions. At the other end of the scale is the skillful farmer who carefully plans his whole crop array in relation to his monetary and labor resources, and then tends the crops in all matters except those requiring large inputs of labor at sowing and harvest. His tools and his situation are more complex. Yet there is no manual for him to follow, and his detailed actions, on this larger scale, attempt to adhere to experience and to apply it in procedures that are always partly new in response to the new aspects of the situation as they emerge.

Rule of Pragmatic Interactional Primacy

The division of labor is similarly complex, and its use is similarly pragmatic. Its general rule of procedure can be described as a rule of "pragmatic interactional primacy," which means that the criterion for acceptability of a given formulation lies not in the way the putative object of the proposition behaves, but rather in the effect it has on the interactional relations between the users of the proposition and people of interest to him. This rule reflects the principal formal difference between the two systems. In the ecology, the putative objects of the information and the basis of the sanctions are identical. The sanctions that stabilize information on wheat, maize, and buffalo milk are wheat, maize, and buffalo milk. In the division of labor the putative referents are in many instances not the sanctioning objects, and are not considered to be. The information on families, caste groups, factional groups, and so forth is sanctioned not by these groups as such, but rather by one's own resources and by the individuals one deals with, by a given householder, by a group that sponsors *diwan* in a given year in the name of a factional cause, and so forth. Individuals, not the groups named, impose the sanctions of the system.

Apart from the locus of sanctions, there is another aspect to the relationships between descriptions and their objects in the division of labor that contrasts sharply and significantly with the ecology. It is that the descriptions within this system are used to exercise a direct influence on the objects described. Speaking to objects to influence their behavior, in ways that would appear "magical" if they occurred in the context of the ecology (such as telling wheat how it grows), is normal and efficacious in this system. In fact, it is often impossible to influence the objects of the system—the units controlling production—without using their descriptions to address people in those units and describe their relations to oneself. In this sense, the "pragmatism" of this system is somewhat different from the pragmatism of the ecology. In the ecology, the verbal formulae are not directly involved in manipulative action and are either changed or stabilized insofar as it is necessary to indicate actions that are in turn efficacious. In the division of labor, formulae are manipulated and changed pragmatically insofar as it is necesary to use them to achieve the desired effect on the objects. Gaining acceptance of one's formulation is, in many cases, a part of causing the desired effects.

Like the rule of objective primacy in the ecology, the rule of interactional primacy can be "followed" at varying levels of effectiveness. It involves manipulating descriptions of individuals to fit the cooperative or competitive situation. Such manipulation is effective if it accomplishes productive ends, and ineffective if it results in a loss of control over one's own resources. Gains or losses can occur in two ways. One can gain by construing the immediate situation in one's own favor, or by construing it to one's long-run advantage. A few villagers tried, for example, to exaggerate their importance and helpfulness to me in the early stages of my field work, to convince me that I was obligated to them in some way, and therefore should reward them. In doing this they made commitments to me that put them in a bad light when the commitments became known, so that their reputations were not enhanced. Other villagers consistently let their short-term interest suffer in the interests of building a generally dependable set of relationships. Still others, notably the factional leaders, made a policy of pushing individual relations almost to the point where they became extractive enough to be damaging to their general reputation, and to the point also of involving them in reciprocal relations with some people that were incompatible with their relationships with others. A few people, one a Brahmin who was mentally deficient, and several old men with small families, consistently lost in both areas, largely because they did not command the economic power either to bend situations to their own advantage or to force others to construe them in a consistent manner. They got neither what was due to them on the basis of long-run reciprocities nor the normal amount of short-run extractive gains that were not due. Sociologists operating in several traditions have described aspects of this process, generally in an American setting (Garfinkel 1967; Goffman 1959; McHugh 1968). Such interaction through negotiating descriptions of mutual power and responsibilities has also been the subject of literary concern by writers as diverse as Damon Runyan and C. P. Snow, and of historians concerned with analysis of intergovernmental communications, such as treaty negotiations.

The rule of interactional primacy, like the rule of objective primacy, is built into the formal characteristics of the system it covers. The pragmatic aspect of the rule, like the pragmatic aspect of the rule of objective primacy, derives from the complexity and size of the system of objects (villagers and effective village groups) in relation to the complexity and power of the codifying concepts. There are many people in many combinations. There are only a few general ways of characterizing them, and these are not developed in a generally accepted detailed scheme. The system is therefore not the same for any two people. Each has to construct it according to his own lights and needs.

Rule of Symbolic Primacy

The economy is used in a way quite different from either of these two systems. Instead of either objective or interactional primacy, its use involves what can be called "symbolic" primacy. That is, the uses of the system are oriented toward maintaining consistency and order in a specifically designated and carefully managed set of conventional symbolic objects—primarily money and secondarily the market conventions. Money embodies the quantitative and comparative logic of the economy in the way that wheat, cattle, wells, disease syndromes, and the rest embody the homeostatic logic of the ecology. The mathematical organization of the quantitative conceptions is imbedded in money, and the established conventional market transactions apply this logic to selected nonmonetary objects. If one simply follows the primary rule of consistently focusing on money as the basis for evaluation and choice in diverse situations, one can operate coherently and maximize one's resources in an orderly pattern. However, as in the other systems, superior knowledge —a more complex and subtle knowledge of money and its significance—can produce a more effective pattern of behavior.

Just as the rule of objective primacy is inherent in the complexity of the ecology, the rule of symbolic primacy is inherent in the simplicity and low information of the economy. Where complexity of a system militates against coherent and widespread consensus on the meaning of any part of it, simplicity does the opposite. It permits, and is in fact an aspect of, wide general consensus. Of course, such wide consensus in so few elements conveys only a single kind of significance, the significance of an object in exchange for money, and then, indirectly, for exchange for other goods not available within the ecology but available within reach of the monetary system.

The market conventions of the economy, in their rigid and well-known prescriptions for a sequence of actions, resemble the rituals associated with systems of low entropy much more than the technical and variable actions of the ecology. So, too, the quantitative system of concepts, in its elegance and logical form, resembles the conscious sociological models more than it does the pragmatic, specialized, and uncodified conceptual apparatus of the ecology and the division of labor. The basic principles of the economy are widely and uniformly known: the uses of money and the major marketing conventions. The principal difference is that money is object-like, not human-like. Although it is an entirely artificial creation, it is artificially physical, inanimate. It has conventionally assigned properties resembling those of uniform beads or bricks, rather than properties like those of ideas, social groups, or biological objects. As such it has no exact parallels in the other systems. The objects of the ecology lack the uniformity of money, while social groups, defined as the "real objects" of the conscious sociological models, lack their resemblance to physical objects. The uniform "brick-like" character of money carries the logic of economic calculation within it, and is maintained through the utilization of that logic.

Conscious sociological models, as we have noted, are systems of extremely high organization and low information. Whether they are all of lower information than the economy is difficult to say in the absence of an agreed-upon scheme for discussing elemental units of systems; but if we provisionally regard each denomination of currency, each market convention, each basic operation of mathematics, and each concept like "rent" and "interest" as a basic element, comparable to the definition of God in the religious system, then the economy would seem to be still more complex than the highly redundant kinship model, which in turn is obviously more complex than the religious model. The economy is apparently just complex enough so that fewer people are aware of all the basic marketing conventions in detail than are aware of the basic kinship or religious ideas.

Rule of Definitional Primacy

The three conscious sociological models are all handled in more or less the same way according to a final rule we can call the "rule of definitional primacy." This rule, like the others, is simple and easy to follow, capable of being employed by people of a wide variety of capacities and inclinations. Also, like the other general rules, it is inherent in the organization of the systems themselves.

Definitional primacy means that whenever there is an apparent contradiction or disjunction between observable phenomena which can be taken as the referent of an idea and the implications of the idea itself, the interpretation of the phenomenon, not the idea, is modified. This rule is institutionalized in such practices as carrying on factional arguments over leadership by arguing explicitly that the person one supported was the "true" Guru and the other person was not, and in the general hortatory use of the ideas of these models. One tells a father, or a son, what *he should be doing*, if his action does not seem to conform to the model; one does not modify the model. Rituals are institutionalized performances, wherein action is specifically constructed to conform only to the dictates of the model. They form the main general means of instruction in the use of the models according to the rule of definitional primacy.

Formal Relations among the Conscious Sociological Models

It is important to review the descriptions of the three conscious models in order to spell out quite clearly how it is that the models attain their characteristics and pervasive importance in behavior even while their users follow the rule of definitional primacy. This is an ancient problem. How do "formal," definitional systems assume their pervasive and immediate importance, their moral force in daily behavior?

The first and simplest reason for the rule of definitional primacy to be tied to the peculiar observable importance of the conscious sociological models is that the definitions include the stipulation that the models describe a "reality." What we objectively call the "putative" referents of the models are described within them as "real" referents. When a villager recounts the kinship terminology, this is not taken as a mechanical learning recitation of a set of interconnected abstract definitions, like a recitation of multiplication tables. Instead, it is taken as speaking "about," as "describing," something. He is taught to act as if the kinship map is in some sense "real," a part of the real world, not the world of imagination. In short, one of the conceptions included in the definition of kinship is the "reality" of kinship. Since kin are real, the argument might run, the kinship map is real and not merely a matter of definition. The same goes for all of the ideas—parties, the Guru, God, friends, and so on—all are understood as being real. They are defined with an idea of "reality." They are not felt to be matters of definition; they are not hypotheses for the natives, but descriptions of the basic elements of social life. It is appropriate that, in having this "reality," conceptions are conceptions "of" kinship, "of" types of people, and "of" groups—in part.

There is no need to engage in metaphysical speculations over what is or is not real, because of this common feature of conscious sociological models. We need only observe that even though the structural ideas are defined as applying to real things, they are standardized and taught only in verbal and other symbolic media. We observe that in practice "reality" is hypothesized of items included in the established ideas of the society. This is the difference between fathers and unicorns.

The hypothesis of reality in conscious models provides an automatic rule of application for the models. It says that ideas are to be connected with various objects in the concrete world. The idea of "father" is to be applied to a single real person, the idea of "kin" to real people, the idea of "God" to concrete books and teachers, and so on. The definitions of the ideas as descriptions of real things implies that we are to see concrete objects in terms of the ideas—they instruct their users to see the world in this way. Since the conceptions are not only "real" but are defined by each other to form closed systems, they provide a fixed choice of categories, one of which will be *by definition* applicable to any concrete object. This is the basic rule for the use of the socially established ideas, and it is established in the formal structure and semantics of the ideas themselves.

Complexity

People can easily link ideas with the concrete situations they need to discriminate, according to the definition of the "reality" of ideas. This is because of the complexity of ideas, along with their elegance or organization. As we have noted, the three major models, religious, social structural, and party, have several component notions. There are enough of these elementary conceptions—terms, rules, and images—to permit a great number of combined notions to be made with a bare minimum of types of combinations. The exact number of combinations in each model is somewhat related to the number of its elemental ideas. In the case of the kinship model, with seventy-two basic kinship positions, ideas quickly become several hundred possible definitions of types of persons in relation to ego through means of simple addition of one or more such derived concepts as "caste" or "family" to each term or group of terms on the basic map. To a lesser extent, the same simple operation of addition operates within the other two broad models for even more combinations, any of which can be applied uniquely to some person. Further, ideas of the three broad categories can be added in practice to ideas of the other categories. As was noted in the division of labor, people are often "described" with some kinship combination, plus some religious combination, plus some party combination. Ego may know A, who is his brother of his caste but not of his household, in his group of actual kin, who is strong and loyal (*nihang*) but not pious or submissive (*bhai*) Sikh, and who is in his party. This description is, to a native, very informative, because the different implications of each idea seem to accumulate in certain directions. But it is made only of simple items of the definitions, added to one another.

The elegance of the organization of the ideas permits the different significances to be known and remembered by people of minimal intelligence. It also permits such combinations to occur where each term adds to each other term's meaning. The order connects the ideas into logical patterns, which at the same time differentiate the elements. Since all terms are understood as "real" things, or descriptions, such combined forms will be "real" descriptions, and will fit concrete persons.

The initial plurality of simple ideas permits the formation of a great number of particular labels for things, people, and objects, through simple operations of addition or, conversely, of subtraction or occlusion (e.g., "They are brothers, but not close"). The number of resulting terms is great enough for any person incapable of more sophisticated manipulations to use in his daily dealings. More intelligent persons, who will want more subtle shades of definition of those they deal with, can accomplish more subtle and numerous combinations, by the addition of more operations and the use of the additional bodies of information.

Structural "space"

A single-term element defined in the models can be used to structure a complete social situation in an area and for a time, when it is invoked with an appropriate symbol in some concrete circumstance. This capability rests heavily on a kind of "space" that is built into the definitions of element in two senses, one literal, the other logical.

Ideas have space in them in the sense in which maps or diagrams have. They are so stated as to conjure up images, in two or three dimensions, in the imagination of the hearer, the learner. It is not accidental that representations of these images, in the form of diagrams, paintings, or sculpture, are among the established representations of each model. The Guru is above the disciple, a person of high rank above one of lower rank. The Khalsa is a large group of men, with a leader in the place of the Guru. Parties are two opposed groups on the same level. The imagery of the kinship ideas has been reviewed in detail, including of course the organization of the kinship map itself.

The grouping of terms into these images is a most important mnemonic device and a fundamental part of the "elegance" of the ideas referred to above. Terms when grouped into images become exclusive systems. Two such arrangements of terms cannot be referred to in the same situation at the same time. Imagistic space thus provides an automatic device for keeping ideas separate from one another but linked to each other's implications in close groups. Transformations from one image to another, when they occur, are generally provided for by recurrent words, not images, as was noted in the chapter on kinship ideas. Thus the kinship term *bap* would appear in the image of the kindred, the *parivar*, the *patti*, the clan, and the caste. In short, the imagery of space provides the means of constructing logical compartments for the ideas of the society. A term may share one or more compartments with some other terms, yet be out of the compartments of still others.

In a looser sense, which encompasses the first, space occurs in the systems of conceptions because some elements are defined in close association with a given term or rule, while others are not. *Bap* and *putar* are close; *nakar dada* and *patija* are not. Property and inheritance are close; property and marriage residence less close; property and respect are not closely related at all. That is, inheritance is invariably a part of the definition of property—they must be mentioned together. It is not necessary to mention "respect" in relation to property in the same way or with the same frequency. Nor is it necessary to mention property in explaining or expressing respect. Some terms may be thought of as "close" to one another in this sense, and others as "far," or "remote." When one term is invoked by some object, terms close to it are closely implied, while those remote are less relevant. If A is the wife of B, B is the husband of A. If A is the wife of B, B may or may not be a pious Sikh.

The nearness of conceptions to one another provides for the richness of situations; the remoteness of ideas from one another provides for the differences between situations. The remoteness of ideas also provides for the richness of the world at large. It provides the multiplicity of possible situations, or the possibility of multiple situations, which is a major part of the pattern in the world which a native feels to exist.

Just as a ball is so formed that it must roll, the presence of "space" within the ideas, in the formation of ideas, includes a basic set of rules for their use. By learning the ideas alone, one automatically learns to use them to pattern immediate situations and to feel that remote situations exist and will also be patterned.

The conceptions are used to define situations because they are suited to the purpose. Indeed, to know them is to be instructed to use them in this way. And they are used because it is expected that other people will adhere to them and recognize them. That is, they are used both because they are suitable and because they are expected.

The expectation of the general acceptance of the ideas is implied by their being defined as "real" descriptions. But, much more obviously and strongly, it is the result of wide publicity, of repeated implicit assurances that the world is as the conceptions say. These occur in rites, as we have noted; in actual situations where the "close" ideas are borne out and distant and irrelevant ideas are not introduced; and in literature and other textual materials current in the society.

The same features of the ideas which lend them to application in defining situations in daily behavior permit them to be invoked in texts, which aids their stabilization and promulgation. The words defined in the ideas "father," "wife," "son," "property," and so on, can appear in texts, and when they do they will naturally call forth other ideas which are "close" in the established ideas of the society, and so on. We have seen this process in the few rituals discussed above. It must be borne in mind that in less literate communities, rites and associated stories and statements of belief constitute an important part of the literature. In written and nonritual material, one can find an example of this in nearly any nontechnical text from any society. The points of jokes, the force of plot situations, and so on are generally lost on people not acquainted with the conscious sociological models of the society. Without the models, one cannot recognize situations in the text and finds the action disjointed and vague, in sharp contrast to equally unimportant literary efforts of one's own society. As in daily life, the socially established ideas give life and richness and considerable meaning to small items of communicative behavior. In literature, by the same token, the meaning of small acts that is developed in the course of a text constitutes a reinstruction in and an affirmation of whatever established ideas are relevant to the situation described. The fund of personal knowledge of lore, stories, and rites, therefore, is automatically a repository of knowledge of the established ideas of one's society. Knowledge that this personal knowledge is shared is automatically knowledge that one's general outlook is shared. The lore reinforces personal confidence in the social information as representing a very basic set of truths about the nature of man and the world. When a person knows the marriage rite and knows that his description is "correct" and commonly held, he automatically knows that the significance of attendance will also be generally acknowledged. He can therefore confidently impute the ideas which underlie the rite to the behavior of those who attend. Everything else that he knows, and knows that others know, will further convince him of the correctness of his approach. The literature of a society, including oral literature and rituals, is at once a repository of its ideas and proof of their general acceptance. It is the source of the social structural information, a source as appropriate to and as tightly bound up with the content and function of this system of conceptions as the sources of the ecological information or the division of labor information are with their respective forms and functions.

Behavioral Situations

If the villagers of Shahidpur can be recognized as counterparts of a group of Americans—or Chinese, or Frenchmen—of similar size, different only in their information systems, the behavior of people in all these groups must be recognized as fundamentally alike in some important way. We would expect some similarity in the way information is used to create order, in the process whereby "physical space and chronological time are transformed into social space and social time" (McHugh 1968, p. 3). We should see something familiar, for example, in the process by which "respect" relations are constructed, as well as in the formation of the elaborate and complex collectivities described in the last section of the preceding chapter.

Through selecting and acting upon information in the several sources, a situation in social space and time is created out of activity in physical space and chronological time. The "duration" of the social situation thus created is as long as the specific choice is manifested. It ends when another point of choice is reached. The "space" taken up by such a "social" behavior (including ecological and division of labor behavior) includes all the significant actions necessary to the manifestation of the choice, and may overlap the space of other manifestations—for example, when a religious idea is used to effect an ecological exchange. But there is no necessary fit or fixed relationship between a behavior distinguished in terms of one system and a behavior distinguished in terms of another. A given relationship between two people in terms of the division of labor can encompass many discrete ecological behaviors, just as the manifestation of a given idea from one of the conscious sociological models can encompass a number of distinct relationships of control in the division of labor. Furthermore, behaviors do not exclusively classify physical actions. That is, if some gesture or movement is identified in terms of one behavior, this does not preclude its being properly and legitimately identified as another, of a wider or a narrower scope, or even of a different system altogether. Cutting a row of wheat is cutting a row of wheat; it may also be part of clearing a holding, and it can also be part of being a tenant or a friend. A given action may even be disputed, with different people assigning it different significance. And finally, the behavioral identification of some physical action can be changed in time. For example, an action once thought of as friendly may retrospectively be considered hostile: a Harijan of the village took a loan from a farmer and then found that the farmer was seeking a pretext to obtain the Harijan's milk-buffalo by demanding a return when the Harijan could not pay it.

The organization of the preceding chapters has necessarily considered most behaviors only in the context of their own systems, yet it should be clear that they do not occur naturally in such isolation. In addition to the structured relationships between behaviors that exist through the choices imposed within the defining message sources, there are what we might call "practical" relationships that exist across message sources.

Although the analyses of single systems should provide an adequate basis for organizing any analysis of single behaviors, it is necessary to have recourse to the comparison of the formal properties of different systems in order to describe the regularities that exist in the relationships between complex behaviors responding to multiple systems.

While there are no direct relationships between one system and another, there are at any one time specific sets of behaviors defined in each system that tend to be associated with a specific set or range of behaviors from one or more others—for example, in the association of factional and religious manifestations with agricultural activities in the ecology, or in the "groups" described in the division of labor. Going beyond the definition of collectivities given in chapter 8, these can now be seen as coordinated choices of elements of several messages sources (complex behaviors) by recognizable sets of persons. In this context, the formal differences between the message sources, with their respective operating rules, provide an infrastructure at the individual level that guarantees instability in the combined behavioral "message" that is the collectivity as a perceived whole that can be referred to in action and communication. The differences between the rules of objective primacy, pragmatic primacy, symbolic primacy, and definitional primacy guarantee that no single behavioral run or object in a collectivity can be interpreted in the same sequence and in the same exact way in two systems at once. This preserves the integrity of the separate systems. But at the same time it requires that any sense of unity across objects with different interpretations, uniting a social definition, an economic situation, and an ecological situation, for example, must be created by deliberate public actions. Such action, of course, is precisely the kind of sanctioning imposition of combined information choices that has been described above, and that pervades the activity of daily life as indicated in the descriptions of the division of labor. These activities in turn, again because of the formal and semantic differences between the systems, reinforce consensus on each message source separately, preserving at once the collectivity and the infrastructure and the requirement for further deliberate action by coordinated individuals in the future. If we assume that some sort of collectivities are required in any community organization, we can see the formal differences between the systems, in this light, as structuring a second major area where free creative activity on the part of members of the community is not only allowed by its structure but is required.

Selection of the specific subset of elements of the several systems that enter into each behavioral complex can be attributed to a process implicit in the foregoing description of the formation of collectivities. To picture this process, imagine several sheets of blotting paper, each representing one information system, laid on top of one another. A behavioral complex can be thought of as a section passing through two or more of them, or more precisely, a stain that has spread from a central line passing through a point on each. The different properties of each sheet may make the edges of the "sandwich" irregular, but the central portion and some space of association around it, which is the part created by the sanctioning activities of concerned individuals, will be clear.

The linkages between elements in each system of information form the "fibers" along which the stain of inclusion into a behavioral complex is spread. Since tasks recur in always slightly different forms that embody elements of nearby related tasks, and since people are often dealt with for repeated tasks or for sequences of work in related tasks, any idea used to organize one event tends to be repeated and to be spread as the event itself is repeated and its outlines blur in time. When factional ideas are used to convey an understanding of reciprocal help in arranging to borrow an ox, it is natural for the same relationship to be chosen to borrow a plow in return. When such an idea is invoked to promise extra consideration in hiring short-term field labor, it is likely that the same or a related idea will be invoked, and thereby slightly reinterpreted, when longer-term labor is sought later in the year, and the circle of related ideas and work will continue to be invoked and expanded as long as the arrangements seem satisfactory. If arrangements are unsatisfactory, which they frequently may be, then the dissimilarity between two ideas or tasks is likely to furnish the basis for disavowing past promises. The configurations of each system contain potential natural limits that can be used to define, or redefine, the boundaries of each complex. As is indicated by the process of formation of the factional groups, there are relatively few areas of firm specific concepts to be associated with specific types of tasks—the central points of contact. Consensus becomes more ephemeral and more a matter of individual relationships as behaviors spread from these points.

Even though there is an obvious logical "fit" between the ideas at the center of such behavioral complexes and the tasks that they organize—such as the Sikh ideas of community and the coordination of water-use behaviors around irrigation facilities—this fit cannot be regarded as a primary explanation of linkages across systems. Elements of the conscious models, in particular, are obviously transmutable, and must take their meaning at any one time from precisely those behaviors that they organize. Could we imagine, for example, that an idea applied to a court case would not be rendered by us as an idea of conflict, or that an idea applied to wells would not be rendered as some form of cooperation? Language is full of terms from conscious sociological models whose meanings have changed as the circumstances of their employment have changed.

Recognized and Unrecognized Behaviors

The direct relationship between formal characteristics of the information systems and the detailed characteristics of behaviors and behavioral complexes permits a formulation, integral to the theory, of the methodology both of testing theoretical hypotheses and of analyzing practical problems in preparation for predicting or attempting to create changes affecting welfare. Since the judgments involved in formulating such policies often involve perceptions that are not defined within the village message sources—resting as they often do on comparisons between cultures and countries—they involve us in the complicated area of assessing local information systems for their contribution to behavioral patterns not recognized by those who use and maintain them. These problems require a technique for working "backwards"—from apparent behaviors to message sources rather than from message source to informational behavior and behavioral complexes.

The first step in analyzing a feature of a community that may be of interest is to determine whether all or part of it is a manifestation of one or more of the formal systems of information, a manifestation of some other systematic influence on human welfare or behavior, a combination of these, or none of them. The mode of analysis appropriate to the behavior, and the kinds of practical uses to which analysis can be applied, are different in each case.

Some systematic constraints on behavior may be found that are not message sources—or at least not similar enough to the present sources to warrant inclusion here. For example, epidemic disease complexes affect behavior and even the pattern of population. So does the skeletal and muscular configuration of the human body as it develops. Descriptive linguistics, chemistry, biochemistry, and genetics have all described systematically interrelated phenomena that affect behavior. They are not, however, the continuing products of conscious choices, and do not operate through cognitive mediation in the same way as do the systems described here.

Consider the problem of "development," or "underdevelopment" of a nation. Intuitively, the problem is that many nations have large populations who are quite poor. But the different ways of defining such poverty have very different implications, both theoretically and in terms of policy to change the condition. Although it is generally discussed in a frame of reference broader than specific villages and regions, this is an important matter upon which the present study has a definite bearing.

The shape that this problem of underdevelopment appears to take when phrased in terms of the multisystemic theory, and the policy recommendations that suggest themselves as leading to "development" in this framework, are rather different in a number of practical respects from the shape that it takes and the recommendations that it suggests in terms of the theoretical framework that has, until quite recently, exercised a preponderant influence both in economic aid planning in the United States and in internal central planning in India and elsewhere.

The "dualistic" theory identifies population, population density, capital, production (usually aggregated nationally), political organization, and ideological values as significant parameters of analysis. Using them, two broad "sectors" of society are defined: an industrial, scientific, "rational" sector with high per capita productivity; and an agricultural, "traditional" sector with low per capita productivity. When these coexist in one nation-state, they constitute a "dual economy."

Each socioeconomic system, as conceived in the dualistic theory, encompasses and directs its characteristic type of behavior, and each behavior perpetuates the system. It is widely held that traditional agriculture, equated with peasant agriculture in India, supports a population over and above what is required on a purely rational economic basis, a "hidden" surplus, which is permitted to exist by adherence to the traditional values, and which, in turn, produces or maintains the poverty, and thereby the rest of the traditional apparatus of the system. For example, the following is taken from Gerald Meier's remarks in his recent synthesizing text that reflects the work of many scholars who share this viewpoint (Meier 1964, pp. 44, 45).

> Unlike the social heritage with which Western countries entered the take-off stage, the social structure and value patterns in many poor

countries are still inimical to development. The structure of social relations tends to be hierarchical, social cleavages remain pronounced, and mobility among groups is limited. Instead of allowing an individual to achieve status by his own efforts and performance, his status may be simply ascribed to him, according to his position in a system of social classification—by age, lineage, clan, or caste. A value system that remains "tradition-oriented" also tends to minimize the importance of economic incentives, material rewards, independence, and rational calculation. . . . Even though they may have latent abilities, individuals may lack the motivations and the stimulations to introduce change; there may not be sufficiently large groups in the society who are "achievement-oriented," concerned with the future, and believers in the rational mastery of nature.

Given the sharp and thoroughgoing contrast between the two socioeconomic systems, the policies that suggest themselves are either to create an expanded industrial sector at the expense of the traditional agricultural system, which would involve a shift in population to urban centers (cf. Viner in Meier 1964, pp. 78–83), or to modify the traditional sector by such measures as birth control programs and expanded and often improved educational facilities (Meier, pp. 265–283). Dualistic economic theory has not encouraged the modification or improvement of agricultural production as such.

Beneath the discussions of values and organization, the basic approach of the dualistic theory to the definition of underdevelopment rests on the Western distinction between capital and labor. As was noted particularly in chapter 3, this is inappropriate to the ecology and economy of Shahidpur and, I presume, to most other Indian villages, in several important respects. It presupposes that people themselves are not "capital" or productive goods, in any important sense. The theory of surplus labor is but one explicit statement of this presupposition.

By contrast, neither "capital" nor "labor" served as explanatory variables in the present analysis. Each of the Western terms suggests elements from more than one information system, combined in unclear or obscure ways. "Labor" seems to involve some aspects of human behavior as part of the ecological productive system, some aspects of the division of labor, and some aspects of the priced labor as it appears in conventional market situations, all merged into one.

Similarly, "capital" combines some elements of the nonhuman populations in the ecology with controlled goods in the division of labor and with the prices that might be paid for some goods in the economy.

If we proceed system by system in Shahidpur, quite different variables suggest themselves to give form to our intuitive sense that the village represents an "underdeveloped," poor, community in some way. First, the systems of high organization can, in their nature, have little directive force or influence on particular patterns of productive behaviors, and they are observedly manipulated in pursuit of perceived competitive options. If they cannot direct particular behaviors, it follows that they cannot direct either productive or unproductive patterns of particular behavior. They are, therefore, not to be seen as essential or determinate elements in the definition of "underdevelopment," although they may provide important means of gaining cooperation in pursuit of new policies to remedy the condition.

The economic message source, too, seems to play no essential role in creating a condition we could see as underdevelopment. In Shahidpur the economic mechanisms clearly are ways of choosing between the exchange values offered by different ecological options, and they seem to be appropriately and efficiently adapted to that purpose. They are not constructed in such a way as to cause hidden consumption of basic factors of production. They do not constitute the productive options, nor do they determine their true productivity. We can easily conceive of the same market mechanism operating in a situation of great and increasing productivity, or in a situation of low or declining productivity.

Aspects of the division of labor may be more essential in underdevelopment. The quotation from Meier recalls suggestions that inequities in the distribution of wealth exist and can lead to decreasing or low productivity through the mismatching of capital and entrepreneurial ability. This has been argued in connection with large absentee landholders and insecure tenure for actual farmers as well as the "burden" of rural debt that was discussed in chapter 5. In Shahidpur, however, the pattern of control seems more to reflect the pattern of productive or managerial efficiency than to determine it. There are no such large absentee landlords; the rents seem reasonable and conducive of productive allocations of resources; and the farmers express a desire to acquire more debt rather than a desire to escape from the debt they have. While there is no reason to doubt that inequities exist and produce inefficiency from time to time and place to place in India, even in Shahidpur, as they do elsewhere, they are not conspicuous in the present case.

The division of labor in Shahidpur does, however, embody what we can regard as underdevelopment in another and important respect—namely, that each productive unit contains a large number of people. The village as a whole has two people per acre; households average seven members each, with farming groups considerably larger.

On the assumption that the division of labor reflects an efficient allocation of resources, the pattern of household populations and the overall large numbers of people can be seen as a managerial arrangement reflecting the basic structure of the ecology. It reflects the high reliance on human labor as a source of mechanical power when compared with draft animals. Animals and men together constitute almost the only power sources.

Although this structural difference can appear as low per capita productivity when cast into a Western frame of reference, it is important to realize that it does not involve either low productivity or low capitalization on other bases. The reported average yields in Shahidpur of wheat, maize, and cotton—approximately 27.5 maunds, 21 maunds, and 23 maunds per acre—compare favorably with the average reported American yields of 18.5, 45.2, and 6.0 maunds per acre, respectively, for the same crops (Bureau of the Census 1969; table 936).

The reported average farm value in the United States in 1964 was $51,000, and the average farm size was 352 acres (table 897). Despite the value per farm, obviously much higher than the average in Shahidpur, the value per acre held was just $146. This is far less than the value per acre in Shahidpur and is a second indication that the land in Shahidpur is more highly capitalized than average land in the United States. If we divide the same average United States farm value by the total "farm population," derived from the same source, the average value is $5,500 per capita. This compares with about $1,500 of equivalent capital value per capita (at the legal exchange rate in 1964) in Shahidpur, according to the rough estimates of chapter 5. That is, the same measures that show the capitalization per acre in Shahidpur to be higher than in the United States show the capitalization per person to be lower.

In the mechanized Western farms, humans primarily provide skill and knowledge to direct the use of energy from nonhuman sources. In Shahidpur, there is less nonhuman power to direct, while human energy itself looms larger as a direct motive force. Heavy reliance on direct human labor is precisely what permits the intensive capitalization that is tied to mixed cropping and ecological self-sufficiency at the village level. The mixed cropping in turn permits a settled population to live on local resources, and this provides a power source that can be readily applied to the many integrated farming tasks in a continuing cycle. The heavy use of human labor goes along with the simple but flexible tool array and the use of draft animals, which themselves require constant attention and regular care.

The ecological system, as a system of low entropy, can be readily altered at many points, and it obviously has been altered continually over time. Accordingly, to provide a corrective to underdevelopment, the general policy that suggests itself is to guide future alteration toward changes that lower the reliance on human labor. This follows if we assume that all the energy now used is necessary, and that a reduction of energy inputs would require that new inputs be developed or located to substitute for the human labor removed from the system.

There are many possible sources of replacements of human power. These might include improved breeds of cattle to provide more energy on the same fodder, improved forms of traditional tools, new labor-saving machines like the mason's threshing machine, new crop varieties that produce the same or more yield with less labor inputs, and labor-saving ways of controlling weeds or pests. Each possibility has its attendant dangers. Satisfactory solutions to the many specific problems in realizing the overall policy without incurring offsetting penalties, such as pollution or increased economic insecurity, cannot be expected to come easily.

Since Independence in 1947, the central government in India has tended to keep for itself a great deal of the power of the highly centralized, almost monolithic, colonial government. This government has directed its attention toward a development effort which, partly in response to the interests of the "westernized intellectuals and industrialists" who guided the Congress party through Independence (Rosen 1967, pp. 121 ff.), has been defined substantially in the terms of the dualistic theory. Private and government firms have been coordinated within a general development scheme under a strictly controlled and comprehensive system of licensing that extends into all aspects of the acquisition of resources, production, and sales. The central policy aim toward which the activities of this formidable apparatus was directed was the development of the industrial sector, which itself centered on the iron and steel industry. Agricultural policies were designed to support industrialization by assuring a supply of low-cost food grains to the urban poor. Beyond price stabilization, the types of programs developed were subsistence oriented rather than development oriented. This general strategy came under increasingly critical review as difficulties developed in both agriculture and industry. In the early 1960s a series of measures were undertaken to strengthen government control over distribution. This did not ameliorate the situation, and dissatisfaction increased. In 1965 a new strategy for development was announced, a program that began to shift primary emphasis to agriculture as a direct recipient of government aid rather than an indirect recipient of this aid through industrialization. "The new strategy, advanced by the Food and Agriculture Ministry, stood in striking contrast to the basic assumptions of past policies. Whereas the older approach had relied mainly on more intensive utilization of traditional inputs, e.g., reclamation of cultivable wasteland and the more efficient application of underemployed labor, the Ministry now urged the utmost importance of applying 'scientific techniques and knowledge of agricultural production at all stages' " (Frankel 1969, pp. 693–694). The new "knowledge" revolved around hopes of spectacular gains from new seeds, in the context of labor-intensive package programs for introduction in irrigated areas (pp. 694–698). Incentives include credit, organized through cooperatives, and the services of the development officers.

This modified policy has encountered difficulties on many levels, from disappointing performance of the new varieties, through political defeats of the Congress party (including the action resulting in the partition of former Punjab State into the new Punjabi and Hindi states of Punjab and Hariana). In response, there has been a general relaxation of the licensing controls that have been used to administer plans in the past, and greater sensitivity toward the felt needs of farmers and other rural groups. But despite these many changes, no specific policy of altering the balance between human and nonhuman sources of power in agriculture has been formulated. The conceptual framework, however relaxed, is still that of the dualistic theory.

The multisystemic theory and its policies suggest many activities that are similar to, some that are identical to, and some that are absolutely distinct from those now pursued.

The effort to introduce new seeds in the package programs was coordinated with an increased program of research publication in agronomy and agricultural economy, including studies of crop rotation and comparisons of the ecological characteristics and economic gains not only of new crops but of many indigenous varieties as well. Such studies are significant for both theories and both concepts of development. Their results can be applied either to the intensification of agriculture in accordance with central policy, or it could be applied to the selection of crops that fit with a labor pattern relying on more nonhuman power sources than are now used.

The development of fertilizers, irrigation facilities, and better cattle, like the development of better seeds, would also have a logical place in a development program under either theory, though, again, with shifting emphasis. The strategy of the Ministry of Food and Agriculture to concentrate development—in the form of "package programs" involving seed, fertilizer, irrigation support, and instructions—in the irrigated areas flows logically and plausibly from a policy conceived in terms of sectors. It is a way to increase productivity of the agricultural sector in pursuit of the realization that "production of an agricultural surplus (is) the key to industrialization" (P. C. Mahalanobis in Frankel 1969, p. 705). It does not, however, follow equally well from the multisystemic definition of the problem as one that changes the structure of power sources in the ecology—indeed, it could be counterproductive. Shahidpur's block was one of the leading irrigation areas and one of the first recipients of the new factors, in the form of irrigation loans and fertilizers. Although other factors, such as the new sugar mill, doubtless made their contribution, there does not seem to be any reason to doubt that these new factors did contribute to the rising labor demand, which is reflected in the rapidly rising rates for daily field help. Other things being equal, such an imbalanced labor price ought to result in villagers spending more of their time working within the village area —more local population on an average day-to-day basis.

Package programs designed to diminish underdevelopment as conceived of in multisystemic terms—as a problem of the structure of farm ecology rather than of the productivity of the agricultural "sector" vis-à-vis the industrial sector—ought to have a component of power inputs. That is, each package ought to contain some device or set of devices to assure that the increased power that it almost always requires can be provided without a proportional increase in the human power that will be needed. One device suggested by improvements already in use is improved bearings and wheels for ox-carts (suggested by a current type of cart utilizing a salvaged automobile differential and tires. Such carts are reported to carry thirty maunds with the same bullocks normally required for eight maunds in a conventional cart). For another instance, combination linkages could enable electric or diesel engines for pumping to be applied to other purposes as well. Farmers with tractors now regularly use them as pumping engines and for threshing, while some others have attached their bullock-powered well wheels to fodder-choppers, so the principle is well established. The mason's thresher is conceived along the same lines. Still other devices suggest themselves on the basis of Western experience, such as better bushings, better and cheaper lubricants, and better sharpening equipment for all cutting edges. It was reported to me recently (1969) that delicensing was followed by the opening of two factories producing small combines and one producing tractors in Punjab. It is difficult to guess what the limits might be on the kinds of labor-saving devices that could be developed under the encouragement of formal policy that recognized their place in village productive activity.

Summary

Differences in entropy and in sanction are interrelated with the different "rules of use" followed in manifesting each system of information. Each rule of use can be followed, as the system is manipulated, at many different levels of general competence or sophistication, and for very different individual purposes, without in any way compromising its integrity or losing its specific and unique character in delineating behaviors.

At each level and in pursuit of each purpose, each system of information delineates behavior by providing socially recognized options that can be manifested in a spatiotemporal setting. By a symbolic act indicating the choice of an element in one system of information, the onset of a behavior is demarcated, and by an act indicating choice of another element in the system, that behavior is terminated.

The different rules of use permit behaviors from more than one system to "overlap" in their spatiotemporal manifestations. One can, either immediately, or in retrospect, or in prospect, attribute behaviors from as many as all of the information systems to a given sequence of actions—subject, of course, to the logic of the systems themselves.

Overlapping behaviors have been defined as "behavioral complexes." Many behavioral complexes are ephemeral, but some are well-established and enduring. A collectivity, as described here, can be conveniently regarded as a behavioral complex about whose character there is some degree of consensus. The consensus may involve a few people, or, for example, factions and religious groups. It may be established far beyond the village community.

Most of what is normally called behavior consists of behavioral complexes, insofar as it comes within the ken of the behavioral sciences (as opposed to the physical sciences or to medicine). The concept of a behavioral complex, therefore, provides a general key to the systematic analysis of matters of policy and to analytic problems, both of which involve segmentation of activity and prediction of the observable states of the analyzed segments.

Some kinds of observations may be described as "intuitive." They are phrased in undefined "ordinary" language, whose implications are not carefully or systematically set down, and they rely on such expectations about human society as are normally embodied in the cultural backgrounds of the author of the description. Such descriptions generally lack operational clarity.

One important example of an intuitive or naïve observation is the observation that India, with a large group of other countries, is "poor," otherwise called "underdeveloped." Numerous, more rigorous and systematic sets of concepts have been developed to give clearer and more operational form to this simple observation; one of the more important of these is the concept of a "dual economy."

The concept of a dual economy is essentially an elaborated version of the organic model discussed briefly in the Introduction. Each of the two "sectors" that exist side by side in a dualistic state constitutes an integral organic structure exhibiting most of the characteristics attributed by Durkheim to the "social division of labor." Each constitutes an integrated and self-perpetuating unit consisting of an economy, a system of production, a system of social organization, and a system of values.

The dualistic theory has apparently provided the principal rationale for the planning policies of the government of India in the recent past, just as it formed an important aspect of foreign aid planning in the United States. It is notable, for example, that W. W. Rostow, one of the major contributors to the current form of theory, served in several important advisory capacities under Presidents Kennedy and Johnson. Since only the "modern" industrial sector was deemed capable of substantial growth in response to the availability of new capital inputs, the theory articulated a system of specific policies designed to advance the development of heavy industry while, in effect, fighting only a holding action in agriculture.

When the naïve perception that India—including Shahidpur—is "poor" is cast into the present framework, it takes a different form from that which it takes in the dualistic theory. The policy implications that pertain to replacing "underdevelopment" with "development" differ correspondingly. Underdevelopment is seen not as a pervasive quality of an organic system, but rather as an aspect of the structure of one particular information source—the ecology. It consists in the low per capita ratios of goods and productivity that are the logical correlates of heavy reliance on human beings as means of producing mechanical power rather than as guides and supervisors of power derived from nonhuman sources. This view of underdevelopment gives no reason to assume that development cannot take place readily and at low cost in peasant agriculture. On the contrary, it suggests numerous specific means by which the balance of human and nonhuman power might be favorably altered without the massive inputs of capital and the long delays between inception and fruition that have characterized schemes for developing heavy industry (cf. Johnson 1966).

The difference between development policies and projects suggested by information-system and dualistic theories is an important indication of the extent and scope of differences that extend beyond policy into all phases of predictive and analytic activity. Any apparent phenomenon of behavioral significance can be compared with the information systems, behaviors, and behavioral complexes revealed by an analysis of the present sort. The phenomenon may be of policy significance to those in the society under study, or may be only of theoretical significance to anthropologists, perhaps on a point affecting the comparison of this theory with some other.

Predictions based on the analysis of information systems of a particular community can point to results of the unmodified operation of the systems and behaviors discovered, or they may point to expected results from deliberate attempts to modify the systems by inputs designed on the basis of the analysis, such as the new ecological inputs suggested to achieve a restructuring of the "underdeveloped" ecologies of villages like Shahidpur.

Analyses in pursuit of policy are just one type of operationally clear analysis the framework permits, and development of new information items in pursuit of policy goals is but one type of operationally clear prediction that it suggests.

Chapter X

Social Organization

*I*t is always in order for one mariner to report to others the reefs and shoals he saw on a specific voyage, and sirens he did not heed. Similarly it would not be far amiss to remark on some expectable problems of our own sort of adventure that have been avoided in this study, and to suggest what the route seems to promise.

To my mind, the anthropological parallel to the song of the sirens is the commonplace that theory is derived in some indirect way from data, but is in its own nature fundamentally unlike data; and the allied belief that "methodology" as an area of concern is different from both theory and fact. This three-way split leaves speculation without substance, observation without explanation, and description without identification. If this trichotomy had guided the present study, the concept of an information source would have lost most of its value, for one of its great advantages is that it points both to a precise range of phenomena and to a pattern of what linguists call "discovery procedures."

A message source, when its implications for behavior are laid out, is not theory *or* fact, but rather theory *and* fact. When we speak of one of the village message sources in terms of its formal properties of entropy and organization, we are only using descriptive terms of more general relevance, potentially useful in many other settings. We are not speaking of any more or less "factual" a thing than if we use the local term: religion, kinship, and so forth; nor are we speaking in any greater or lesser detail. We are, more accurately, speaking in two different ways about the same thing.

One of the principal reasons for adding the general terms to the local terms is precisely to indicate the method by which the thing named and described is to be discovered. The theoretical concepts of "freedom of choice" and organization indicate that it is patterns of relationships among choices we are to look at, while the concept of "information" itself suggests that these choices, and the patterns, are to be consciously recognized and contextually situated by those who make them. Indeed, one of the methodological and descriptive procedures that I used consistently—and indicated specifically in describing the division of labor and the kinship and political models —was to put myself in the way of making these choices as a villager would, tracing the form of the systems by tracing the pattern of factors that affect the choice, or use, of each of its elements (a method that might be described as "observant participation" rather than "participant observation"). A second method was to ask directly for the relevances: to ask, in unambiguous contexts, what affects thus and such an action, and why. And finally, a procedure systematically used was to play the fool, to "crosswire" the system by using elements from one system as if they pertained to choices defined in the context of another. Even though the villagers naturally were not aware of the formal criteria for differentiating one information system from another, they responded operationally to questions and silly suggestions with words to the same effect: "That is another matter," or "That is not important here." An understanding of the formal properties of information systems (theory) is integral to our ability to trace their use in all aspects of behavior (fact) and to establish procedures for validating our analysis by detached observation and by interacting with informants and knowing how to apply their responses to our problems (method). Theory, fact, and method, as they pertain to the use of information systems in Shahidpur, are three aspects of the analysis of one phenomenon.

On the basis of the integration of theory, fact, and method, in speaking of those six information systems and their use, it is possible to see a parallel between certain important practical problems faced and resolved by the villagers of Shahidpur and certain equally important "theoretical" problems in the social sciences. Within the village these are the problems that arise for those who would use their cultural resources as fully as possible while seeking as much freedom as possible from the restraints the systems impose on them. They are the problems of reconciling self-interest with the social good, freedom for oneself with control of others, and social stability with social adaptability.

Even though these problems, and others like them, obviously pit two aspects of every individual against each other, as well as pit the individual against "society" or the community in some general sense, they have been conceptualized in Western social science largely in terms of the dichotomy between individual and society alone. Unfortunately, the form of the conceptualization has largely been one of a conflict between two overdrawn or partial positions— the one concentrating on individuals and seeing them as free and creative, the other concentrating on society and seeing it as integrated and deterministic. The great modern proponents of each of the positions in the social sciences are G. H. Mead on the side of the individual and Durkheim and Weber on the side of society. Each of these men, however, operated in a much broader tradition of debate going back to the beginnings of the nineteenth century. Mead drew support from the ideas of perception and learning of the American philosophical pragmatists, from biological evolution, and ultimately from Immanuel Kant's conception of the individual basis of what he called "practical reason" and morality. Weber, and more obviously Durkheim, by contrast, relied upon the tradition of sociological positivism derived from Comte's "organic" state, coupled with a Spencerian conception of social evolution that in turn went back to Hegel's concept of a disembodied and deterministic "world reason" that acted through history regardless of individual minds or wills.

The upshot is that Mead's description of "emergent evolution" comprehensively portrays the manipulative ways individuals create their roles and collective memberships by symbolic processes, but he does not describe the nature or structure of the symbols used. Durkheim, and those who have come after him, provides a comprehensive analysis of societal symbol systems and their use in such stereotyped activities as rituals, but his Hegelian idea that these all form one system in a community that impresses itself on individuals by its own "authority" leaves us no useful conception of individual behavior. These peculiarly complementary but opposed positions have been carried into social anthropology without substantial modification, even though the conflict between them has come under increasingly critical review in recent years. Boas's conception of culture as the material and practical embodiment of mental states was basically Kantian, and suffered from the same ultimate weakness in dealing with extra-individual order as did Mead's more psychological position. Modern "Durkheimians," like Max Gluckman and C. Levi-Strauss, have added an "idealistic" theory of theories—the idea that theory is a logically integrated system or network of statements that *is* inherently different and remote from fact. This view, of course, only further reduces the capacity of their theory to deal with individual action.

At a practical level, in Shahidpur, the conflicting demands for freedom and control and for order and flexibility are all articulated and met through message sources. Each source, within itself, provides areas of freedom and of constraint, resources to use, ways to control useful objects, and ways to be controlled in turn. At a higher level, the relative information values of the several systems guarantee that order in behavior is never determinate and always entails—even requires—free choice and resourcefulness.

If we recognize that the theoretical conflict between individual and societal orientations reflects such practical conflicts between individual freedom and control as we find in Shahidpur, then we must be prepared to recognize that message sources as items of theory provide a middle ground between the two theoretical camps—a way of recognizing the central concerns, and positive contributions, of each without being forced by extraneous "theoretical" considerations to reject those of the other. Leaving aside Durkheim's too simple concept of a straight-line social causality, we can easily see an information source as a system of general categories that embodies patterns for behavior and yet is "a reality *sui generis*" that is not simply a sum of individual opinion, and actions (Durkheim 1957, p. 29). At the same time, however, we can look at the use of these systems in creating collective behaviors and agree with Mead (as paraphrased succinctly by Anselm Strauss) that "group membership is thus a symbolic, not a physical, matter, and the symbols which arise during the life of the group are, in turn, internalized by the members and affect their individual acts" (Strauss 1956, xxii).

On a wider scale, the concept of a message source has an obvious bearing on those issues in social and moral philosophy and in the philosophy of science that frame the disputes between Mead and Durkheim, while in a more restricted compass it can influence the relationships between the positions in social anthropology and other fields that have been shaped by the larger arguments. In this sense, the concept, in the form presented here, is "new" only in the narrow sense in which a single specific crop or tool might be new to Shahid-pur's ecology, or a theological interpretation to its religion. It is here where there was nothing "objectively" like it before. But its context and utility is derived from ideas and issues developed within the field long before its advent, by the working of many minds, with much care, over a long period of time.

Appendix

Anthropological Background to the Study

*T*he theoretical framework used in this study incorporates responses to many developments throughout anthropology in this century. These developments are at what may seem to be isolated points. But the more they are examined, the more clearly it will appear that the isolation exists not for empirical reasons but because of unwarranted conceptions accepted from the past without adequate consideration, conceptions that are in fact inappropriate to the needs of social theory in today's world. The relevant developments have been matters of both commission and omission. They have consisted in the persistent occurrence of recognized findings with no theoretical base and of recognized recurrent difficulties in theory without clear empirical consequences. They were, generally speaking, the same developments that led Leach to see a need for "rethinking" anthropology (1961), and Schneider and others to propose a departure from attempts to find "total system models" and seek instead a "model of defined parts" (1965b, p. 78)—which may be one way to describe what has been done here. Pressure has been building for a restructuring of our thinking for some time, and the outline of the present theory has already begun to emerge. But it could not be fully articulated so long as those who tried to advance it conceived of theory itself on a pattern that obscured the differences between essentially different classes of phenomena with radically different relations to behavior.

One major focus of the general readjustment has been in the complex evolution of social structural theory proper. It is illustrated by Leach's conclusion that the Sinhalese village he studied was "a society in which locality and not descent forms the basis of corporate grouping" (1968, p. 301)—that the composition of family farming groups first reflects ecological and economic adjustments, and secondly is rationalized in terms of the putative "prescriptions" for kinship groups. This spelled out more fully on a largescale analysis what had previously been suggested for residence in Polynesian kinship groups by the complementary analyses both of Ward Goodenough (1956) and of Raymond Firth (1957). It challenged the widely held conception, deriving from Spencer and Comte and inherited directly through Durkheim and Radcliffe-Brown, that social structures alone embody and control patterns of behavior, and it opened two major doors to the present theory. It established, within the context of the modern literature, that social structure was manipulated in behavior, not determinative of it, and it also implied that social structure was but one of several factors that behavior reflected. When social structure is seen as a totality encompassing and determining behavior, social structural theorists have to argue that different, nonstructural factors do not similarly control or influence behavior. But to see social structure as Firth and Leach suggest, as a conceptual model or system of rules applied after other forces have been at work, implies recognition of nonstructural factors affecting the order of behavior. So conceived, social structural analyses should complement, not conflict with, other analyses.

Similar suggestions made their appearance in economic and ecological studies. Clifford Geertz, in *Agricultural Involution* (1966), follows a pattern earlier established in Murphy and Steward's (1955) description of the responses of small communities to imposed opportunities for new forms of trade. He describes interplay between colonial policy, ecology, and economics that enforced new patterns of behavior and workaday activity, which were in time reflected in new forms of social structure and culture. Michael Moerman's (1968) monographic account of "peasant choice" in an agricultural village in northern Thailand points up the same sort of dynamic and changing relationship between the technological and economic opportunities and resources and pays particular attention to its implication for a theory of behavior. Although he emphasizes that manipulations in the ecology and economy are guided by seemingly enduring "cultural values," he is emphatic in portraying the natives as "cultural sharpies" manipulating both cultural ideals and material resources to suit their individual purposes. So described, the actor is a creative force in his own right, like the "rational man" of economic theory. Moerman's view closely parallels the conception expressed as a positive thesis by Theodore Schultz in his analysis of economics in Indian agriculture (1964). It is clearly implied in his conclusion that education is one of the most potent factors to invest in, to bring about change in the rural economy and agricultural system (pp. 205–206). These developments reinforce the need for structural theory to include a description of manipulated cultural systems that can bring social structure into explicitly defined perspective with other systems or entities with similar functions in relation to behavior, and they add a direct stress on behavior itself that extends the concerns reflected in the more esoteric structural studies.

In what is now called "symbolic anthropology," analysts like Max Gluckman and Victor Turner provided accounts of behavior that fill out the picture still further. In elaborate and convincing detail they showed social structural themes to be represented over and over in a vast array of interrelated forms of ritual and in the daily usages that ritual shades into: standardized usages, old saws, significant phrases, manners, placement of utensils, and so forth. The list of potentially "symbolic" elements that can be used is endless, one feels. Whether the theme was that of a king as the embodiment of tribal cohesion and morality (Gluckman 1963) or the more abstract concepts of ritual and sexual purity, pollution, neutrality, fecundity, and barrenness (Turner 1968), these analyses demonstrated the conscious attention people pay to bringing overt behaviors into line with an apparent requirement of consistency in explicitly and openly representing widely shared social ideas, down to the smallest details of individual actions. They documented something for social structure that paralleled what had long been established in ecology, economics, technology, and several other areas, and they removed some of the mystery of the relationship between social structure and behavior that had shrouded Durkheim's idealistic determinism.

For the record, I should say that I see no reason to assume, in reading these studies (as Bateson at times seems to assume in his analyses, which are closely analogous to Turner's), that the social structural conception a given behavior may represent does in fact control that behavior. Not only does the evidence of ecological and economic influence on detailed behavior weigh against such an assumption, with the documentation that Schultz and others produce (Paglin 1965; Neale 1962), but direct accounts give impressive evidence of choices made between different social structural conceptions to be represented in any given segment of activity. For example, Geertz, in 1957, provided a brief study of a conflict between two politico-religious groups—one Islamicly oriented, the other "Javanese," Marxist, and anti-Moslem—each of whom attempted to claim the deceased as a member in order to use the funeral to advance their conceptions.

More recently, and closer to the geographical area of Shahidpur, Cristoph von Furer Haimendorf edited a volume of studies of social mobility (and social activity) along the border between the South Asian Hindu area and its neighboring Ceylonese and Tibetan Buddhist cultures. These studies confirm graphically what was suggested by Ibbetson many years before. Ibbetson (1916) proposed a regular sequence of castes that any given group might go through in the course of time in a village, starting at the lowly position of sweeper and moving up through each caste—each of whose occupation traditionally requires a more valuable basic capital good—to farmer (pp. 3, 4). He had noticed that many groups in the villages of north India claim more than one caste, and he drew the obvious conclusion that the system is regularly manipulated. Haimendorf, Rosser, and the others in the volume go beyond Ibbetson in pointing out the rapidity of change, and in pointing out that it occurs at an individual family level as well as at the level of larger corporate village groups. In addition, the examples from the border regions show people moving from positions in a Buddhist milieu to positions in a Hindu one, and sometimes back again, or back and forth as opportunities warrant. In such cases, no credibility can be attached to the claim naturally made by a person moving from one caste position to another: that they have "really" always been whatever they are becoming. The clarity with which the technique of looking at border areas exposes the process of manipulation leads Rosser, in one of the essays, to draw a sharp line between the "static stereotype of caste" as an ideological model people use, and the "system of status and power" in which actual people operate with the stereotype as it may suit them. The manipulative process is so clear to Rosser that he concludes that in societies whose system of status and power is highly stratified, with great differences in power and little real opportunity to alter one's position, any one of a wide variety of ideologies would be equally serviceable, "from the caste system to the divine right of kings" (p. 136). The ideology, in his view, merely "reinforces" and is "not a vital characteristic of" the system of economic and political power (p. 136).

Rosser's distinction recalls and adds a measure of clarity to Firth's similar but more general distinction between social structure and social organization, and F. G. Bailey's distinction between "structure" and the "social field" it affects (1960, p. 9). It also recalls the recent conclusion of D. M. Schneider, in analyzing American kinship, that the kinship system was a "cultural system," a phenomenon of a different order, different in kind, from patterns of behavior (1968, pp. 7, 9 ff).

Manipulation of social structure by natives to suit their purposes—purposes that may be defined by reference to matters other than structure—is compatible with the presence of multiple structural models. Manipulation implies choice, and multiple models provide choices (although choices can also, logically, be made between parts of models and between interpretations of models). Evidence of multiple models is widespread, even though (again because of the influence of the deterministic conception of theory) the orientation toward choice of models does not always accompany it as a theoretical perspective.

From Africa come many instances of age grades "crosscutting" lineage systems, and of household organization involving members of lineal groups in a way that cannot be predicted from the lineal rules. In India, there are repeated analyses which speak of the faction organization of a village as crosscutting kinship; of religion and caste that sometimes coincide and sometimes do not; of political organization at higher levels that has no regular relation to caste or religious organization in villages; and, finally, of obvious discrepancies between the stereotypic occupational model involved in the various forms of the jajmani system and the actual occupational order. F. G. Bailey made an important move in the present direction by recognizing that such irregular relations are not merely aspects of one underlying structure, whose real connection can be shown by improved or more abstract theory. He described them instead as representing "incompatible" social structures. They are incompatible because a person's relation to another in terms of one structure does not determine his relationship in terms of another (1960, pp. 7, 8). He also recognized that such incompatible systems indicate the "need to see individuals not as passive actors exhibiting for our benefit regularities in behavior, but as actors who may not only choose between systems but may attempt to twist and amend these systems to their own advantage" (p. 271). From the point of view of native choice, we can easily see the social advantage to opportunistic, manipulative actors in having such incompatible structures. They allow a freedom of action and a freedom to combine systems of unrelated role conceptions that a single model would not allow, even while each separate relation may remain perfectly clear and well defined.

These formulations, and others too scattered to draw together here, all indicate a breakthrough in the line that had been drawn between "savage" societies, or savage behavior, and our own. To see the behavior of Indian peasants or African tribesmen as responding to multiple systems, and to see the peasants or tribesmen as having a limited creative role in each—ecology, social structure, economics, ritual, and so on—is to see them essentially as we ourselves operate in our own societies. A complete theory embodying this view will be the whole of which the present study is a part. In the end, it will be able to document what we have long felt, and now label the "psychic unity" of man. The whole promises greater generality and explanatory power than other formulations which distinguish some type of "savage thought" from our own, or which assume that peasants and tribesmen respond to "laws" or motivational stimulae we ourselves would not respond to under similar circumstances.

The present concept of a message source is a generalized analytical model that applies to the alternative social systems Bailey recognized as well as to economic and ecological structures whose relation to behavior is essentially similar, and which are similarly "twisted and amended" by individuals pursuing their purposes. The related concept of a constructed message, the vehicle of such manipulations, is a generalized model that applies to such symbolic activities as Gluckman and Turner have described, as well as to communications by means of market transactions referring to the economic system, and communications by similarly detailed overt and consciously directed actions defined by other sources.

Bibliography

Bailey, F. G.
   1957   *Caste and the Economic Frontier.* Manchester: Manchester University Press.
   1960   *Tribe, Caste, and Nation.* Manchester: Manchester University Press.
Barth, Frederick
   1959   Segmentary Opposition and the Theory of Games: A Study of Pathan Organization. *Journal of the Royal Anthropological Institute of Great Britain and Ireland* 89:5–21.
   1966   Models of Social Organization. Occasional Paper No. 23, *Royal Anthropological Institute of Great Britain and Ireland.*
Bateson, G.
   1958   Naven. 2d ed. Stanford: Stanford University Press.
Belshaw, Cyril
   1956   *Traditional Exchange and Modern Markets.* Englewood Cliffs, N.J.: Prentice-Hall.
Bennett, Robert L.
   1967   "Surplus" Labor and Agricultural Development—Facts and Theories. Comment, *American Economic Review* 57:194–202.
Beteille, Andre
   1965   *Caste, Class, and Power.* Berkeley and Los Angeles: University of California Press.
Biedelman, Thomas O.
   1959   *A Comparative Analysis of the Jajmani System.* Ann Arbor, Michigan: Association for Asian Studies, Monograph No. 8.
Boserup, Ester
   1965   *The Conditions of Agriculture Growth.* Chicago: Aldine.
Buchler, Ira A., and Henry Selby
   1968   *Kinship and Social Organization: An Introduction to Theory and Method.* New York: Macmillan Company.

Bureau of the Census (U.S.A.)
  1969   *The American Almanac: The U.S. Book of Facts and Information* (being) *The Statistical Abstract of the U.S.* New York: Grosset and Dunlap.
Caprihan, P. P.
  1962a *Assessment Report of the Rupar Tehsil (Ambala District).* Chandigarh: Controller of Printing and Stationery of Punjab.
  1962b *Statements Relating to the Assessment Report of Rupar Tehsil.* Chandigarh: Controller of Printing and Stationery of Punjab.
Codere, Helen
  1968   Money-Exchange Systems and a Theory of Money. *Man* 3:557–577.
Conklin, H.
  1964   Ethnogenealogical Method. In *Explorations in Cultural Anthropology*, ed. Ward H. Goodenough. New York: McGraw-Hill.
Cook, Scott
  1966   The Obsolete Anti-Market Mentality: A Critique of the Substantive Approach to Economic Anthropology. *American Anthropologist* 68:323–345.
Darling, Malcolm
  1947   *The Punjab Peasant In Prosperity and Debt.* London: Oxford University Press.
Das, Tarak Chandra
  1939   Clan Monopoly of Personal Names Among the Purum Kukis. *Man* 39:3–7.
  1945   *The Purums: An Old Kuki Tribe of Manipur.* Calcutta: University of Calcutta.
Dayal, Rajbans, with Gurmel Singh and R. C. Sharma
  1967   Growing of Legume and Cereal Mixture Under Dry Farming Conditions. *Indian Journal of Agronomy* 12:126–131.
Duesenberry, James S.
  1967   *Income, Saving, and the Theory of Consumer Behavior.* New York: Oxford University Press.
Durkheim, Emile
  1957   *The Elementary Forms of the Religious Life.* 4th ed. London: George Allen & Unwin, Ltd.
Epstein, Scarlett
  1967   Productive Efficiency and Customary Systems of Rewards in Rural South India. In *Themes in Economic Anthropology*, Association of Social Anthropologists Monograph No. 6. New York: Tavistock.
Evans-Pritchard, E. E.
  1962   *Social Anthropology.* Evanston: Free Press.

Bibliography

Firth, Raymond
  1957   A Note on Descent Groups in Polynesia. *Man* 57:4–8.
Forde, D.
  1965   *African Worlds.* London: Oxford University Press.
Fortes, Meyer
  1962   Ritual and Office in Tribal Society. In *Essays On the Ritual of Social Relations,* ed. M. Gluckman. Manchester: Manchester University Press.
Frankel, Francine R.
  1969   India's New Strategy of Agricultural Development. *Journal of Asian Studies* 28:693–710.
Garfinkel, Harold
  1967   *Studies in Ethnomethodology.* Englewood Cliffs, N.J.: Prentice-Hall.
Geertz, Clifford
  1957   Ritual and Social Change: A Javanese Example. *American Anthropologist* 59:32–54.
  1966   *Agricultural Involution.* 2d printing. Berkeley and Los Angeles: University of California Press.
Gluckman, Max
  1963   *Order and Rebellion in Tribal Africa.* New York: The Free Press of Glencoe.
Goffman, Erving
  1959   *The Presentation of Self in Everyday Life.* Garden City, N.Y.: Doubleday, Anchor Books.
Goodenough, Ward
  1956   Residence Rules. *Southwestern Journal of Anthropology* 12:22–37.
Goody, Jack, editor
  1958   *The Development Cycle in Domestic Groups.* Cambridge Papers in Social Anthropology, No. 1. Cambridge: Cambridge University Press.
Haimendorf, Cristoph von Fürer, editor
  1966   *Caste and Kin in Nepal, India, and Ceylon.* New York: Asia Publishing House.
Hammel, Eugene A.
  1968   *Alternative Social Structures and Ritual Relations in the Balkans.* Englewood Cliffs, N.J.: Prentice-Hall
Herskovitz, Melville
  1952   *Economic Anthropology.* New York: W. W. Norton, Norton Library.
Ibbetson, Sir Denzil
  1916   *Punjab Castes.* Lahore: Punjab Government Press.

Ishwaran, K.
  1966   *Tradition and Economy in Village India.* New York: Humanities Press; and London: Routledge & Kegan Paul.
Johnson, William A.
  1966   *The Steel Industry of India.* Cambridge, Mass.: Harvard University Press.
Kluckhohn, Clyde, and D. Leighton
  1956   *The Navaho.* Cambridge, Mass.: Harvard University Press.
Kolenda, Pauline M.
  1963   Toward a Model of the Hindu Jajmani System. *Human Organization* 22:11–31.
Kroeber, A. L.
  1957   *The Nature of Culture.* Chicago: University of Chicago Press.
Kuhn, Thomas S.
  1962   *The Structure of Scientific Revolution.* Chicago: University of Chicago Press.
Leach, E. R.
  1951   The Structural Implications of Matrilateral Cross-Cousin Marriage. *Journal of the Royal Anthropological Institute of Great Britain and Ireland* 81:23–55.
  1961   *Rethinking Anthropology.* London School of Economics Monographs on Social Anthropology, No. 22.
  1962   What Would We Mean by Caste. In *Aspects of Caste in South India, Nepal, and Ceylon,* ed. E. R. Leach. Cambridge Papers in Social Anthropology, No. 2.
  1967   *The Structural Study of Myth.* Cambridge Papers in Social Anthropology, No. 4.
  1968   *Pul Eliya: A Village in Ceylon.* New York: Oxford University Press.
Leaf, Murray J.
  1963   "Age" in Purum Social Structure. Master's Paper, Department of Anthropology, University of Chicago.
Levi-Strauss, C.
  1955   The Structural Study of Myth. *Journal of American Folklore* 68:428–444.
  1960   On Manipulated Sociological Models. *Bijdragen* 1163.
  1962   Social Structure. In *Anthropology Today,* ed. Sol Tax. Chicago: University of Chicago Press.
  1966   *Totemism.* Boston: Beacon Press.
Macauliffe, Sir Max Arthur
  1963   *The Sikh Religion,* 6 vols. Bombay: S. Chand and Co., by arrangement with Oxford University Press.
McHugh, Peter
  1968   *Defining the Situation.* New York: Bobbs-Merrill Co.

Malinowski, B.
1935   *The Coral Gardens and Their Magic*. London and New York: American Book.
Meier, Gerald M.
1964   *Leading Issues in Development Economics*. New York: Oxford University Press.
Miller, James G.
1965   Living Systems: Basic Concepts. *Behavioral Science* 10:193–237.
Moerman, Michael
1968   *Agricultural Change and Peasant Choice in a Thai Village*. Berkeley and Los Angeles: University of California Press.
Murdock, G. P.
1949   *Social Structure*. New York: Macmillan.
Murphy, R. F., and Julian Steward
1955   Tappers and Trappers: Parallel Processes in Acculturation. *Economic Development and Culture Change* 4:335–355.
Nadel, S. F.
1951   *The Foundations of Social Anthropology*. London: Cohen and West.
Nash, Manning
1958   *Machine Age Maya*. Glencoe: Free Press.
1966   *Primitive and Peasant Economic Systems*. San Francisco: Chandler.
Neale, Walter C.
1962   *Economic Change in Rural India*. New Haven and London: Yale University Press.
Needham, Rodney
1958   A Structural Analysis of Purum Society. *American Anthropologist* 60:75–101.
Nie, Norman, Dale H. Bent, and C. Hadlai Hull
1970   SPSS: Statistical Package for the Social Sciences. New York: McGraw Hill.
Paglin, Morton
1965   Surplus Labor and Agricultural Development: Facts and Theories. *American Economic Review* 55:815–833.
1967   "Reply" to Bennett. *American Economic Review* 57:202–209.
Parsons, Talcott, and Edward A. Shils, editors
1959   *Toward a General Theory of Action*. Cambridge, Mass.: Harvard University Press.
Pillai, K. M.
1967   *Crop Nutrition*. London: Asia Publishing House.
Potter, David
1964   *Local Government in India*. London: G. Bell and Sons, Ltd.

Prashar, C. K.
   1965   Some Problems in Irrigated Lands. *Indian Journal of Agronomy* 10:18–22.
Punjab Government. Agricultural Information Service.
   1964   *Economic Cultivation of Cotton in Punjab*, Publication No. 170. Chandigarh: Controller of Printing and Stationery.
Punjab Government. Board of Economic Inquiry. Publications of the Economic and Statistical Organization.
   1953   *Family Budgets 1951–1952 of Eleven Cultivators in Punjab.* Pub. No. 23.
   1957   *Farm Accounts in the Punjab 1955–56.* Pub. No. 45.
   1961   *Farm Accounts in the Punjab 1958–59.* Pub. No. 72.
   1962   *Farm Accounts in the Punjab 1960–61.* Pub. No. 86.
Quine, W. V. O.
   1953   *From a Logical Point of View.* Cambridge, Mass.: Harvard University Press.
Radcliffe-Brown, A. R.
   1961   *Structure and Function in Primitive Society.* London: Cohen and West.
Radhakrishnan, K., and Charles A. Moore
   1967   *Sourcebook in Indian Philosophy.* Princeton: Princeton University Press.
Randhawa, M. S., and Prem Nath
   1957   *Farmers of India. Vol. 1: Punjab, Himachal Pradesh, Jammu and Kashmir.* New Delhi: Indian Council of Agricultural Research.
Read, Kenneth
   1959   Leadership and Consensus in New Guinea Society. *American Anthropologist* 61:425–436.
Reichard, Gladys
   1928   *Social Life of the Navaho Indians.* Columbia University Contributions to Anthropology, No. 7. New York: Columbia University.
Richards, A. I.
   1948   *Hunger and Work in a Savage Community.* Glencoe: Free Press.
Rivers, W. H. R.
   1968   *Kinship and Social Organization.* Oxford: Athlone Press.
Rosen, George
   1967   *Democracy and Economic Change in India.* Berkeley and Los Angeles: University of California Press.
Sahlins, Marshall
   1961   The Segmentary Lineage: An Organization of Predatory Expansion. *American Anthropologist* 63:322–345.

Bibliography

Sahlins, Marshall, and E. Service
  1960   *Evolution and Culture.* Ann Arbor: University of Michigan Press.

Schneider, David M.
  1965a Kinship and Biology. In *Aspects of the Analysis of Family Structure.* A. J. Coale, L. A. Fallers, Marion Levy, Schneider, and S. Tomkins, editors. Princeton: Princeton University Press.
  1965b Some Muddles in the Models. In *The Relevance of Models for Social Anthropology.* Association of Social Anthropologists Monograph, No. 1. New York: Taplinger.
  1968   *American Kinship: A Cultural Account.* Englewood Cliffs, N.J.: Prentice-Hall.

Schultz, Theodore
  1964   *Transforming Traditional Agriculture.* New Haven: Yale University Press.

Shannon, C., and Warren Weaver
  1964   *The Mathematical Theory of Communication.* Urbana: University of Illinois Press.

Singh, Narain
  undated (c. 1965) *Our Heritage.* Amritsar: The Chief Khalsa Diwan.

Steward, Julian
  1955   *Theory of Culture Change.* Urbana: University of Illinois Press.

Stocking, George N.
  1968   *Race, Culture and Evolution.* New York: Free Press.

Strauss, Anselm
  1956   *George Herbert Mead on Social Psychology.* Chicago: University of Chicago Press.

Tharp, W. H.
  1965   *The Cotton Plant.* Agriculture Handbook No. 178. Washington, D. C.: U.S.D.A.

Turner, Victor
  1966   Color Classification in Ndembu Ritual. In *Anthropological Approaches to the Study of Religion.* Association of Social Anthropologists Monograph No. 3. New York: Praeger.
  1968   *The Drums of Affliction.* Oxford: Clarendon Press.

Wallace, Anthony F. C., and John Atkins
  1960   The Meaning of Kinship Terms. *American Anthropologist* 62:58–80.

Ward, Barbara
  1965   Varieties of the Conscious Model: The Fisherman of South China. In *The Relevance of Models for Social Anthropology.* Association of Social Anthropologists Monograph No. 1. New York: Taplinger.

Watt, Bernice, and Annabel Merrill
1963   *Composition of Foods.* Agriculture Handbook No. 8. Washington, D.C.: U.S.D.A.
Wiener, Norbert
1961   *Cybernetics.* Cambridge, Mass.: M.I.T. Press.
Wiser, William
1939   *The Hindu Jajmani System.* Lucknow: Lucknow Publishing House.
Wittgenstein, Ludwig
1965   *Philosophical Investigations.* New York: Macmillan.
Wolf, Eric
1966   *Peasants.* Englewood Cliffs, N.J.: Prentice-Hall.
Yadava, J. S.
1968   Factionalism in a Haryana Village. *American Anthropologist* 70:898–910.
Yalman, Nur
1967   *Under the Bo Tree.* Chicago: University of Chicago Press.

Index

abadi: defined, 28, 65; two sides of, 65; map of, 65; and flooding, 70
Absentee landowners, 81, 85, 91, 253
Agricultural development loans, 18
Agricultural labor: done by Goldsmiths, 94; done by Potters, 96; done by Water-carrier, 97; done by Cotton-ginners, 98; Harijans involved in, 91, 102, 104; done by Sweepers, 103; wage rates, 125, 138–140. *See also* Labor
Agricultural policies, 256–257
akhandpat ritual, 159, 218
Alliance theory, 171
Ambala: rainfall, 16
Ambala District: rainfall, 16; tehsil a subdivision of, 18
Amrit, 153, 154
Amritsar: Golden Temple in, 155; ni-hang gurdwara in, 158
Anandpur Sahib: Baisakhi day celebration at, 159
Ancestral property, 74–75, 77, 184–185
Arjuna, 150, 151, 152
Atkins, John, 170
Augury: and castes, 199

Bagpipes: of Sweeper, 103
Bailey, F. G., 6, 17, 271, 272
Baisakhi day, 153, 159
Bajra: cultivation of linked to Hindu-ism, 216, 217
Balmik, 103. *See also* Sweeper caste
Banks: villagers avoid saving in, 127
Barber caste, 94–95; village census fig-ures, 51; houses of, 66, 67; household size and structure, 73; role in mar-riage ritual, 190
Barley: distribution over land types, 38; as fodder, 39; grown with gram, 39

Barns, 68, 69, 71, 75
barsheen, 40
Barth, Frederick: generative theory, 6
batai rent, 121
behairi ritual, 191, 192–193, 219
Behavior, 230–261; locus of interaction of message sources, 14; relationship of religious model to, 164, 167; choices of, 177; as symbolic process, 177, 228, 229; sometimes ordered by caste, 202; defined in relation to conscious socio-logical models, 226; and sanctions, 227–229; relation to message source, 231; systematic constraints on, 250; assessing contributions of information systems to, 250. *See also* Behavioral complexes; Behavioral situations; Col-lectivities
Behavioral complexes, 248–249, 250, 259. *See also* Collectivities
Behavioral situations, 246–250
Bhagavad Gita, 150, 154
bhai: as kinship term, 174; as Sikh term of address, 156, 157, 158, 160
Bhakra canal: canal road links Shahid-pur to other roads, 20–21; effect on water table, 27; fee assessment, 28
Bhakti: reform movement, 150; the-ology, 150, 151
Biological laws, 27; and structure of ecology as a message source, 32; and choices, 32; and surpluses, 56
Biology: in kin-type approach to kin-ship terminology, 169, 182, 183; in Schneider's view of kinship analysis, 171; in present analysis of kinship, 176, 182–183
Blacksmith (caste group), 94
Blacksmith (occupation group): work done by Masons, 93, 142

Block Development Officer, 18, 19; source of loans, 18, 120; in court case, 215

Boas, Franz, 231, 265

bradari. *See* Caste; Caste groups

Brahmanic Hinduism: and bhakti movement, 150

Brahmins: village census figures, 51; housing of, 66, 67, 68; household size and structure, 73; in division of labor, 90–91

Brickmaking, 96

Buffaloes, 42–47. *See also* Fodder; Milk

Bullocks: ownership distribution, 41–43; ratio to land, 42; census of, 42; correlation to crop income, 43; selective retention, 43; fodder needs, 46; price, consumption and yield, 47

Buses: serving villages near Shahidpur, 20

Butter: in basic diet, 53, 54

Camels: pulse as fodder, 37; in village cattle census, 42; popularity as draft animals, 44–45; fodder requirements, 46, 47; price, consumption, and yield, 47

Canal department: maintains canal roads, 21

Canal-irrigated land: in kharif crop pattern, 31; sorghum grown on, 36; use for rabi crops, 38; strategy of use for income, 83–85; and land prices, 116

Canal roads: link Shahidpur to other roads, 20–21; maintenance of, 21

Canal system, 16; roads associated with, 20–21; effect on water table, 21, 27; fee assessment, 28. *See also* Canal-irrigated land; Well-canal irrigated land

Cane. *See* Sugarcane

Capital, return to: and new well construction, 120; equilibrium in cropping, 129–130

Capital expenditures: and land rental practices, 122; decision-making, 129

Capital goods: and marketable surpluses, 57

Capital improvements: loans available for, 18

Capitalization in agriculture: India and U.S.A. compared, 254–255

Carbohydrates: in village diet, 55

Carpenter (caste group), 93

Carpentry: done by Masons, 93; rate of pay, 142, 143

Caste: and Sikh religion, 154; in kinship, 183, 196–199; defined, in kinship, 197, 199; equality within, 198; in folklore,

199; in perceived behavior, 202; in Hinduism, 220; Ibbetson on, 270; Rosser on, 271. *See also* Caste groups; Caste occupation

Caste groups: defined, 41, 89; and cattle ownership, table of, 42; census of village by, 50–52, 105; demographic structure of, 52; in descriptions of division of labor, 63–64; and distribution of houses, 65–67; variation of household size and structure,72–73; property rights, 74; in division of labor, 89–90, 105. *See also* Barber; Brahmin; Cotton-ginner; Farmer; Goldsmith; Harijan; Mason; Potter; Sadhu; Sweeper; Water-carrier

Caste occupation: as establishing legal presumption of ancestral status of property, 74; fulfillment of traditional callings, 89, 105. *See also* Caste groups

Cattle, 41–49; census, by caste of household, 42; selective retention of, 43, 44; importance and scarcity of, 45–46; relevance for structure of ecology, 46; ideal feeding pattern, 46; method of feeding, 46–48; price, consumption and yield of major species compared, 47; ideal behavior toward, 48; milk, importance for family growth, 53, 82; fodder needs of, related to production of surplus, 56; pattern of care, 75; human labor required by, 75; barn facilities, 75; density, related to Sikhism, 216, 217

Cattle market: at Kurali, 19, 20

Census: of village cattle, 42; of human population, 50–52, 106

Centrifuge (for sugar refining), 86, 87; in cane strike, 117

Chamkaur, 18, 20; and *diwan* ritual, 210, 211

Chicken: in diet, 55

Chick-pea. *See* Gram

Child mortality rate, 52–53

Children: importance of, 52, 53. *See also* Child mortality rate; Infant diet

Chilis: distribution over land types, 31, 36; in diet, 36, 53

Choices: and entropy of message source, 8, 110; structured by elements of village ecology, 25, 27, 41, 46, 57, 107–108; and biological law, 32; and surpluses, 41, 56; structured by fodder scarcity, 46; in selection of fodder crops, 49; in crop distribution, 56; structured by economic information, 57–58; and financial risk of innovation, 59; in landholding patterns, 76;

Index

Ecology, 24–59; defined, 24; cultural, 25; as system of symbols, 25–26; biological relationships as underlying sanctions, 26; and surpluses, 41, 56; importance of cattle in, 53, 56; and choices, 107–108; relation to land prices, 116; and land rental conventions, 121–122; close fit with economy and division of labor, 123; rule of objective primacy, 233–236; sanctions in, 236; as locus of underdevelopment, 255
—as message source, 24–25, 165; crops in structure of, 30, 40; in distribution of cattle, 46, 48; human population as element in, 50; structures choices, 57, 58, 59. *See also* Freedom of choice
Economic behavior: Duesenberry's view of, 114
Economic choice, 122, 146
Economic model: for acquisition and use of capital, 129
Economic rationality: as rationality of the economy, 114, 125, 140; as aspect of individual behavior, 114–115
Economy, 111–146; and choice in the village, 58; defined, 111; close fit with ecology and division of labor, 123; mathematics and organization of, 144, 145; low information, 144, 145, 146; compared with ecology and division of labor, 145; relation to "society," 146; compared with religious ideology, 147; rule of symbolic primacy, 238–240; unrelated to underdevelopment, 253. *See also* Economic behavior; Economic choice; Economic model; Economic rationality
Educational system: and Sikh religion, 20. *See also* Schools
Eggs: in diet, 55
Emergent evolution: Mead's concept of, 264
Entropy: concept of, 6; in Weaver's information theory, 7–8; of message source, 8; high, distinguished from disorganization, 107, 110. *See also* Message source
Equality: theme in Sikh religion, 154, 156, 159; political interpretation of, 212
Exports. *See* Surpluses

Fact, concepts of, 262
Factions: called parties in village, 91, 203; Brahmins in, 90; Farmers in, 91, 92; reflect ecological conditions, 92;

Harijans involved in, 101; activity in, related to dependency on agriculture, 105; use of term to suggest cleavage, 203–204; analysis of interests, 221, 225; landholding patterns related to, 221–224; income comparisons, 223–224. *See also* Parties
Fairs: and Kurali cattle market, 19; on Sikh religious occasions, 159; gurdwaras attract, 166; associated with *diwan* ritual, 210, 211
Fallowing: seldom used, 24
Family: importance of growth of, related to milk cattle, 52; composition and size, 71–75; size correlated with number of cattle, 82. *See also* Domestic groups; Households; *parivar*
Farm accounts, 124
Farmers (caste group), 50, 91–93; village census figures, 51; houses of, 66, 67, 68, 69; capital of, 69; land as inherited right, 72; in division of labor, 91–93, 105; factionalism of, 91–92; dues paid to Harijans, 102
Farmers (occupational group): bullock ownership, 41–42; family size, 71; diversification of occupation, 71; and education, 71; alliances with other households, 88; non-monetary benefits of farming, 125
"Farmer side" of village, 65, 67, 68
Fategarh: *diwan* ritual at, 211
Fats: in diet, 55
Feeds: distributed by Block Development Office, 18
Ferozepore: rainfall, 16
Fertilizers: distributed by Block Development Officer, 18; and village soil, 29; in land rental practices, 121; village production and use of, 135
Field map, 78–79
Firth, Raymond, 268
Fish: in diet, 55
Flooding: and village roads, 21; and village soil, 29; *abadi* protects houses from, 65, 70; and rats, 70
Fodder: distribution over land types, 31, 38; percentage of land devoted to, 31; maize as source of, 32, 33; in relation to cane crop, 35; rainfall land used for production, 33–34; sorghum millet for, 35, 36; green, 35; for camels, 37; wheat as source of, 38; mustard as, 39; barley as, 39; scarcity of, in village ecology, 46, 56; village requirements, 46–47, 55; as fuel, 47; forms of, 48; by-products of growing, 48–49; selecting crops for, 49; related

See also Conscious sociological models: kinship model; Kinship groups; Kinship terminology; Kin-types

Kinship groups: meanings of names of, 199; conceptions used by villagers in organization, 200; uses of concepts, 201

Kinship terminology: Kroeber's view of, 168–169; methods of analysis, 169–171; kin terms as sets of kin-types, 169–170; psychologically real analysis, 170; different treatments of, 171; basic patterns of definitions, 172; construction of semantic maps, 172–176; semantic map of main terms, 173; semantic map of terms for affinal kin of male, 174; standard, distinguished from colloquial terms, 174; map of terms for affinal kin of female, 175; uses of the map, 176, 178–183; distinguished from genealogy, 177; and definition of caste, 197; as message source, compared with religion, 200; relation to kinship system, 201. *See also* Caste; Caste groups; Clan; Genealogy; *pattis*

Kinship theory: present approach, 168–169; structural analysis of, 171. See also Conscious sociological models: kinship model; Kinship analysis; Kinship terminology

Kin type patterns: in componential analysis, 170, 183

Kin-types: Murdock's, 169–170

Kirpan, 153, 156, 157

Knight-Herskovitz controversy, 113

krapreshad, 157

Krishna, 150, 151

Kroeber, A. L., 168–169, 170, 182–183

Kuhn, Thomas: view of theory, 4–5; concept of paradigm, 5, 6

kumbal looms, 86–88, 101

Kurali, 19–20

Labor: required for cattle care, 75; return to, in farming, 124; wage rates, 127, 138; market conventions, 138; skilled, 140–143; heavy reliance on human, 255. *See also* Agricultural labor

lag: defined, 95. *See also* Traditional dues

Land, return to: interest rates reflect, 126; related to crop patterns, 130

Landholding, patterns of, 76; related to factionalism, 91–92; statistics by faction group in Shahidpur, 221–222. *See also* Property rights

Land ownership: records of, 18, 19, 76, 77; sale of, 76; holders of rights, statistics, 79; types of rights in relation to income, 80; reasons for manipulation of rights, 81; tendency to retain, 84; and land use, 84; statistics, by faction group, 221–223; related to Sant faction, 223–224. *See also* Property rights

Land prices, 116–119; relation to productivity, 117–119; related to cane prices, 118, 129–130; and village of buyer and seller, 119; relation to division of labor, 119; and cost of wells, 119; and out-migration, 120; and inflation, 126; and crop income, 128

Land rental. *See* Rental of land

Land tenure, 75–78; types of rights, 76, 77–78; absentee owners, 81; and household resources, statistics, 82; income related to irrigation types, 83, 84. *See also* Land ownership; Land use; Mortgage arrangement; Rental of land; Tenancy arrangement

Land types (classified by irrigation source): kharif crop pattern by, 31; and maize cropping strategy, 33–34; rabi crop pattern by, 38; and lentil cropping, 40; strategy of use for income, 83, 84–85; and land prices, 116–117. *See also* Irrigation

Land use: statistical analysis, 78–80; rights-holding groups, 79–80; pattern of arrangements, 81, 83; interchange of rights, 81; strategies, 82; and land ownership, 84. *See also* Cropping strategy; Land tenure

Land use (for crops). *See* Cropping strategy

Land valuation: rate of appreciation, 123

langar, 212

Language: defined in present treatment, 11; and cultural ecologies, 25

"Language game": Wittgenstein's concept of, 3–4, 9, 149

Laws: and division of labor, 77

Leach, E. R., 171, 267, 268

Leather worker (caste group), 99–100, 102, 103. *See also* Harijan caste

Leather worker (occupation), 100

Legal disputes. *See* Court cases

Legumes: in cropping strategy, 56

Lentils, 38, 39; distribution over land types, 38; in diet, 40, 53, 55; cropping strategy, 40

Levi-Strauss, C.: and organic theory, 3; idealistic theory of theories, 265

Life cycles, 187–195

Index

Literature: as symbolic expression of consensus on message sources, 245–246

Loans. *See under* Government of India

Logical positivism, 4

Looms, 86–88, 100–101

lori ritual: in relation to male life cycle, 189–190; in relation to village factions, 209–210; and participants in court cases, 215

Machli (*pseud.*): links Shahidpur with metaled road, 20; shares panchayat with Dinpur, 20; canal road to, 20, 21

Macroecology, 49–50

Maize, 32–34; cropping pattern, by land type, 31; in diet, 32; cropping strategies, 33; growth cycle, 34; relation to wheat crop, 34; relation to cane crop, 35; economic characteristics of, 132; income from, 134

mandi: defined, 19; at Rupar, 19; at Kurali, 19; at Morinda, 20

Manure: ban on sale outside of village, 92, 136

Market committee, 19

Market conventions, 144–145, 146, 238, 239

Marketing information: jobber a source of, 19

Market mechanisms, 115

Markets, economic: defined, 112, 115, 116; in land, 116; others related to market in land through cropping patterns, 128

Market towns: legal designation, 19

Marriage: importance of, 52; and equality within caste, 198. *See also* Marriage rituals; Marriage rule; Weddings

Marriage rituals, 190–191. *See also* Weddings

Marriage rule: requires exogamy, 188, 199; and property concept, 197; in caste definition, 197

Marshall, Alfred, 146

Martyrdom: theme of in Sikh religion, 153, 154, 156, 159, 164, 166, 220; political interpretation of, 212

Mash (*Phaseolus radiatus*), 31, 34, 39

Masonry, 93, 142

Masons (caste group), 93–94; village census figures, 51; houses of, 66, 67, 68; household size and structure, 73; principal occupations, 93; 141–143; income of, 141–143

Masons (occupational group), 93, 142–143

Master Tara Singh, 160–161; as "issue" in village politics, 205. *See also* Master Tara Singh party

Master Tara Singh party; aligned with Congress party, 213; correlation with types of landholding, 221, 222

mata rani, 193–194

Matrilateral kin terms, 179, 180, 182, 199

Mead, G. H., 231, 264, 265–266

Meals: in payment for labor, 126, 139

Meat: in diet, 44, 55

Meier, Gerald, 251–252

Message source: in Weaver's model, 6; definition in present approach, 7, 262; entropy as information in, 8; as social structure, 9; use in present analysis, 10–12, 266, 272–273; division of labor as, 60, 89, 105–106; specialization in use of, 110; and market in land, 116; economy as, 144; religion as, 154, 200; problem of maintenance of integrity of, 230–233, 248; application to social behavior, 231; fit between elements of, 249; relation to free choice, 265. *See also* Conscious sociological models; Entropy; Freedom of choice; Information theory

—ecology as, 26–27, 30, 58, 165; structures choices, 26, 27, 56, 58; cropping strategy illustrates, 30, 32, 40; importance of cattle an element in, 46; human population an element in, 50; and isolation of village, 57–58; incentive for utilization of, 165

Microecology: distinguished from macroecology, 49, 50

Migration out of village, 23, 91; and land prices, 120

Militancy: in Sikh religion, 152, 153, 154

Milk: buffaloes popular source of, 43–44; dietary importance, 43, 45, 54; goat, 44; value of, 45; yield, of buffalo cow, 47; milk cattle, correlation to family growth, 52, 53, 82; use in basic diet, 54, 55

Miller, 86

Milling: done by Masons, 93

Minerals: in basic diet, 55

Model of defined parts, 267

Models. *See* Conscious sociological models

Models, total system, 267

Moerman, Michael, 268–269

Monetary system of evaluation: basis for, 112; relation to consumption, 113; and definition of markets, 115

Money: and land rights, 76; as system